Catholic, Lutheran, Protestant

by
Pastor Gregory L. Jackson, STM (Yale University),
PhD (University of Notre Dame)
Illustrated by Norma Boeckler

Martin Chemnitz Press
Glendale, Arizona 85304

Copyright Notice

Individual copies of this book may be ordered from:

Christian News

573-237-3110

684 Luther Lane

New Haven, MO 63068

A pdf file of this book or the paperback version can be ordered from http://www.lulu.com, and from bookstore chains.

Discounted large orders may be sent to:

Gregory L. Jackson

6421 W. Poinsettia Drive

Glendale, AZ 85304

Acknowledgements and Dedication

Many people contribute to the final text of a book. Norma Boeckler took the time to illustrate this edition, as she did with the text and website for *Jesus, Lord of Creation* and the book *Jesus, Priceless Treasure*. Raymond Klatt, Martin H. Jackson, and others offered many valuable suggestions in proofreading the text. The final edit was executed without mercy by Mark Ochasankehl, who would make any publishing enterprise proud.

During the period when *CLP* was being re-written, our dear friend Christian Bruce Wenger passed from this life into eternal life. Bruce earned an M.D. and Ph.D. from Yale University, working at the famed J. B. Pierce Lab and later for the government in Boston. He was a friend who never hesitated to question liberal theories of the Bible, confirming in conversation what the conservative Biblical scholars of Yale laid bare. We continued to see Bruce over the years, the last times at the Ad Fontes conference in Pennsylvania and at Cape Cod. Melanoma took him away from his dear wife and children, medical science, and us. Nevertheless, his personal, professional, and confessional influence remains.

My wife Christina was diagnosed when *CLP* was first being written. She has been the most significant force behind my ceaseless writing efforts. Although we deal with medical issues all the time, we also enjoy the blessing of Martin's marriage to Tammy, and their three delightful children: Josie, Danielle, and Alexander. Grandchildren are God's confirmation of that first love, which began in English class at a school named for the Augsburg Confession – Augustana College. Therefore, this edition is dedicated to my wife Christina:

> Her children arise up, and call her blessed; her husband *also*, and he praiseth her. Many daughters have done virtuously, but thou excellest them all. Proverbs 31:28-29

Preface

My autobiography involves many of the authors listed in the bibliography. At Waterloo Lutheran Seminary, Otto Heick began my interest in comparative dogmatics and Christology. Paul Holmer was instrumental in getting me accepted at Yale, where I learned careful exegesis in Hebrew and Greek from Robert Wilson, Abraham Malherbe, and Nils A. Dahl. George Lindbeck was a regular at the small, early morning chapel services at Bethesda Lutheran Church, New Haven, where I helped as a student assistant. We often saw the late Jaroslav Pelikan at the coffee hour at Bethesda. I attended lectures by Roland Bainton, who was retired. Bainton helped me later with my dissertation and sent me a drawing of Luther holding our son Martin and our daughter Bethany. Father Henri Nouwen was shocked to learn that I actually knew who Thomas Merton was. I saw him again at Notre Dame, when he lectured there. I often wrote to Richard J. Neuhaus, when he was complaining about the Lutheran Church in America. I met Neuhaus and Leonard Klein before they became Roman Catholic priests. At Notre Dame, Robert Wilken was the head of the graduate school in theology. He became a Roman Catholic afterwards. Two of my professors at Notre Dame, Francis and Elisabeth Schussler-Fiorenza, found their way to endowed chairs at Harvard University. Some of the Evangelical leaders I heard speak at conferences were: Billy Graham, D. James Kennedy, Paul Y. Cho, and Charles Colson. In my transition to the Synodical Conference I attended lectures by the late Kurt Marquart, the late Robert Preus, David Scaer, and Klemet Preus. I met the late Jack Preus at the Indianapolis Missouri Synod convention, where he signed my copy of Chemnitz' *Two Natures of Christ*. He had just denounced Herman Otten, whose *Christian News* was soon dotted with many of my articles. My wife Christina and I often saw the Otten family in New Haven, Missouri. Their son Timothy was instrumental in getting *Catholic, Lutheran, Protestant* in print the first time. Tim was also a great help with *Angel Joy* and *The Wormhaven Gardening Book*. At Mequon I attended a number of classes on an involuntary basis, the best of which was church history, taught by the late Edward C. Fredrich. Many phone conversations and email discussions with Lutheran laity have increased my interest in doctrinal matters and my knowledge of local or synodical issues.

Books Frequently Cited

The books cited most often in this work are listed below, after the abbreviated title.

Birth of Purgatory – Jacques Le Goff. *The Birth of Purgatory*. trans. Arthur Goldhammar, Chicago: University of Chicago Press, 1984.

Examination – Martin Chemnitz. *Examination of the Council of Trent*, trans., Fred Kramer, St. Louis: Concordia Publishing House, 1986.

Hasler – August Bernhard Hasler. *How the Pope Became Infallible, Pius IX and the Politics of Persuasion.* Garden City: Doubleday and Company, 1981.

Hudson – Henry T. Hudson. *Papal Power, Its Orgins and Development.* Hertfordshire, England: Evangelical Press, 1981.

Jugie, *Purgatory* – Martin Jugie. *Purgatory and the Means to Avoid It*, New York: Spiritual Book Associates, 1959.

Mariology – Juniper B. Carol, O.F.M., ed. *Mariology*, 3 vols., Milwaukee: The Bruce Publishing Company, 1961.

Sermons – *Sermons of Martin Luther*, 8 vols. ed. John Nicolas Lenker, Grand Rapids: Baker Book House, 1983.

Tappert – *The Book of Concord*, translated by Theodore Tappert, Philadelphia: Fortress Press.

Triglotta – *Concordia Triglotta*, St. Louis: Concordia Publishing House,

What Luther Says – Ewald Plass, ed., *What Luther Says*, 3 vols., St. Louis: Concordia Publishing House.

Table of Contents

Part One: Areas of Agreement

1

Chapter One: The Scriptures, the Trinity, Natural Law

Introduction

Only one, true Christian Church exists, and that Church is made up of all those who sincerely believe in Christ as their Savior. The true Church, then, is invisible, including members of all denominations, even those without a denomination or formal affiliation. Only God can judge the heart, so one cannot judge whether a person has saving faith from his membership in one denomination or another. However, people should affiliate with those who teach the truth of God's Word, since false doctrine appeals to human reason and undermines our faith in God's saving work in Christ. Visible churches are those denominations that have a history, a confession of faith, property, members, income and expenditures. God allows divisions among Christians in order to test what is pure in doctrine.

> 1 Corinthians 11:18 For first of all, when ye come together in the church, I hear that there be divisions among you; and I partly believe it. 19 For there must be also heresies among you, that they which are approved may be made manifest among you.

We must distinguish between primary and secondary doctrines in order to understand how God could allow so many differences in doctrine and yet offer salvation in those conflicting confessions of faith. The primary doctrines teach what we must believe and understand in order to have saving faith. For instance, the Trinity, the Incarnation, the Atonement, and the Resurrection of Christ are all essential for trusting in the Savior's mercy. Considering Jesus a mere man, as some do, simply cancels the meaning of the Christian faith. In contrast, one may not know or understand the doctrine of the Antichrist, yet hold fast to salvation through grace alone. In addition, the Sacraments may be misunderstood or misused, yet faith in the Gospel remains. Many people in America hear sermons from ministers who deny the central doctrines of the faith, yet the Holy Spirit continues to work through the Scriptures to create and sustain faith, in spite of man's efforts to supplant those truths.

These examples are not offered to suggest that any false teaching is harmless. Many have used the so-called contradictions in the Bible to deny the central doctrines of the Scriptures, to undermine people's faith in God's Word, and to promote human wisdom. Through one error an entire nation can be lost, as Luther observed, since the unity of the faith is destroyed and errors multiply. Nevertheless, one cannot correctly identify one denomination as the only soul-saving church, nor condemn all members of another confession to eternal damnation. Although people argue heatedly over football teams, many find discussing Christian doctrine the mark of a primitive mindset. The widely heralded tolerance, which allows Christians to worship with Muslims, is not a sign of love, but proof of doctrinal indifference. Those who love the Scriptures will benefit from knowing how Christian doctrine is taught in the Bible.

Agreement among Catholics, Lutherans, and Protestants

Catholics, Lutherans, and Protestants agree that:

1. The Bible is the revealed Word of God, inspired by the Holy Spirit, without any contradictions or errors.

2. God has revealed Himself as Triune, Three-in-One: Father, Son, and Holy Spirit.

3. The Son of God was conceived by the Holy Spirit and born of the Virgin Mary, having Two Natures, divine and human, united in One Person, Christ.

4. Jesus, the Son of God, died on the cross to pay for our sins, and rose bodily from the dead, as the first of all to conquer death.

5. Faith in Christ is the basis for salvation.

6. The soul is immortal.

7. Christ will return.

Catholic and Lutheran Agreement

Catholics and Lutherans agree about the importance of:

a. The Ecumenical Creeds

b. The Church Fathers

c. The Sacraments

d. The historic liturgy

e. Doctrinal harmony.

Lutheran and Protestant Agreement

Lutherans and Protestants (commonly called Evangelicals today) agree about the importance of:

a. The Bible as the sole authority for teaching

b. The inspiration and inerrancy of the Scriptures

c. Salvation as a gift, received through faith.

Scriptures: The Measuring Rod

Every study has a standard of measurement that is used for comparison. Catholics, Lutherans, and Protestants agree that the Bible is the Word of God, revealed by the Holy Spirit. Liberal theologians influenced by rationalism have tried to subordinate the Bible to the 19th century view of science. Liberals will concede that the Bible "contains the Word of God," to use their words, but they deny the Bible is the Word of God. The liberal position allows almost any interpretation, except that of historic Christianity. Liberals seldom admit that their position is new, alien to Catholicism, Lutheranism, and Protestantism. One of the best descriptions of the Bible is by Pope Pius XII (1876-1958), who said:

> As the Word, the Second Person of the Trinity, being of the same essence with God, became true man in Jesus, but without sin, so also God's word in Scripture is truly human in its various forms of speech with the exception of errors and mistakes *(quoad omnia humani sermoni assimilia facta sunt, excepto errore).*[1]

Jesus Himself said, "The Scripture cannot be broken." (John 10:35)

Biblical Testimonies

Lutherans and Protestants are familiar with the many passages in the Bible which speak of the Scriptures as a unity, inspired by the Holy Spirit, clear, trustworthy, and without error. Some of them are listed below:

---

[1] *Acta Apostolicae Sedia. Commentarium officiale, 25, 943,* p. 315, cited in Uuras Saarnivaara, *Can the Bible Be Trusted? Old and New Testament Introduction and Interpretation,* Minneapolis: Osterhus Publishing House, 1983, p. 39. Roman Catholic acceptance of the Historical-Critical Method, *Divino afflante,* 1943, and in *Verbum Dei, Documents of Vatican II,* has changed the interpretation of Scriptures. Pope Pius IX (1792-1878) condemned the Historical-Critical Method in the Syllabus of Errors, 1864. The use of tradition in Roman Catholic interpretation is another matter, discussed in a later chapter.

Numbers 23:19 God *is* not a man, that he should lie; neither the son of man, that he should repent: hath he said, and shall he not do *it*? or hath he spoken, and shall he not make it good?

Isaiah 55:8 For my thoughts *are* not your thoughts, neither *are* your ways my ways, saith the LORD. 9 For *as* the heavens are higher than the earth, so are my ways higher than your ways, and my thoughts than your thoughts. 10 For as the rain cometh down, and the snow from heaven, and returneth not thither, but watereth the earth, and maketh it bring forth and bud, that it may give seed to the sower, and bread to the eater: 11 So shall my word be that goeth forth out of my mouth: it shall not return unto me void, but it shall accomplish that which I please, and it shall prosper *in the thing* whereto I sent it. 12 For ye shall go out with joy, and be led forth with peace: the mountains and the hills shall break forth before you into singing, and all the trees of the field shall clap *their* hands.

Jeremiah 14:14 Then the LORD said unto me, The prophets prophesy lies in my name: I sent them not, neither have I commanded them, neither spake unto them: they prophesy unto you a false vision and divination, and a thing of nought, and the deceit of their heart.

John 5:39 Search the scriptures; for in them ye think ye have eternal life: and they are they which testify of me.

John 17:17 Sanctify them through thy truth: thy word is truth.

2 Timothy 3:16 All scripture *is* given by inspiration of God, and *is* profitable for doctrine, for reproof, for correction, for instruction in righteousness: 17 That the man of God may be perfect, throughly furnished unto all good works.

2 Peter 1:21 For the prophecy came not in old time by the will of man: but holy men of God spake *as they were* moved by the Holy Ghost.

Hebrews 4:12 For the word of God *is* quick, and powerful, and sharper than any twoedged sword, piercing even to the dividing asunder of soul and spirit, and of the joints and marrow, and *is* a discerner of the thoughts and intents of the heart.

1 Thessalonians 2:13 For this cause also thank we God without ceasing, because, when ye received the word of God which ye heard of us, ye received *it* not *as* the word of men, but as it is in truth, the word of God, which effectually worketh also in you that believe.

Jude 1:4 For there are certain men crept in unawares, who were before of old ordained to this condemnation, ungodly men, turning the grace of our God into lasciviousness, and denying the only Lord God, and our Lord Jesus Christ.

The Early Church

Some Catholics, Lutherans, and Protestants may well be ignorant that the Scriptures served as the infallible rule for all matters of faith and practice in the early Church. In the first four centuries after Christ, many Christian leaders wrote about the faith because of doctrinal struggles against the false teaching of their time. These men are commonly called Church Fathers, and the period of time in which they lived is called the Patristic Era. The better known leaders are such men as Augustine, Ambrose, and Jerome. Others include Chrysostom, Cyprian, Tertullian, and Origen. Some of these Church Fathers promoted one error or another, but we still honor and study their orthodox writings. Protestants often ignore this era altogether. One Baptist seminary had courses in church history that skipped from the Apostolic Era to the Reformation, as if nothing worthwhile had happened in the 14 centuries between. Lutherans today slight the Church Fathers, but the Lutheran Reformers paid close attention to them. The testimony of the Patristic writers remains a reflection of God's work in their day and supports His work in our day as well.

Church Fathers

Lutherans and Protestants look at the Reformation as a turning point in church history, a fact acknowledged by Roman Catholics as well. All three confessions must understand how Christians dealt with error in the first few centuries of the Church, how they viewed the Scriptures. When Church Fathers are quoted for their support of Purgatory, the intercession of Mary, and the infallibility of the pope, they should also be cited for their view of the Bible's authority. Even if we remain ignorant of the Patristic Era, the participants in the Reformation and Counter-Reformation were not. Theologians of all three groups used the Fathers as authorities for their arguments.

One of the most important questions to answer in dealing with a comparison of doctrine is: "How did the Church Fathers view the authority of the Bible, their confessions, and other theological works." Knowing this material is a special area of theology and requires fluency in Latin and Greek. One of the most prolific authors during the Reformation, Martin Chemnitz (1522-1586), studied under Martin Luther and Philip Melanchthon. Consequently, he saw Lutheranism fall into disunity after Luther's death, and then worked with several leaders to write the Formula of Concord and compile the *Book of Concord* in 1580. Fortunately, Chemnitz' flair for calculating horoscopes landed him in a royal library where he had access to the Patristic Fathers and took careful notes. This experience was his Harvard and Yale. He lost interest in astrology, which is not Christian, and served the Church faithfully. His four-volume *Examination of the Council of Trent*, 1565-1573, is the key work used to study the issues in this book. All Roman Catholic doctrines today are consistent with and based upon the Council of Trent.

The citations gathered by Chemnitz to illustrate the attitude of the Church Fathers toward the Scriptures may be verified through other studies.[2] Catholics, Lutheran, and Protestants cannot disown these Church Fathers any more than they can disown their parents and grandparents. Church doctrine is derived solely from the Bible, but refined in the doctrinal conflicts, confessions, books, and articles of the participants through the ages. Church history is not a dusty, dry document to examine, but a brightly woven tapestry, vividly illustrated with the drama of persecutions, executions, betrayals, sacrifices,

---

[2] John D. Hannah, ed. *Inerrancy and the Church*, Chicago: Moody Press, 1984. Briefly, the inerrancy of the Bible was not debated until the Age of Rationalism, the 18th century, when scoffers found apparent contradictions in the Bible (most of them known and explained adequately since the earliest days of the Church) and decided the Bible was purely a human creation. An excellent discussion of these Biblical problems can be found in William Arndt, *Bible Difficulties and Seeming Contradictions*, ed. Robert G. Hoerber and Walter Roehrs, St. Louis: Concordia Publishing House, 1987. The Lutheran Church used *infallible* for the Scriptures until the liberals limited the term to *infallible in doctrine but full of other errors. Inerrant* became a new word in English out of necessity, but Luther used the term in the Large Catechism.

benevolent works, tragedies, miracles, and blessings, which only come through God's grace in Christ Jesus.

What happened when synods or councils were held in the early Church to work out doctrinal conflicts? What was the highest authority for these discussions? Chemnitz informs us:

> And Cusanus writes that the custom of the ancient ecumenical synods was to place the holy Gospels in their midst.[3]

St. Augustine, whose voluminous writings have been probed to support the weakest arguments in favor of extra-Biblical doctrines, clearly spoke of the primacy of the Scriptures:

> Wherever the place has been determined, let us see to it that the canonical codices are on hand and if any proofs can be produced on either side, let us set everything else aside and bring so important a matter to a conclusion.[4]

Although the creeds and confessions of the day were important in determining what would be taught, St. Augustine did not want to start with current confessions and work back to the Scriptures for support, but instead to begin with the Word of God and set aside any previous statements. Denominations today honor the recent dead by making mediocre theologians the primary authority in a disputed issue. Augustine's statement would be good for all groups to study and apply to themselves:

> But now I ought not to quote the Nicean, nor you the Ariminensian Council, as if to judge beforehand. I will not be bound by the authority of this, nor you by the authority of that. On the authority of the Scriptures and not on anyone's own, but

---

[3] *Examination*, I, p. 154.

[4] *Ibid.*, Augustine, Letter 163, about private disputations concerning religion.

on the common witnesses of both, let matter contend with matter, cause with cause, reason with reason.[5]

St. Jerome, who lived at the same time as Augustine and produced the Vulgate (Latin version of the Bible), also made the Scriptures the highest authority, the ruling norm that judges all others:

> It is the doctrine of the Holy Spirit which is set forth in the canonical writings, and if the councils declare anything against it, I hold it to be wicked.[6]

John Chrysostom's last name was really a nickname earned for his fine sermons, "Golden Mouth" in Greek. He confirmed the authority of the Bible and the effectiveness of the Word of God as the Means of Grace:

> If anything is said without Scripture, the thinking on the hearers limps. But where the testimony proceeds from the divinely given Scripture, it confirms both the speech of the preacher and the soul of the hearer.[7]

Chrysostom also wrote:

> They say that we are to understand the things concerning Paradise not as they are written but in a different way. But when Scripture wants to teach us something like that, it interprets itself and does not permit the hearer to err. I therefore beg and entreat that we close our ears to all these things and follow the canon of Holy Scripture exactly.[8]

---

[5] *Ibid.*, p. 155. Augustine, *Contra Maximum*, Book 3, chapter 14.

[6] *Ibid.*, Jerome, commenting on Galatians.

[7] *Ibid.*, p. 156. Chrysostom, commenting on Psalm 95.

[8] *Ibid.*, p. 154. Chrysostom, Homily 13, on Genesis.

Those who think that *sola scriptura* (Latin for the Scriptures alone) is a slogan confined to the Reformation and new to the Church, should consider what Cyprian (ca. 200-258) said:

> There is a short way for pious minds both to dethrone error and to find and bring out the truth. For when we return to the source and origin of the divine tradition, human error ceases.[9]

Athanasius wrote another version of *sola scriptura:*

> The holy and divinely inspired Scriptures suffice for all instruction in the truth.[10]

Many other examples could be quoted, to show the unanimity of the Church Fathers in considering the canonical Scriptures to be the very Word of God and the sole authority for determining doctrine. Opposing views belonged to the heretics whose views were condemned, not for lack of cleverness, nor for want of charming and skillful advocates, but only for the absence of Biblical support. The Emperor Constantine attended the Council of Nicea, which gave us the Nicene Creed, and urged the participants to settle the controversy over the divinity of Christ according to the Scriptures:

> For the book of the evangelist and apostles and the oracles of the ancient prophets plainly teach us what we are to think concerning divine matters. Therefore let us cease our hostile discord and take the solutions of the questions out of the divinely inspired sayings.[11]

This must be our own attitude today.

---

[9] *Ibid.*, p. 158. Cyprian, *Ad Pompejum.*

[10] *Ibid.*, p. 152. Athanasius, *Contra gentes.*

[11] *Ibid.*, p. 154. Constantine at Nicea.

Clarity of the Scriptures

Some who confess the authority and inerrancy of the Scriptures will nevertheless take refuge in newly discovered "grey areas" of the Bible where they agonize over several opinions, as if God were the author of confusion. Arguing for the lack of clarity in the Bible is nothing new: it is the first resort of scoundrels. Refuting this charge against God's Word is just as ancient as the error. St. Augustine was first a scoffer who thought the plain, simple language of the Scriptures beneath him. He was the greatest intellect of his era, at the peak of Roman culture. God gave Augustine the grace to become one of the greatest theologians of the Church and a superb expositor of the Bible. Converted by a verse from the Bible, Augustine wrote:

> God wanted this same word to be complete and brief, and not obscure: brief, lest men should not have time to read it; clear, lest someone might say: I could not understand it.[12]

St. Ambrose also advocated the clarity of the Scriptures.

> He speaks with us in this way, that we may understand his speech.[13]

Chrysostom found the same clarity in Holy Writ:

> All things are clear and plain from the divine Scriptures; whatever things are necessary are manifest.[14]

---

[12] *Ibid.* , p. 167.

"What more shall I teach you than what we read in the apostle? For Holy Scripture fixes the rule for our doctrine, lest we dare to be wiser than we ought. Therefore I should not teach you anything else except to expound to you the words of the Teacher." *Ibid.*, p. 152. Augustine, *De bono viduitatis*, chapter 2.

[13] *Ibid.*, p. 167. Ambrose, Book 3, Letter 5.

[14] *Ibid.*, p. 152. Chrysostom, commenting on 2 Thessalonians 2.

Sufficiency of the Scriptures

When certain teachers cannot convince their audiences that the Scriptures are unclear, they argue with great force that the Bible is incomplete or insufficient. Indeed, the climax of St. John's Gospel states:

> John 21:25 And there are also many other things which Jesus did, the which, if they should be written every one, I suppose that even the world itself could not contain the books that should be written. Amen.

However, the Bible contains everything we need to know about salvation and remains our only constant in a world of inconsistencies, man-made traditions, fads, and fallacies. The tactic of arguing for the insufficiency of Scripture (and therefore the necessity of another source, whether it be the Book of Mormon or Mary Baker Eddy's *Science and Health*) is old rather than new, and countered long ago. Irenaeus, a 2nd century theologian famous for his work *Against Heresies*, wrote:

> When they are proved wrong from the Scriptures, they turn and accuse the Scriptures themselves, as if they were not correct and were without authority, both because they speak now one way, now another, and also because the truth cannot be found from Scripture by those who do not know the tradition; for (so they say) the truth was not given through epistles, but through the living voice, etc.[15]

Chrysostom stated:

> Whatever is required for salvation is already completely fulfilled in the Scriptures.[16]

---

[15] *Ibid.*, p. 82. Irenaeus. *Contra haereses.* Chapter 2.

[16] *Ibid.*, p. 157. Chrysostom, commenting on Matthew 22.

St. Augustine did not display restraint and patience toward the false teachers of his day, but instead rebuked them (the Manicheans in this case) with the Scriptures:

> If you believe the report about Christ, see whether this is a proper witness; consider what disaster you are headed for. You reject the Scriptures which are confirmed and commended by such great authority; you perform no miracles, and if you performed any, we would shun even those in your case according to the Lord's instruction, Matthew 24:24. He wanted absolutely nothing to be believed against the confirmed authority of the Scriptures, etc.[17]

Scriptures during the Reformation

The Reformation of the 16th century brought about sharp doctrinal distinctions between Lutherans, Protestants, and Roman Catholics. However, at no time did any religious leader of these groups teach that the Bible was anything other than the Word of God. Although the Roman party did introduce a new method for allowing tradition and papal authority to supplant Scripture as the primary rule of faith, by declaring that the Bible was not completely clear nor sufficient in its teaching, no one thought to make the Bible equal to a story, a poem, or an entertaining Greek myth. The latter view developed during the 18th century Age of Rationalism, when literary criticism was used dishonestly to discover (as they claimed) apparent errors and contradictions of the

---

[17] *Ibid.*, p. 172. Augustine, *Contra Faustum*, Book 13.

Bible. In fact, most of these problems were known for centuries and answered sufficiently. Nevertheless, the spirit of doubt, scorn, and mockery became institutionalized in the Historical-Critical Method of studying the Bible.[18] This method gradually took over mainline seminaries and—last of all—became accepted in the Roman Catholic Church. The implications of accepting the Historical-Critical Method will be discussed later.

Harold Lindsell has shown in *The Battle for the Bible* that many Protestant seminaries once known for a conservative position of the Scriptures, such as his former school, Fuller Seminary in Pasadena, have accepted the rationalistic view of the Bible and rejected the historic position of the Christian Church outlined above.[19] The Historical-Critical Method has done its damage across Christianity and left many Christian leaders of all confessions treating the Word of God as merely a human book written by ordinary men. Needless to say, this method proved to be quite sterile in gaining any spiritual wisdom from the Bible. Even though this fad has had a long and successful run, Christian leaders still exist who teach the historic view of the Scriptures. Unless one accepts the Bible as the standard (or rule) of faith and practice, discussions about the Christian faith are fruitless exchanges. Most laity still accept the Bible as God's inspired and inerrant Word, although some have been trained to question the truth, authority, and clarity of the Scriptures.

---

[18] This is discussed at length in the author's *Liberalism: Its Cause and Cure*, Milwaukee: Northwestern Publishing House, 1991.

[19] Grand Rapids: Zondervan, 1976. Lindsell's book shocked Evangelicals by revealing the deliberate rejection of inerrancy by Fuller Theological Seminary, a school he helped establish. Lindsell and others worked to maintain the original stance of Fuller, but failed. The Church Growth Movement flourished at Fuller after inerrancy was rejected, yet leaders of the Missouri Synod, Wisconsin Synod, and Evangelical Lutheran Synod (all pledged to inerrancy) flocked to Fuller and forced this alien religion of statistics, marketing, and pop music on their abused flocks.

The Holy Trinity: the Father, the Son, and the Holy Spirit

...There is one divine essence, which is called and which is God, eternal, incorporeal, indivisible, of infinite power, wisdom, and goodness, the maker and preserver of all things, visible and invisible. Yet there are three persons, of the same essence and power, who are also coeternal: the Father, the Son, and the Holy Spirit.[20]

The Holy Trinity is one doctrine that distinguishes the Christian faith from all other religions and from pseudo-Christian cults. The Trinity (Triune God) is shorthand for the Biblical revelation that God is One in essence but Three in Persons. The Bible specifically names the Father, the Son, and the Holy Spirit as the members of the Trinity. Catholics, Lutherans, and Protestants agree about the Trinity. Cults such as Jehovah's Witnesses, the Latter Day Saints (Mormons), and the United Pentecostal Church deny and distort the historic teaching of the Trinity. Other religions, such as Judaism and Islam, acknowledge Jesus as a teacher, but deny He is the pre-existent Son of God and the Savior of the world.

Scoffers, liberal theologians, and cult leaders have claimed to find no references to the Trinity in the Bible. The word Trinity cannot be found in the Bible, since the term was created in the early Church to express a truth already known and taught, but under attack at the time. Many theological terms are shorthand expressions for distant and lengthy controversies: Real Presence, Sacrament, non-reciprocity. Many

---

[20] Augsburg Confession, Article I, God, Latin translation,. Tappert, p. 27f.

Trinitarian references can be found in the Old and New Testaments. Most Christians are familiar with the Great Commission in Matthew:

> Matthew 28:19 Go ye therefore, and teach all nations, baptizing them in the name of the Father, and of the Son, and of the Holy Ghost: 20 Teaching them to observe all things whatsoever I have commanded you: and, lo, I am with you alway, *even* unto the end of the world. Amen.

When Jesus was baptized in Matthew, Mark, and Luke, the Father spoke, saying, "This is My beloved Son, in whom I am well pleased," and the Holy Spirit descended. Therefore, within a few verses, all Three Persons of the Holy Trinity are revealed.

Old Testament

References to the Trinity in the Old Testament indicate what will be fully revealed at the coming of Christ. The Creation hymn of Genesis opens with the Father commanding through the Word and the Holy Spirit moving across the face of the deep.

> Genesis 1:1 In the beginning God created the heaven and the earth. 2 And the earth was without form, and void; and darkness *was* upon the face of the deep. And the Spirit of God moved upon the face of the waters. 3 And God said, Let there be light: and there was light.

The Trinitarian nature of the Creation is confirmed in the Gospel of John, where the Logos Hymn (John 1:1-17) replicates the first words of Genesis and reveals the true nature of the Word. As Lenski noted, Word is used three times, like the tolling of a great bell, reminding us of the three-fold nature of God. Verses 2-3 also have a triadic structure.

> John 1:1 In the beginning was the Word, and the Word was with God, and the Word was God. 2 The same was in the beginning

with God. 3 All things were made by him; and without him was not any thing made that was made.

The three-fold use of the Lord in the Aaronic benediction implies the Trinity without expanding on the doctrine. In the same way, the many messianic prophecies of the Old Testament prepared believers for Christ without stating exactly how He would die on the cross for the sins of the world.

Numbers 6:24 The LORD bless thee, and keep thee:

25 The LORD make his face shine upon thee, and be gracious unto thee:

6 The LORD lift up his countenance upon thee, and give thee peace.

A skeptic is inclined to dismiss what God said at the Creation, "Let us make man in our own image, in our likeness" (Genesis 1:26), as an example of the first person plural being used in formal speech. However, the Bible is completely consistent, with an extraordinary unity of expression that defies all human explanation. One human author cannot achieve the unity in a single book that is revealed in canonical books of the Bible. A group of theological writers, working within the same denomination, cannot edit a single book with the miraculous unity revealed in the Bible.

The Scriptures express God's revealed truths through human authors, giving the Bible its dual nature of human expression and divine infallibility. Since God is Triune from all eternity, it would be contradictory for Genesis to reveal God saying, "I will make man in My image." The best way to understand the Trinitarian indications of the Old Testament is to remember how episodes in the past suddenly make sense later when all the facts are known. For instance, one college girl mysteriously signed up for an English section that no one took voluntarily, freely confessing that she did not like the professor. This puzzled her fellow student, until he realized in time that her blunder was not without cause. They were married one week after graduation, and many small episodes leading up to that special day made perfect sense. The former college president, Conrad Bergendoff, even declared, "It was foreordained." Without these events, this book could not have been written.

Trinitarian references are easy to discover throughout the Bible. Isaiah's vision of God, with its three-fold use of "holy," one of the divine attributes, foreshadowed the complete revelation which would come about through Christ:

> Isaiah 6:3 And one cried unto another, and said, Holy, holy, holy, *is* the LORD of hosts: the whole earth *is* full of his glory.

New Testament

Some of the New Testament references to the Trinity have a three-fold structure, so that God is described and revealed as Triune. St. Paul wrote:

> Romans 11:33 O the depth of the riches both of the wisdom and knowledge of God! how unsearchable *are* his judgments, and his ways past finding out! 34

> For **who** hath known the mind of the Lord? or **who** hath been his counsellor? 35 Or **who** hath first given to him, and it shall be recompensed unto him again? 36

> For **of him**, and **through him**, and **to him**, *are* all things: to whom *be* glory for ever. Amen.

Verse 33 is also triadic in the original Greek: "O the depth of the **riches** and **wisdom** and **knowledge** of God." Emphasis has been added to show three examples of triadic structure in three verses. This majestic passage expresses the unity of God and His three-fold nature, with three references to Him and not to Them.

Other references to the Trinity are in the clearest possible language. The Trinity is named in Ephesians 4:4-6, and another triadic structure defines God, as emphasized below:

Ephesians 4:4 *There is* one body, and one Spirit, even as ye are called in one hope of your calling; 5 One Lord, one faith, one baptism, 6 One God and Father of all, who *is* **above all**, and **through all**, and **in you all**.

Additional examples show how clearly the members of the Trinity are named in various New Testament books.

Ephesians 1:17 That the God of our Lord Jesus Christ, the Father of glory, may give unto you the Spirit of wisdom and revelation in the knowledge of him:

2 Corinthians 13:14 The grace of the Lord Jesus Christ, and the love of God, and the communion of the Holy Ghost, *be* with you all. Amen.

John 15:26 But when the Comforter is come, whom I will send unto you from the Father, *even* the Spirit of truth, which proceedeth from the Father, he shall testify of me:

Without doubt, the Bible teaches that God is One in Three, yet Three in One. "Hear, O Israel: the LORD our God, the LORD is one." (Deuteronomy 6:4) Deuteronomy teaches God's oneness in 6:4 and His three-ness in 6:24-26. St. Paul, who often used specific three-part language in describing God, also wrote: "There is no God but one." (1 Corinthians 8:4) Jesus made it impossible to claim many gods (the Mormon view) or to deny the Trinity (Unitarianism) when He said,

John 10:30 I and the Father, we are one. (author's translation)

John 10:30 I and *my* Father are one. (KJV)

John 10:30 I and the Father one we are. (Literal, Greek word order)

Nor could someone use John 10:30 to defend the Modalist position, which holds that God has three forms, like ice, water, and steam) a subtle way of denying the Three Persons.

The Trinity in the Early Church

The Trinity came under attack in the early Church, specifically the relationship between the Son and the Father. The Arians tried with great charm and intellectual adroitness, to teach that Jesus was almost but not quite equal to the Father. The Church's answer to the Arian heresy was the Nicene Creed, which we call ecumenical because the entire Christian Church agrees with and confesses the Nicene Creed, even if some denominations are not keen about creeds.

I believe in one God, the Father Almighty, Maker of heaven and earth and of all things visible and invisible.

And in one Lord Jesus Christ, the only-begotten Son of God, begotten of His Father before all worlds, God of God, Light of Light, Very God of Very God, Begotten, not made, Being of one substance with the Father, By whom all things were made; Who for us men and for our salvation came down from heaven And was incarnate by the Holy Ghost of the Virgin Mary And was made man; And was crucified also for us under Pontius Pilate. He suffered and was buried; And the third day He rose again according to the Scriptures; And ascended into heaven, And sitteth on the right hand of the Father; And He shall come again with glory to judge both the quick and the dead; Whose kingdom shall have no end.

And I believe in the Holy Ghost, The Lord and Giver of Life, Who proceedeth from the Father and the Son, Who with the Father and the Son together is worshiped and glorified, Who spake by the Prophets. And I believe one holy Christian and Apostolic Church. I acknowledge one Baptism for the remission of sins, And I look for the resurrection of the dead, And the life of the world to come. Amen.[21]

This creed was hammered out at Nicea in 325 AD and represents the triumph of orthodox Christianity after years of conflict. Scoffers like to say that the difference between the orthodox view and the Arian view was limited to one tiny letter, the letter "i" or iota in Greek, (*homoousios* vs. *homoiousios*). The first word in Greek means "the same substance" with the Father. The second word means "similar substance." The precise word used makes a considerable difference. For instance, in identifying a getaway car spotted at a gangland murder, the police would want to know if the car identified is the "same" car or just "similar" to the one seen – an SUV, for example. The difference would not be a few letters, but life and death. In the same way, when we speak of being confessional Christians, these creeds make a difference, not to fuel or rehash a theological dispute, but to clarify what the Scriptures actually say, since they are the source and origin of our faith in Christ. Creeds do not cause confusion, but help resolve confusion and conflict, as long as the Bible is the ruling norm of the statement. The truth revealed by the Word of God is a matter of eternal life and death.

Two other Trinitarian creeds, in addition to the Nicene Creed, are important for Catholics, Lutherans, and Protestants. One is the Apostles' Creed, which has an unknown but ancient origin.

I believe in God the Father Almighty, Maker of heaven and earth.

And in Jesus Christ, His only Son, our Lord; Who was conceived by the Holy Ghost, Born of the Virgin Mary, Suffered under Pontius Pilate, Was crucified, dead, and buried; He descended into hell; The third day He rose again from the dead; He ascended into heaven And sitteth on the right hand of God the Father Almighty, From thence He shall come to judge the quick and the dead.

---

[21] *The Lutheran Hymnal*, St. Louis: Concordia Publishing House, 1941, p. 22.

I believe in the Holy Ghost; the holy Christian Church, the communion of saints; The forgiveness of sins; The resurrection of the body; And the life everlasting. Amen.[22]

The Nicene Creed, in comparison, is obviously arguing against another position. The creed offers a positive and negative statement (begotten, not made). The second article of the Nicene Creed is especially long because the relationship of the Father and Son was being disputed at the time. The Nicene Creed is still used in Catholic and Lutheran worship services, not for antiquarian interest, but to guard against the repetition of those earlier errors. The Arian error was revived in the Reformation as Socinianism and rebuked in the Augsburg Confession. Two recent manifestations of this error are the musical play and movie *Jesus Christ Superstar,* and the book and movie *The Last Temptation of Christ.*

Another creed used by the Church is the Athanasian Creed, which was also forged to guard against errors about the Trinity. The Athanasian Creed is much lengthier than the Nicene, but is used in Catholic and Lutheran services, especially on Trinity Sunday. Most Protestant churches do not use the Three Ecumenical Creeds (Apostles', Nicene, Athanasian), the historic liturgy, or a cycle of Scriptural readings in their worship services. However, some are beginning to emulate the liturgical worship shared by Lutherans, Anglicans, Roman Catholics, and Eastern Orthodox communions. On the other hand, some Lutherans and Catholics have tried to modernize their services and to make them more attractive by adding entertainment, removing the creeds, the liturgy, and traditional hymns, often with disastrous results.

Hymnic Confessions

Although Protestants have a commonly acknowledged dislike of creeds and liturgy, hymn singing is universal and never likely to fade away. The Book of Psalms is the hymnal of the Bible, and many early hymns or confessions are included in the New Testament, especially in Revelation, but also in other passages. We can see the poetic structure and style of proclamation that indicates a hymnic confession:

---

[22] *Ibid.*, p. 12.

Philippians 2:5 Let this mind be in you, which was also in Christ Jesus:

> 6 Who, being in the form of God,
>> thought it not robbery to be equal with God:
>
> 7 But made himself of no reputation,
>> and took upon him the form of a servant,
>> and was made in the likeness of men:
>
> 8 And being found in fashion as a man,
>> he humbled himself,
>> and became obedient unto death, even the death of the cross.
>
> 9 Wherefore God also hath highly exalted him,
>> and given him a name which is above every name:
>
> 10 That at the name of Jesus every knee should bow,
>> of *things* in heaven, and *things* in earth, and *things* under the earth;
>
> 11 And *that* every tongue should confess
>> that Jesus Christ *is* Lord, to the glory of God the Father.

Verses 7, 8, and 10 have a triadic structure, suggesting the Trinity. The concise phrases are descriptive, poetic, and easy to memorize. Within the Trinitarian structure of the passage is also a declaration of the Two Natures of Christ, Whose death on the cross shows His human nature, Whose exaltation shows His divine nature.

The one-verse creed in 1 Timothy is comprised of six aorist passive verbs. Lenski calls them: "Six tremendous facts, heaped one upon another, all soteriological, all infinitely blessed."[23] The work of God is almost always described in the New Testament in groups of three.

---

[23] R. C. H. Lenski, *Interpretation of Timothy*, Columbus: Wartburg Press, 1937, p. 609.

1 Timothy 3:16 And without controversy great is the mystery of godliness:

God was

> manifest in the flesh,
>
> justified in the Spirit,
>
> seen of angels,
>
> preached unto the Gentiles,
>
> believed on in the world,
>
> received up into glory.

The passage is introduced as a creed in the original Greek, although the KJV chose to use "without controversy" instead of "we confess" or "as confessed."

Many of our favorite hymns are creeds confessing a Biblical truth that has come under fire. St. Ambrose's hymn, "Splendor of the Father's Light," (*Lutheran Worship*, #481) is a Trinitarian confession written in reaction to the Arian controversy at the time. A better known creedal hymn is "Rock of Ages," written by Augustus M. Toplady (1740-1778) to dispute the emotional extremes of revivalism:

> Not the labors of my hands can fulfill thy Law's demands;
>
> Could my zeal no respite know, could my tears forever flow,
>
> All for sin could not atone;
>
> Thou must save, and Thou alone. (*The Lutheran Hymnal*, #376)

Some hymnic confessions are so clear that subsequent versions are edited for a particular audience. Frederick W. Faber, who left the Church of England to become a Roman Catholic priest, wrote this hymn with a verse unfamiliar to most Protestants:

> Faith of our fathers, Mary's prayers
>
> Shall win our country back to Thee;

And through the truth that comes from God,

England shall then indeed be free.

Protestants sing "Faith of our fathers living still, in spite of fire, dungeon, sword," not thinking that the original hymn spoke of Protestant dungeons and swords, Roman Catholic priests as fathers, Mary as the Intercessor for England. Likewise, "Amazing Grace" contains a typical Calvinist sentiment, "t'was grace that taught my heart to fear," a line that cannot be sung by Lutherans, since God's grace does not induce fear. The Law creates contrition through the work of the Holy Spirit, and God's grace comes to us through the Gospel promises. Grace teaches our hearts to love God, not to fear Him.

"No creed but the Bible!" is a popular Protestant slogan because many are wary of having a denominational creed. Hymns and worship do constitute a type of confession or a proclamation of doctrinal principles, because worship expresses the faith of a communion. Lifting hands up in prayer and speaking in tongues are typical expressions of Pentecostalism, carefully taught to new adherents. Likewise, the final stage of corruption in a Protestant service is manifested in clowns, balloons, pop music, non-sermons, and antagonism toward the historic, Biblical forms of worship.

In contrast, the Lutheran service, which emphasizes the Means of Grace, worships God in the beauty of His holiness, through preaching, teaching the Word and administering the Sacraments. This emphasis on the Means of Grace shapes the design of the church interior, as a Lutheran professor of worship wrote:

> In the Church of the Reformation however, in the course of years the font has come to occupy a position in the chancel end of the church. The desire to present to the faithful the close association of the two Sacraments and to centralize at one place every emphasis on the Means of Grace, inspired the location of the font at the front center of the chancel, immediately at the entrance thereto.[24]

---

[24] Paul Zeller Strodach, *A Manual on Worship, Venite Adoremus*, Philadelphia: The United Lutheran Publishing House, 1930, p. 47. Contrast Strodach's statement with Pope Leo XIII's: "O Virgin most holy, none abounds in the knowledge of God except through thee; none, O Mother of God, obtains salvation except through three, none receives a gift from the throne of mercy except through thee." Encyclical, *Adiutricem populem*, September 5, 1895. *Mary, Mother of the Church*, p. 12.

Those who reject the Means of Grace tend to have auditoriums and lecterns, not altars and pulpits, and they view the cross as having a harmful effect on the success of their operation. This anti-cross attitude is frequently mentioned in articles about Willow Creek Community Church, an icon of the Church Growth Movement. Would the Willow Creek disciples agree with Paul?

> Galatians 6:14 But God forbid that I should glory, save in the cross of our Lord Jesus Christ, by whom the world is crucified unto me, and I unto the world.

The Trinitarian battles that gave us the Athanasian and Nicene Creeds have been viewed as the senseless warfare of contentious Christians. However, the conflicts are properly seen as our confessional foundation built upon the cornerstone that the builders rejected, Christ Jesus, true God and true man, our Savior, our Redeemer, the King of Kings and Lord of Lords. The ancient battles fought and won, at great cost, not only teach us more about the historic Christian faith, but also warn us not to repeat the errors of the past. Tragically, church history records the same errors repeating themselves in various forms. Salvation by works is as old as Pelagius, who lived at the time of St. Augustine (354-430 AD) and Pentecostalism is as old as Montanus (2nd century), who distinguished between "Spirit-filled" Christians and ordinary Christians.

The Two Natures of Christ

Christology, the teaching about Christ, is extremely important for the nurturing of the faith, since we are saved through Christ's death on the cross for our sins. Our hope of eternal life rests upon His bodily resurrection. Protestants and Lutherans have some significant differences in Christology, which will be fully explained in the section dealing with Holy Communion. Protestants and Lutherans do not disagree about the basics of Christology (the two natures, the atoning death, the bodily resurrection) but about the relationship between the two natures of Christ. Roman Catholics and Lutherans agree about Christology but disagree about certain aspects of Holy Communion. One example of this agreement is an excellent book called *Luther's Catholic Christology*, written by a Roman Catholic and published by the Wisconsin Evangelical Lutheran Synod.[25]

The doctrine of the Two Natures of Christ relates to all issues of the Christian faith. If Christ were only a man, as various liberals and Unitarians have taught, then His death on the cross was meaningless, except for showing His "solidarity with the poor," as Walter Rauschenbusch taught in his *Theology of the Social Gospel*, 1917. If Christ were only divine, as some early heretics taught, then He could not have undergone temptation in the desert, suffered, and died on the cross. In some passages of the Bible, one nature is emphasized, but both natures have always been united in Christ from the moment the Word became flesh (Incarnation), when the Virgin Mary conceived through the Holy Spirit. The birth of Christ was both human and divine – human in the way He was born, divine in the way He was conceived through the power of the Holy Spirit. The Two Natures, human and divine, remain united in Christ. When St. Paul wrote his most important apostolic letter, he began with the Two Natures of Christ and related that truth to justification by faith:

> Romans 1:1 Paul, a servant of Jesus Christ, called *to be* an apostle, separated unto the gospel of God, 2 (Which he had promised afore by his prophets in the holy scriptures,) 3 Concerning his Son Jesus Christ our Lord, which was made of the seed of David **according to the flesh**; 4 And declared *to be* the **Son of God** with power, according to the spirit of holiness, by the resurrection from the dead: 5 By whom we have received grace and apostleship, for obedience to the faith among all nations, for his name: (emphasis added)

The Two Natures did not mix to become a hybrid, nor was one nature diminished in favor of the other, as if Christ were half man and half god. The early Church fathers spoke of the Hypostatic Union of the Two Natures, a term they used to guard against the many heresies that disputed the clear, Scriptural truth. John Schaller's *Biblical Christology* is a brief summary of these issues, while Martin Chemnitz' *The Two Natures of*

---

[25] Franz Posset, *Luther's Catholic Christology, According to His Johannine Lectures of 1527*, Milwaukee: 1988.

Christ offers an encyclopedic explanation of the controversy with a clear Christian confession of Scriptural truths.[26]

The Scriptures were written so that God's message would be taught in His words, not filtered through cultural norms, temporary fads, and personal opinions. We do not have a Biblical passage that discusses the Hypostatic Union of the Two Natures using that technical term, but we do have many passages revealing the doctrine to us. To show that Christ Jesus was completely human, the Bible offers many examples, such as when He was tempted by Satan in the desert after His baptism. His final temptation came when He faced brutal torture and death on the cross, asking that "this cup be taken from Me." If Jesus had seen His agonizing death and humiliation with cold indifference, He could not have been completely human. He also prayed, "Not My will, but Thine be done," revealing His divine nature and sinlessness. Hebrews teaches us that Jesus helps us in our temptations because He was tempted in every way.

Hebrews 4:15 For we have not an high priest which cannot be touched with the feeling of our infirmities; but was in all points tempted like as *we are, yet* without sin.

Human Nature of Christ

Some of the revelations of Jesus' humanity are when:

1) He reacted to His friend Lazarus' death by weeping at the tomb, even though He knew He would raise him from the dead (John 11:35).

2) He asked the woman at the well for water because of His thirst (John 4:7).

3) The sight of moneychangers in the Temple made Him angry (John 2:15).

4) Jesus walked, slept, ate, displayed human emotions or refrained from using His divine power. His divine nature was

---

[26] *Biblical Christology, A Study in Lutheran Doctrine*, Milwaukee: Northwestern Publishing House, 1919. *The Two Natures of Christ*, trans. J. A. O. Preus, St. Louis: Concordia Publishing House, 1971.

never absent or impaired in any way, but He did not display this power during His trial and crucifixion, except for the cursing of the fig tree (Mark 11:12-14).

Luther wrote about Genesis 6:5-6:

> The incarnate Son of God is the cloak in which the Divine Majesty with all His gifts presents Himself to us. Therefore no sinner is so miserable that he dare not venture to present himself before God with the certain confidence of attaining forgiveness. This is the only view of the Godhead which is easy and possible in this life.[27]

In the weak and crying Newborn of Bethlehem, we see the mercy and love of God, giving us forgiveness through this Child, so that no one is afraid, intimidated by wealth, power, and majesty but drawn by the meekness, frailty, and mystery of a baby born of a Virgin laid in a manger, surrounded by animals, and worshiped by poor shepherds.

Divine Nature of Christ

The divine nature of Christ has been a fatal trap for rationalists, especially since the 18th century, when they began treating the Bible as another book produced by man, although they allowed it was better than the average novel. Many excuses have been invented to explain away the miracles:

1) People thought they were sick, then thought they were cured when Jesus spoke to them or touched them.

2) Jesus walked near but not on the water, or cleverly maneuvered His way along sand bars on the Sea of Galilee.

3) The crowd suddenly shared their hidden lunches when moved by the generosity of the boy who shared his food during the Feeding

---

[27] *What Luther Says*, I, p. 160.

of the Five Thousand, which (according to the liberals) should be renamed the Sharing of the Five Thousand.

4) St. Paul, through his genius in marketing, turned a failed rabbi (Jesus) into a cosmic Savior thanks to his uncommon zeal. The apostle's conversion is difficult to explain.

Miracles do abound when rationalists find insights in the Scriptures unsupported by a single word of text, such as the hidden lunch wonder, while claiming their methods are scientific and objective. As comical as these attempts may be, they have confused people about the Two Natures and left them doubting the infinite power of God.

Nevertheless, the divinity of Christ is established by Old Testament prophecies of the Messiah and the New Testament fulfillment of the Scriptures. Psalm 2 is quoted 18 times in the New Testament.

Psalm 2

Psalm 2:1 Why do the heathen rage, and the people imagine a vain thing? 2 The kings of the earth set themselves, and the rulers take counsel together, against the LORD, and against his anointed, *saying*, 3 Let us break their bands asunder, and cast away their cords from us. 4 He that sitteth in the heavens shall laugh: the Lord shall have them in derision. 5 Then shall he speak unto them in his wrath, and vex them in his sore displeasure. 6 Yet have I set my king upon my holy hill of Zion. 7 I will declare the decree: the LORD hath said unto me, Thou *art* my Son; this day have I begotten thee. 8 Ask of me, and I shall give *thee* the heathen *for* thine inheritance, and the uttermost parts of the earth *for* thy possession. 9 Thou shalt break them with a rod of iron; thou shalt dash them in pieces like a potter's vessel. 10 Be wise now therefore, O ye kings: be instructed, ye judges of the earth. 11 Serve the LORD with fear, and rejoice with trembling. 12 Kiss the Son, lest he be angry, and ye perish *from* the way, when his wrath is kindled but a little. Blessed *are* all they that put their trust in him.

Verse 7 is quoted 10 times (Matthew 3:17; 17:5; Mark 1:11; 9:7; Luke 3:22; 9:35; John 1:49; Acts 13:33; Hebrews 1:5; 5:5). Psalm 110 is quoted

25 times in the New Testament, referring to versus 1 and 4 printed below.

Psalm 110

1 The LORD said unto my Lord, Sit thou at my right hand, until I make thine enemies thy footstool.

4 The LORD hath sworn, and will not repent, Thou *art* a priest for ever after the order of Melchizedek.

Jesus used verse Psalm 110:1 against the Pharisees, puzzling and enraging them, since only the divine Messiah could fulfill God (the LORD) saying to King David's Lord (Christ Jesus), "Sit at My right hand." Indeed, only Jesus, the Son of God, could be a priest forever, offering Himself for the sins of the world and opening forever the Holy of Holies through the shedding of His blood.

Isaiah 7

The prophecy of the Virgin Birth in Isaiah 7 illustrates how God reveals His loving purpose in history, even when the promised event is centuries in the future. Just as Adam and Eve were promised the Messiah in the midst of the expulsion from the Garden of Eden (Genesis 3:15), so an evil king was given a promise in the face of his opposition to God. In Isaiah, King Ahaz promoted idolatry (2 Chronicles 28:1-5). Ahaz was taken captive but released because of the prophet Oded. However, when Ahaz learned that his enemies were mustering against him, he was consumed with fear. Rather than trust God, Ahaz tried to make an alliance with Tiglath-Pileser, the Assyrian king. Nevertheless, God sent Isaiah to Ahaz to promise deliverance.

Isaiah 7:5 Because Syria, Ephraim, and the son of Remaliah, have taken evil counsel against thee, saying, 6 Let us go up against Judah, and vex it, and let us make a breach therein for us, and set a king in the midst of it, *even* the son of Tabeal: 7 Thus saith the

Lord GOD, It shall not stand, neither shall it come to pass. 8 For the head of Syria *is* Damascus, and the head of Damascus *is* Rezin; and within threescore and five years shall Ephraim be broken, that it be not a people.

Showing His steadfast love and mercy, God commanded Ahaz through the prophet to ask for a sign of His power, whether on earth or in heaven (Isaiah 7:10). Ahaz covered up his doubt with hypocritical sanctimony:

Isaiah 7:12 But Ahaz said, I will not ask, neither will I tempt the LORD.

Angry at the rejection of His gracious command, God told Ahaz and the house of David through Isaiah:

Isaiah 7:13 And he said, Hear ye now, O house of David; *Is it* a small thing for you to weary men, but will ye weary my God also? 14 Therefore the Lord himself shall give you a sign; Behold, a virgin shall conceive, and bear a son, and shall call his name Immanuel.

The context of this passage clarifies several issues:

1. This passage does not concern an ordinary king who will soon rule over Israel, but a great and mighty wonder.
2. The promised Son will be born of a Virgin (*almah*), not merely a young girl. Moreover, only a Virgin birth could be a miraculous sign from God.
3. This sign will be God-with-us, Immanuel. Isaiah promised the Incarnation centuries before the event. Isaiah states this promise again, below.[28]

---

[28] *Almah* issue, *Christian News. Christian News Encyclopedia*, pp. 634, 1666, 2665, 3322, 3324.

Isaiah 9:6 For unto us a child is born, unto us a son is given: and the government shall be upon his shoulder: and his name shall be called Wonderful, Counsellor, The mighty God, The everlasting Father, The Prince of Peace.

Attempts to make this a prediction of a new earthly king, born the natural way, clash with the inner harmony of the prophecy. Isaiah 7:14 speaks of God working with less than ideal material, as He did with Jacob. God is so powerful that He can use the evil King Ahaz to promise the Messiah.

The Son of God has always existed from eternity, and God knew He would fulfill His plan. Therefore, God chose to reveal the Incarnation in a way that would show His power in the midst of man's rationalism, doubt, and fear, accomplishing two things are once –

1. Filling His people with faith and hope through the Gospel promise of the Son;

2. Causing each new Ahaz to stumble and puzzle over how God could possibly perform such a miracle.

The Scriptures reveal the divinity of Christ in such a way that each person must stop and consider how God transcends all human understanding. One person will balk at Jesus walking on water. Another will accept that miracle but question Peter being able to walk on the water through Christ's help. One person will believe every word of Scripture except "This is My body" (Mark 14:22) and "Baptism now saves you" (1 Peter 3:21). We study the Scriptures all our lives, to nurture the faith according to God's promise, that His Word always accomplishes His will (Isaiah 55:8-10). We hear the Word of God, to have our sins rebuked and our sins forgiven. The divinity of Christ assures us that God can accomplish anything and that He cares about every single person. No miracle is more wonderful than God becoming man, dying on the cross for our sins, and rising from the dead to give us eternal life. When we are tempted by Satan to think that God no longer cares about us, the Gospel shows us three times for emphasis, that God did not spare His own Son, but gave Him for us, when we were still weak with sin, when we were still sinners, when we were enemies of God (Romans 5: 6, 8, 10).

Romans 5:6 For when we were yet without strength, in due time Christ died for the ungodly.

Romans 5:8 But God commendeth his love toward us, in that, while we were yet sinners, Christ died for us.

Romans 5:10 For if, when we were enemies, we were reconciled to God by the death of his Son, much more, being reconciled, we shall be saved by his life.

Natural Law

Considering the modern secular assault against the Christian faith, the basic unity sensed by Catholics, Lutherans, and Protestants concerning morality, right and wrong, law and justice, and the sanctity of human life is not surprising. In spite of confessional differences, all Christians have a basic grasp of natural law, which is not limited to Christianity but still plays a significant role in our government and justice system. When Judge Clarence Thomas was questioned by the U. S. Congress about his nomination to the Supreme Court, his attitude toward the issue of natural law was discussed in the press.

Natural law is the concept that right and wrong were established by a divine Creator. Although the United States was not founded exclusively by orthodox Christians, our country was established by people who believed in the Creator. Anyone who believes in the Creator must also understand that right and wrong are based upon the principles inherent in the work of Creation. For example, a car engine is a man-made creation that works only when certain rules are understood and obeyed. When someone fails to maintain or repair the engine, the mechanic says, "Your car was not made to be abused." The repair manual for the car, written by the manufacturer, states what must be done to maintain the car properly, such as undergoing routine oil changes. The auto manual teaches the owner what is good for the car, even if it imposes difficulties and cost on the owner. *Mutatis mutandis*, the Bible is the Creator's manual, commanding what is good for us. Understanding this was a problem even in Luther's day.

Today nothing is so common as turning right into wrong and wrong into right by employing all sorts of clever expedients and strange tricks.[29]

Declaration of Independence

In the same way, natural law states that God commands what is good. God created us and therefore knows what we need in order to serve useful, productive lives. Natural law is universal, not just Christian, because all people who believe in a divine Creator also believe in right or wrong being based upon that Creation. Natural law would still be true, even if no one believed in the concept. A deist believes that God created the world and then left it to run itself. Therefore, the God of deism does not intervene in people's lives, redeem the human race through the cross, and forgive sins. One does not need to be a Christian to state in the words of the Declaration of Independence:

> We hold these truths to be self-evident, that all men are created equal, that they are endowed by their Creator with certain unalienable Rights that among these are Life, Liberty and the pursuit of Happiness.[30]

The Declaration concludes:

> And for the support of this Declaration, with a firm reliance on the Protection of Divine Providence, we mutually pledge to each other our Lives, our Fortune, and our sacred Honor.[31]

In an age of religious apostasy and virulent attacks upon any form of faith in Divine Providence, the Declaration of Independence reminds us of our country's religious origin. Respect for God and the Christian faith

---

[29] *What Luther Says*, III, p. 1294.

[30] Declaration of Independence, cited in John A. Garraty, *The American Nation, A History of the United States*, New York: Harper and Row, 1966, p. 880.

[31] *Ibid.*, p. 881.

caused our Founding Fathers to call chaplains to the House and Senate, to pay them with government funds, which is still being done today.

Social Structure

Natural law means that the Second Table of the Ten Commandments (concerning our relationship with other people – "Honor your father and mother," etc.) is universal rather than cultural in its application. One cannot name a single law or regulation in any country that does not reflect these commandments, whether it is a speed limit (Thou shalt not kill) or a law governing commerce (Thou shalt not steal). Governments do pass oppressive laws and twist the meaning of justice in many circumstances, but their very existence is an acknowledgement of natural law and the divine establishment of natural order. A tyrant is a servant of God, since tyranny is a better form of government than anarchy.

All people rebel against the law, even when they know it is good and spiritual. Natural law allows a Christian to argue against abortion by appealing to the common good. Compassion for helpless, unborn children is not limited to Christian believers but should be the proper response for everyone who values human life, the family unit, and the suffering caused by any form of murder. Some have piously argued in favor of abortion as a religious right guaranteed by the First Amendment, stating "The origin of life is a religious issue where I must have freedom of action!"[32] They are arguing against natural law, not Christianity. The United States protected unborn babies from abortion on demand for almost 200 years, until the *Roe vs. Wade* Supreme Court decision of 1973 set aside the consensus that killing children was bad for society, bad for families, and heartless toward the weakest of the weak, the poorest of the poor, a wrongful usurpation of God's power over life and death.

Natural law does not agonize over various theories of Biblical interpretation in order to settle the issue of homosexuality. The human body was not designed for homosexual sex, a fact proved beyond doubt by medical specialists who treat the dozens of disorders caused by homosexuality, AIDS being the worst of many maladies. When the Creator's plan for the family is followed, sex is confined to husband and

---

[32] Many liberal denominations and some Roman Catholic groups support the Religious Coalition for Abortion Rights.

wife within the divine institution and social contract that is called marriage. In the past, America has recognized proper marital relations as healthy and good for society, while prohibited or at least inhibiting alternate lifestyles that were formerly called perversions. The Supreme Court supported the concept of natural law (1986) when it recognized that a state may enforce the laws against sodomy but reversed itself later in the *Lawrence* case, 2003.

When a Christian relies on natural law to distinguish between right and wrong, he is not abandoning the faith, but speaking from the perspective that God commands what is good. Therefore, good results will follow from obedience to His commands. For instance, the original safe sex program was instituted by God. A man and woman would pledge their love and seal their commitment in a religious ceremony, then live together and enjoy the blessings that God grants through marriage. Then, God willing, they would raise their children, which are the blessed fruit of marriage. When sex is limited to marriage, no venereal diseases can spread to ruin people's lives. Emotional entanglements from living together without a public commitment are avoided. The potential for divorce is greatly reduced. The social structure is stronger and healthier because the members of that family are secure, loved, protected, and honored. When sex is limited to marriage, crisis pregnancies and the subsequent pressure for abortions are eliminated. The need to escape emotional pain through drugs and alcohol is reduced. No court, government, or church will ever eradicate sin, but our society was indeed much stronger and healthier when natural law was the norm rather than a fading ideal of the past. Catholics, Lutherans, and Protestants agree about this.

Part Two: Areas of Partial Agreement

Chapter Two: The Sacraments

When Roman Catholics attend a service of Holy Communion at a Lutheran church for the first time, they are struck by the similarity in the worship services, the respect shown for the Sacraments, and the emphasis upon the grace and power of God. Sacraments are defined by Lutherans as sacred acts having the command of Christ and an earthly element, their power of forgiveness coming from the Holy Spirit active in the Word. Therefore, Lutherans commonly name two Sacraments: Holy Baptism and Holy Communion, including the third, absolution, listed in the Apology of the Augsburg Confession, as associated with the other two. The Lutheran Reformation emphasized doctrine, which modified certain aspects of the worship service, but did not jettison the liturgy, the Sacraments, the Creeds, or the vestments. In contrast, the Swiss Protestant Reformation, led by Huldrich Zwingli (1484-1531) at first, later by John Calvin (1509-1564), began almost at once with the rejection of the Sacraments and a revolutionary change in worship.

Luther protested against Rome's soul-destroying teachings and reformed the Church by restoring the pure doctrine of God's Word. Zwingli hoped to reform the Church by abolishing Rome's superstitious practices. Calvin believed that a complete reformation implied two things: First, it was necessary to abolish all ceremonies, even those which were in use in the ancient Church, such as the liturgy, the church year, pulpits, altars; secondly, a truly reformed Church must follow the pattern of the

Apostolic Church in all its church practices and adopt the form of church government given to Israel in the Old Testament.[33]

J. T Mueller stated:

Calvinism rejects the Means of Grace as unnecessary; it holds that the Holy Spirit requires no escort or vehicle by which to enter human hearts.[34]

The Swiss Protestants erred when they equated worship forms with false doctrine, made the Sacraments symbolic ordinances of man, and separated the Holy Spirit from the Means of Grace. Mueller wrote:

The doctrine of the means of grace is a peculiar glory of Lutheran theology. To this central teaching it owes its sanity and strong appeal, its freedom from sectarian tendencies and morbid fanaticism, its coherence and practicalness, and its adaptation to men of every race and every degree of culture. The Lutheran Confessions bring out with great clearness the thought of the Reformers upon this subject.[35]

Without overlooking significant differences, we can say that Lutheran and Roman Catholic worship services have had many elements in common: the chanted liturgy, the Creeds, the cycle of Scripture readings, vestments, and the centrality of the Sacraments. American Lutherans have been influenced by Protestant revivalism and Pietism,

---

[33] F. E. Meyer, *American Churches, Beliefs and Practices*, St. Louis: Concordia Publishing House, 1946, p. 24. F. Pieper stated: "Zwingli is a good example of those who separate grace from the Means of Grace. His assertion that the Holy Ghost needs no vehicle (*vehiculum*) is well known. And this rule he applies not only to the Sacraments (*Fidei Ratio*, ed. Niemeyer, p. 241, but to the Word of the Gospel as well. Zwingli asserts emphatically that faith does not come through the outward Word, but through the immediate operation of the Holy Spirit: *ipse tractus internus* (through which we are converted to God) *immediate operantis est Spiritus*. [Zwingli, *Opp.*, ed. Schulthess, IV, 125] F. Pieper, *Christian Dogmatics*, 3 vol., St. Louis: Concordia Publishing House, 1953, III, p. 127

[34] John T. Mueller, "Grace, Means of," *Lutheran Cyclopedia*, ed. Erwin L. Lucker, St. Louis: Concordia Publishing House, 1975, p. 344.

[35] "Grace, Means of," *The Concordia Cyclopedia*, L. Fuerbringer, Th. Engelder, P. E. Kretzmann, St. Louis: Concordia Publishing House, 1927, p. 299.

causing some to emulate their Protestant peers, eliminating the liturgy, downplaying the Sacraments, and wearing black Geneva academic gowns instead of historically correct liturgical vestments. In fact, the American Lutheran movement that rose up before the Civil War promoted revivalism, the mourner's bench, decisions for Christ, and the elimination of those doctrines in the Lutheran Confessions distinguishing Lutherans from Protestants: baptismal regeneration and the Real Presence of Christ's body and blood in Holy Communion. Historically, all of these are Protestant, Pentecostal, and rationalistic influences, alien to the Lutheran Reformation, which was conservative and decidedly Catholic in nature.

> Since the age of Rationalism and Lutheran Pietism a new spirit has crept into the life of the church which is un-Lutheran, un-Evangelical, and un-biblical. The Sacraments have been neglected at the expense of the Word.[36]

C. F. W. Walther, a founder of the Lutheran-Church Missouri Synod and a church musician, found it difficult to establish genuine Lutheran worship in America.

> It was not easy to maintain confessional worship practices in the midst of Protestant America, however. Accusations of "Romanism" and "Puseyism" were not unusual, even from clergy and laity within the synod. Individual absolution, statues, candles, and even the simplest vestments were misunderstood."[37]

Because Protestantism differs from Lutheranism to such a degree, these problems will be considered before Lutheran and Roman Catholic differences are discussed.

---

[36] Walter G. Tillmanns, "Means of Grace: Use of," *The Encyclopedia of the Lutheran Church*, 3 vols., Julius Bodensieck, Minneapolis: Augsburg Publishing House, 1965, II, p. 1505.

[37] Dennis Marzolf, "C. F.W. Walther: The Musician and Liturgiologist," in *C. F. W. Walther: The American Luther*, ed. Arthur Drevlow, John Drickamer, Glenn Reichwald, Mankato: Walther Press, 1987, p. 89.

The Lutheran term for the Biblical doctrine concerning the way in which we receive forgiveness is the Means of Grace.

> Whoever is baptized in Christ is baptized through His suffering and blood or, to state it more clearly, through Baptism he is bathed in the blood of Christ and is cleansed from sins. For this reason St. Paul calls Baptism a "washing of regeneration" (Titus 3:5); and according to what Christians say and picture, the Sacraments flow from the wounds of Christ. And what they say and picture is right.[38]

The term Means of Grace is used among Roman Catholics, referring to seven Sacraments, but rarely among Protestants. Simply stated, from the Lutheran perspective, with overwhelming evidence from the Bible and Church fathers, we receive forgiveness of sin by the grace of God:

a. Through the Word spoken and written, and

b. From the Word connected with the earthly elements in the Sacraments of Holy Baptism and Holy Communion. The Church was created by Christ to offer the Means of Grace, as Luther taught:

> The church is recognized, not by external peace but by the Word and the Sacraments. For wherever you see a small group that has the true Word and the Sacraments, there the church is if only the pulpit and the baptismal font are pure. The church does not stand on the holiness of any one person but solely on the holiness and righteousness of the Lord Christ, for He has sanctified her by Word and Sacrament.[39]

The Formula of Concord states:

---

[38] Plass footnote: "Thus Jerome (d. 420) sees the Sacrament symbolized by the blood and water that flowed from the side of the dead Christ (John 19:34). Similarly St. Augustine (d. 430). In Luther's day pictures and woodcuts presented the same view." See W 30, II, 527, note; SL 13a, 491f *What Luther Says*, I, p. 46. To Duke George, 1533 John 19:34; Titus 3:5.

[39] *What Luther Says*, I, p. 263. Matthew 24:4-7.

It is not God's will that anyone should be damned but that all men should turn themselves to Him and be saved forever...To this end, in His boundless kindness and mercy, God provides for the public proclamation of His divine, eternal law and the wonderful counsel concerning our redemption, namely, the holy and only saving Gospel of His eternal Son, our only Savior and Redeemer, Jesus Christ. Thereby He gathers an eternal church for Himself out of the human race and works in the hearts of men true repentance and knowledge of their sins and true faith in the Son of God, Jesus Christ. And it is God's will to call men to eternal salvation, to draw them to Himself, convert them, beget them anew, and sanctify them through this means and in no other way—namely, through His holy Word (when one hears it preached or reads it) and the Sacraments (when they are used according to His Word).[40]

To understand the Means of Grace properly, the doctrine can be sub-divided into elements for separate treatment, although they belong together and relate to one another:

1. The Holy Spirit is active through the Word.

2. The work of the Holy Spirit exclusively through the Means of Grace.

3. The Word active in baptismal regeneration.

4. The Word active in Holy Communion.

---

[40] Formula of Concord, Solid Declaration, Article II, Free Will, #50, Tappert, p. 530f.

To distinguish it from Christ as the Logos or Word of God, the proclaimed Word is sometimes called the external Word. Luther warned:

> From this it follows that they act foolishly, yea, against God's order and institution, who despise and reject the external Word, thinking that the Holy Spirit and faith should come to them without means. It will indeed be a long time before that happens.[41]

Another distinction might be Christ as the personal Word and the Scriptures as the written Word. Christ is God in the flesh, while the Scriptures are the revelation of what God has done. The Word of God is powerful by itself, without any need for improvement or protection by man, whether to make it attractive, germane, or reasonable. The Word of God can convert a person from unbelief to faith in Christ by being read, by being heard, by being remembered, and by the Sacrament of Holy Baptism. Luther taught:

> But here it is written [John 1:30-32] that when Christ was baptized, all three Persons of the Trinity were present--God the Father, God the Son, God the Holy Spirit...and that the heavens stood open, too. In fact, God the Father, Son, and Holy Spirit daily stand about and at the side of our own Baptism....For this

---

41 *What Luther Says*, II, p. 915.

reason we should highly esteem and honor Baptism and say: Baptism was not devised by any human being, but God instituted it; and it is not simple water, but God's Word is in it and with it, which makes of its water a washing of the soul and a washing of regeneration.[42]

The Word also continues its divine work in the life of the believer, by producing contrition and forgiveness of sin, by nurturing faith and motivating good works. The Word of God can never fail to bring about God's gracious will, as He promised in Isaiah:

Isaiah 55:10 For as the rain cometh down, and the snow from heaven, and returneth not thither, but watereth the earth, and maketh it bring forth and bud, that it may give seed to the sower, and bread to the eater: 11 So shall my word be that goeth forth out of my mouth: it shall not return unto me void, but it shall accomplish that which I please, and it shall prosper *in the thing* whereto I sent it.

Although this great passage is read in all denominations, people still stumble over its clear meaning and application: God's Word will always accomplish His will and never depends upon any human effort to improve it. Christians are to be faithful followers of the Messiah and remain in the Word the way a baby rests in the cradle. They are not expected to be slick salesmen with a sure-fire pitch and a dynamite close. The only thing that can detract from the Word of God is to add human opinion or to delete certain unfashionable doctrines, for then the Word of God is perverted to become the word of man, which dupes and deceives. Luther pointed out that the proclaimed or external Word is essential, because faith comes from hearing the Word (Romans 10:17) and not by making a decision.

The first and highest work of love a Christian ought to do when he has become a believer, is to bring others also to believe in the

---

[42]*What Luther Says*, I, p. 45. John 1:30-32.

way he himself came to believe. And here you notice Christ begins and institutes the office of the ministry of the external Word in every Christian; for He Himself came with this office and the external Word.[43]

The divine power of the Word is never absent, and our greatest comfort is that God accomplishes His will in us apart from any merit or worthiness. Taking away this power clearly meant giving to man the ability to make the Word effective or to make the correct decision about the Gospel, both of which are impossible and unscriptural, as Luther understood so well.

> It is ridiculous to want to deduce from passages such as this that power exists in us to convert ourselves to God without grace. For God gives to those to whom He communicates this Word of His the ability to believe the Word. The Word of God is not taught in vain and without bearing fruit, but the Holy Spirit is with the Word, and through the Word He moves hearts to believe.[44]

The divine power of the Word is clear in many passages of Scripture, none of which expects or demands human assistance. Christ taught the power of the external Word in creating eternal life when He said:

> John 6:63 It is the spirit that quickeneth [gives life]; the flesh profiteth nothing: the words that I speak unto you, *they* are spirit, and *they* are life.

St. Paul wrote that the Gospel itself contained divine power to create faith and offer salvation.

---

[43] *Sermons of Martin Luther*, II, p. 359. First Sunday after Easter, John 20:19-31.

[44] *What Luther Says, An Anthology*, I, p. 346. Isaiah 44:22.

Romans 1:16 For I am not ashamed of the gospel of Christ: for it is the power of God unto salvation to every one that believeth; to the Jew first, and also to the Greek.

St. Paul also wrote about the continuing power of the Word in sustaining faith:

1 Thessalonians 2:13 For this cause also thank we God without ceasing, because, when ye received the word of God which ye heard of us, ye received *it* not *as* the word of men, but as it is in truth, the word of God, which effectually worketh also in you that believe.

The author of Hebrews described the Word of God in a way which should give pause to anyone who thinks that popular programs, methods, and theories are the answer to a particular problem:

Hebrews 4:12 For the word of God *is* quick, and powerful, and sharper than any twoedged sword, piercing even to the dividing asunder of soul and spirit, and of the joints and marrow, and *is* a discerner of the thoughts and intents of the heart.

St. Peter taught his audience about being born again, not through a decision for Christ, but through the power of the Word:

1 Peter 1:23 Being born again, not of corruptible seed, but of incorruptible, by the word of God, which liveth and abideth for ever.

James urged his people to turn away from sin because of the Word planted in their hearts, the saving Word of the Gospel:

James 1:21 Wherefore lay apart all filthiness and superfluity of naughtiness, and receive with meekness the engrafted word, which is able to save your souls.

Throughout the Bible, we find consistent teaching that the proclamation of the Word accomplishes God's will through the power of the Holy Spirit.

The Holy Spirit and the Means of Grace

Protestants agree that teaching and preaching the Word of God is extremely important, but they reject the Lutheran understanding that the Holy Spirit works exclusively through the Means of Grace. Heinrich Schmid wrote about this distinction being a major difference between the Lutherans and the Protestants:

> The Lutheran theologians, in general, had reason to illustrate very particularly the doctrine of the operation of the Word of God, in order to oppose the Enthusiasts and Mystics, who held that the Holy Spirit operated rather irrespectively of the Word than through it; and to oppose also the Calvinists, who, led by their doctrine of predestination, would not grant that the Word possessed this power *per se*, but only in such cases where God chose....[45]

Although Protestantism takes on many forms, from the emphasis upon double predestination in Calvinism to the tongue-speaking of Pentecostalism, all Protestant groups teach an independent working of the Holy Spirit apart from the Means of Grace.

---

[45] Heinrich Schmid, *The Doctrinal Theology of the Evangelical Lutheran Church*, trans., Charles A. Hay, Henry E. Jacobs, Philadelphia: Lutheran Publication Society, 1889, p. 511. Hereafter cited as Schmid, *Doctrinal Theology*. "On the other side, we unanimously reject and condemn all the following errors...6. That bread and wine in the Holy Supper are no more than tokens whereby Christians recognize one another. 7. That the bread and wine are only figures, images, and types of the far-distant body and blood of Christ. 8. That the bread and wine are no more than reminders, seals, and pledges to assure us that when our faith ascends into heaven, it there partakes of the Body and Blood of Christ as truly as we eat and drink bread and wine in the Supper." [Tappert note – View of Calvin 1 Corinthians 11:23. C.R. 49:483] Formula of Concord, Epitome, Article VII, The Lord's Supper, Tappert, p. 485.

The term "Reformed" has therefore become a distinctive name and denotes all those church bodies which follow the theology and particularly the church practices of Zwingli and John Calvin. It is correct when Lutherans insist that there are three large groups of Christians: the Catholics, the Lutherans, and the Reformed.[46]

The Smalcald Articles of the *Book of Concord* state:

Accordingly, we should and must constantly maintain that God will not deal with us except through His external Word and Sacrament. Whatever is attributed to the Spirit apart from such Word and Sacrament is of the devil.[47]

The Formula of Concord is equally forceful:

Likewise, we reject and condemn the error of the Enthusiasts who imagine that God draws men to Himself, enlightens them, justifies them, and saves them without means, without the hearing of God's Word and without the use of the holy Sacraments.[48]

This was taught in the beginning among Lutherans, as stated in the Augsburg Confession, 1530:

It is also taught among us that man possesses some measure of freedom of the will which enables him to live an outwardly honorable life and to make choices among the things that reason comprehends. But without the grace, help, and activity of the

---

[46] F. E. Mayer, *American Churches, Beliefs and Practices*, St. Louis: Concordia Publishing House, 1946, p. 24.

[47] Smalcald Articles, Part III, Article VIII, Confession, Tappert, p. 313. This one statement alone repudiates the crafts and assaults of the Church Growth Movement.

[48] Formula of Concord, Epitome, Article II, Free Will, Tappert, p. 471. Tappert note: "A marginal note at this point reads: 'Enthusiasts is the term for people who expect the Spirit's heavenly illumination without the preaching of God's Word.'"

Holy Spirit man is not capable of making himself acceptable to God, of fearing God and believing in God with his whole heart, or of expelling inborn evil lusts from his heart. This is accomplished by the Holy Spirit, who is given through the Word of God, for Paul says in 1 Corinthians 2:14, "Natural man does not receive the gifts of the Spirit of God."[49]

An interesting variation upon this doctrine is found in a Catholic dictionary, which states that God's grace comes to people:

> ...immediately ("No man cometh to me, except the Father...draw him, " John 6:44), or mediately, on the occasion of a reading of Scripture or the hearing of a sermon, from a joy or sorrow, a dream, a sunset, or a song.[50]

Lutherans, as stated before, teach that God's grace comes only through the Word and Sacraments, never through a dream nor a sunset.

The Protestant view of the work of the Holy Spirit is derived from Zwingli and Calvin. Zwingli did not accept the teaching that God works through the Sacraments:

> Zwingli said, "I believe, yea I know, that all the Sacraments are so far from conferring grace that they do not even convey or distribute it. In this, most powerful Emperor, I may perhaps appear too bold to thee. But I am firmly convinced that I am right. For as grace is produced or given by the divine Spirit (I am using the term 'grace' in its Latin meaning of pardon, indulgence, gracious favor), so this gift reaches only the spirit. The Spirit, however, needs no guide or vehicle, for He Himself is the Power and Energy by which all things are borne and has no need of being borne. Nor have we ever read in the Holy Scriptures that

---

[49] Augsburg Confession, Article XVIII, Freedom of the Will, *Ibid.*, p. 39. The passage cites Augustine, *Hypognosticon contra Palaginos*.

[50] "Grace, Actual," in *A Catholic Dictionary*, ed. Donald Attwater, New York: Macmillan Company, 1949, p. 216.

perceptible things like the Sacraments certainly bring with them the Spirit.[51]

Zwingli and Calvin both taught that the Sacraments were symbolic, not able to confer forgiveness through the Word and Holy Spirit, but mere ordinances to be obeyed as a seal of one's faith. Thus, for Zwingli and Calvin, the Sacraments were not God's work for man, but man's work for God. Calvin, not unlike Zwingli, wrote of the Sacraments being offered without effect because of the lack of the Holy Spirit.

> If the Spirit be lacking, the sacraments can accomplish nothing more in our minds than the splendor of the sun shining upon blind eyes, or a voice sounding in deaf ears.[52]

Such passages from the Reformed, which can be reproduced by the hundreds, illustrate why C. F. W. Walther saw in their scorn a profound confusion about how people come to faith.

> Observe, then, the depreciative, contemptuous, and scorning ring in the words of the Reformed when they speak of the sacred Means of Grace, the Word and the Sacraments, and the grand majestic ring in the words of the Lord and the apostles when they speak of these matters...The true reason for the Reformed view is this: They do not know how a person is to come into possession of the divine grace, the forgiveness of sin, righteousness in the sight of God, and eternal salvation. Spurning the way which God has appointed, they are pointing another way, in accordance with new devices which they have invented.[53]

---

51 *Fidei Ratio*, ed. Niemeyer p. 24; Jacobs, *Book of Concord*, II, 68). Quoted in Francis Pieper, *Christian Dogmatics*, III, p. 132f.

52 John Calvin, *Institutes*, IV, xiv, 9. Quoted in Benjamin Milner, *Calvin's Doctrine of the Church*, Heicko A.Oberman, Leiden: E. J. Brill, 1970, p. 119.

53 C. F. W. Walther, *The Proper Distinction Between Law and Gospel*, trans., W. H. T. Dau, St. Louis: Concordia Publishing House, 1928, p. 152f

The result of Protestant teaching against the work of the Holy Spirit in the Means of Grace is a universal uncertainty that may be found in each Reformed sect, coupled with a new, man-made Sacrament promising to supply the confidence lacking in the Word and Sacraments. The clearest examples are: tongue-speaking of the Pentecostals, which proves to them that they are indeed Spirit-filled Christians; the cell, prayer, *koinonia* or affinity groups of the Pietists, which offer a visible Church they can distinguish from those who only worship on Sunday; and the political lobbies of mainline Christians, who thereby know God's Word is effective because society is being changed by their concerted efforts through the law.

To some, the Lutheran doctrine of the Means of Grace seems to limit God, by tying the work of the Holy Spirit to the Word and Sacraments. But, in fact, the Protestant rejection of the Means of Grace makes one doubt the effectiveness of preaching, teaching, and administering the Sacraments. From the Protestant point of view, one is never completely sure when God in His sovereignty will be present to work His will. Both minister and laity are left in doubt about salvation and the means by which salvation is received. One of the great Lutheran writers of the last century, Herman Sasse, noted this about Karl Barth, the Swiss Protestant theologian admired by liberals and Fuller Seminary:

> The means of grace are thus limited for Barth. The preacher descending from the pulpit can never quote Luther and say with joyful assurance that he has preached the Word of God. Of course, he can hope and pray; but he can never know whether the Holy Spirit has accompanied the preached Word, and hence whether his words were the Word of God. To know this, or even to wish to know it, would be a presumptuous encroachment of man upon the sovereign freedom of God.[54]

Barth has had a powerful, destructive influence on Christianity in America. Known for his Marxism and adultery, Barth and his live-in mistress, Charlotte Kirschbaum, wrote the *Church Dogmatics*. His theology

---

[54] Hermann Sasse, *Here We Stand*, trans. Theodore G. Tappert, Minneapolis: Augsburg Publishing House, 1946, p. 161. George Hunsinger dealt with Barth's Marxism in *Karl Barth and Radical Politics*, Westminster Press, 1976. Eberhard Busch discussed Barth's adultery in *Karl Barth: His Life from Letters and Autobiographical Texts*, translated by John Bowden, Philadelphia: Fortress Press, 1975.

profoundly influenced one of the key figures at Fuller Seminary, leading to the repudiation of inerrancy at the school. Recruiting the leadership of all the denominations (Catholic, Protestant, *and* Lutheran), Fuller imbued church executives with a business marketing model based on numbers rather than fidelity to Scriptures or any confession. From this spiritual adultery has come dozens of examples of the more commonplace variety.

Since nothing is certain for the Reformed, one must offer a standard by which the fruits of faith are judged. Since the objective means are rejected, one must have a subjective standard. That explains the peculiar emphasis upon knowing the date of one's conversion and identifying the born-again experience among many Protestants. Beyond this level—an even higher level of uncertainty—is the necessity of being baptized by the Holy Spirit and speaking in tongues, instead of realizing that there is only one baptism (Ephesians 4:5) and the Holy Spirit is always at work through the appointed Means of Grace. As Hoenecke wrote, "The Holy Spirit never without the Scripture, the Scripture never without the Holy Spirit – that is sound doctrine."[55]

The Word Active in Baptism

The Scriptures teach us that Holy Baptism is one of the most important aids given by God to Christians in their life of grace. Christ commanded baptism, but the Scriptures do not teach the absolute necessity of baptism. Instead, the Bible teaches that unbelief condemns, that we are justified by faith. The thief on the cross believed in Christ and received the promise of eternal life without being baptized. That event does not make Holy Baptism a mere symbol or an ordinance.

Protestant objections to baptism are threefold:

1. Baptism is an ordinance rather than a Sacrament and does not offer forgiveness of sin; baptismal regeneration (rebirth) is considered a Roman Catholic heresy.

2. Baptism is limited to adults who can make a decision for Christ (believers' baptism); related to this is the claim that infants should not be baptized and were not baptized in the New Testament. Infants cannot have faith in God. This claim is made by Baptists,

---

[55] *Dogmatik*, IV, p. 17.

Mennonites, and Pentecostals, all groups related to the Radical Reformation, which parted company with Zwingli and Calvin.

3. Water baptism is not sufficient; one must also have a born-again experience (Evangelicals) or experience baptism in the Holy Spirit (Pentecostals), accompanied by speaking in tongues.

Biblical Answers to Objections

The fundamental objection, which is related to rejection of the Holy Spirit active in the Word, is that baptism itself does not do anything. Lutherans see in the Scriptures a clear portrayal of God at work in baptism, the Word serving as the active power of God, the instrument of His Holy Spirit. Luther compared the Sacraments to an iron glowing with heat, able to ignite an object, not with the iron, but with the energy of the heat active in the iron.

> One must not make the sweeping assertion: God is not worshiped by anything external. Therefore we should not ridicule all things that are external in the worship of God. For when God speaks about a splinter, His Word makes the splinter as important as the sun. It is, therefore, profane language to say that the water of Baptism is only water; for the water of Baptism has the Word added to it. Therefore it is like a glowing or fiery iron, which is as truly fire as it is iron and does all that fire usually does. But only the pious see and appreciate the Word in the water; a cow or a dog sees only water.[56]

In the same way, the Word is present in Holy Baptism, carrying out God's will, so that we see the water but also the effect of the Holy Spirit.

One Protestant objection is that God does not need to use means or instruments, which is true, as Luther observed. God can save the world in an instant without the Means of Grace. But God has chosen to use these appointed means and revealed them to us through the Scriptures, which we are not to despise or alter to suit our personal philosophies. Matthias Loy, an American Lutheran hymn writer and

---

[56] *What Luther Says*, I, p. 45. Psalm 122:3.

leader of the Ohio Synod (American Lutheran Church, now part of the Evangelical Lutheran Church in America) wrote in his book of sermons:

> The Christian's faith trusts in the ordinary means. Prayer is not a means of grace. Means of grace are divine appointments through which God uniformly offers blessings to all who use them. Faith is the means by which the blessings are received and appropriated. God gives us bread, when we ask it, not through the channel of prayer, but through the ordinary channels of His providence. He gives us grace when we ask it, not through prayer, but through the ordinary means appointed for this end, namely the Word and Sacraments. He who despises these will as little have grace as he who refuses to accept bread produced in the ordinary way of nature. Faith asks with confidence, and trusts in the ordinary means of God's appointment for the blessings asked.[57]

If Holy Baptism does not accomplish anything through the power of the Holy Spirit, we have to explain why the Scriptures teach otherwise. If the apostles did not believe that baptism accomplished God's will and removed sin, then it is puzzling that Luke recorded this about Paul's conversion:

> Acts 22:16 [Ananias said] "And now why tarriest thou? arise, and be baptized, and wash away thy sins, calling on the name of the Lord."

Being born again (regeneration) is accomplished through baptism, according to St. Paul:

> Titus 3:4 But after that the kindness and love of God our Saviour toward man appeared, 5 Not by works of righteousness which we have done, but according to his mercy he saved us, by the washing of regeneration, and renewing of the Holy Ghost; 6 Which he shed on us abundantly through Jesus Christ our

---

[57] Matthias Loy, *Sermons on the Gospels*, Columbus: Lutheran Book Concern, 1888, p. 387.

Saviour; 7 That being justified by his grace, we should be made heirs according to the hope of eternal life.

If someone objects that the washing mentioned in the above passage is not baptism, one must ask about the washing that is baptism in St. Paul's own autobiography in Acts 22. One of the apostle's threefold associations, reminding us of the Trinity's work, reveals God's activity. The Word of God has the power to remove sin (Holy Baptism), to declare them innocent through faith (justification) and to make them holy (sanctification).

> 1 Corinthians 6:11 And such were some of you: but ye are washed, but ye are sanctified, but ye are justified in the name of the Lord Jesus, and by the Spirit of our God.

St. Paul's point here is to declare that some Corinthian members had been fornicators, idolaters, adulterers, pedophiles, thieves, and drunkards, but gave up their sinful ways when they received the implanted Word. For adults, faith comes through hearing the Word and Holy Baptism seals God's covenant with the believer, so that a visible sign of His invisible grace always comforts the believer with the knowledge that the Holy Spirit dwells in him. Therefore, St. Paul urged the Corinthians not to fall back into their evil ways, using the objective fact of their baptism, justification, and sanctification by the Holy Spirit as Gospel motivation. Similarly, the command that husbands love their wives is joined with the proclamation of Christ's love for the Church and the work of the Holy Spirit in the Church through the Means of Grace:

> Ephesians 5:25 Husbands, love your wives, even as Christ also loved the church, and gave himself for it; 26 That he might sanctify and cleanse it with the washing of water by the word, 27 That he might present it to himself a glorious church, not having spot, or wrinkle, or any such thing; but that it should be holy and without blemish.

Consequently, we must conclude that Holy Baptism does accomplish God's will, as Isaiah 55 promises, and must have the power of the Holy

Spirit to do this. Jesus Himself taught that to be born again means being born of water and Spirit. The Greek text in John 3:5 connects water and Spirit through a construction called anarthrous, which means without the article – the. Lenski wrote:

> The absence of the Greek articles with the two nouns makes their unity more apparent.[58]

The original text makes it impossible to separate water baptism from Holy Spirit baptism.

> John 3:5 Jesus answered, Verily, verily, I say unto thee, Except a man be born of water and *of* the Spirit, he cannot enter into the kingdom of God. (KJV)
>
> Unless a man is water-Spirit born...(author's literal translation)

Jesus' admonition, "You must be born again," does not teach the necessity of an adult conversion experience, but the importance of Holy Baptism as a Sacrament, the work of the Holy Spirit. The Word is the divine element in conversion, so we should not allow the proper emphasis upon faith to detract from the significance of baptism, since lack of faith—not lack of baptism—condemns.

Infant Faith

Another fatal trap for Protestants is the issue of whether infants should be baptized, whether infants can believe in God. Those who question infant baptism are descended from the followers of Zwingli (Blaurock, Grebel, and others) who began to teach believer's or adult baptism and were dubbed Anabaptists (rebaptizers, a term which they rejected), since they did not accept infant baptism as valid.[59] This controversy erupted during the Reformation and separated the Anabaptists from the Swiss Protestant Reformation. Felix Mantz was

---

[58] R. C. H. Lenski, *The Interpretation of John*, Columbus: Lutheran Book Concern, 1931, p. 229.

[59] Hans J. Hillerbrand, *The Reformation, A Narrative History Related by Contemporary Observers and Participants*, New York: Harper and Row, 1964, p. 217, 234. Hereafter cited as Hillerbrand.

ordered drowned by the Zurich city council for advocating believer's baptism. Blaurock was banished from the city on the same day, January 5, 1527. The Lutherans were also attacked for teaching baptismal regeneration and infant baptism.

One claim made by opponents of infant baptism is that infants cannot believe, an error easily rebutted by Scripture. The Psalmist wrote:

> Psalm 22:9 But thou *art* he that took me out of the womb: thou didst make me hope *when I was* upon my mother's breasts. 10 I was cast upon thee from the womb: thou *art* my God from my mother's belly. (KJV)

The favorite Bible of the Protestants, the New International Version, has this reading:

> Psalm 22:9 Yet you brought me out of the womb; you made me trust in you even at my mother's breast. 10 From birth I was cast upon you; from my mother's womb you have been my God. (NIV)

Even more importantly, a certain type of faith was commended by Jesus when the disciples tried to keep small children from their Master.

> Mark 10:14 But when Jesus saw *it*, he was much displeased, and said unto them, Suffer the little children to come unto me, and forbid them not: for of such is the kingdom of God. 15 Verily I say unto you, Whosoever shall not receive the kingdom of God as a little child, he shall not enter therein. 16 And he took them up in his arms, put *his* hands upon them, and blessed them.

> Mark 9:37 Whosoever shall receive one of such children in my name, receiveth me: and whosoever shall receive me, receiveth not me, but him that sent me.

The Greek words for preventing (forbid them not) and welcoming (whoever shall receive one) are also used in other passages in connection with removing people from the Church and welcoming them as members.[60]

> Matthew 18:1 At the same time came the disciples unto Jesus, saying, Who is the greatest in the kingdom of heaven? 2 And Jesus called a little child unto him, and set him in the midst of them, 3 And said, Verily I say unto you, Except ye be converted, and become as little children, ye shall not enter into the kingdom of heaven. 4 Whosoever therefore shall humble himself as this little child, the same is greatest in the kingdom of heaven. 5 And whoso shall receive one such little child in my name receiveth me.

We are forced to ask, "If children cannot believe, then why are adults supposed to have a child-like faith, which is identified by Christ as saving faith?" St. Matthew records:

> Matthew 11:25 At that time Jesus answered and said, I thank thee, O Father, Lord of heaven and earth, because thou hast hid these things from the wise and prudent, and hast revealed them unto babes.

Although the use of babes in this passage is symbolic, the term points once again to the ideal of child-like faith, which is supposed to be impossible for those who oppose infant baptism. Children in the crowd praised Jesus as He entered Jerusalem, irritating the scribes and chief priests:

> Matthew 21:16 And said unto him, Hearest thou what these say? And Jesus saith unto them, Yea; have ye never read, Out of the mouth of babes and sucklings thou hast perfected praise?

---

[60] Oscar Cullman, *Baptism in the New Testament*, London: SCM Press, 1950, pp. 71-80. Edmund Schlink, *The Doctrine of Baptism*, trans. J. A. Bauman, St. Louis: Concordia Publishing House, 1972.

Psalm 8:2 Out of the mouth of babes and sucklings hast thou ordained strength because of thine enemies, that thou mightest still the enemy and the avenger.

A nursing child (suckling) is a tiny baby, so the Apostolic Church had no reason to exclude babies from Holy Baptism. The unborn baby John leaped in his mother's womb at the presence of Christ:

Luke 1:41 And it came to pass, that, when Elisabeth heard the salutation of Mary, the babe leaped in her womb; and Elisabeth was filled with the Holy Ghost:

In spite of overwhelming evidence that children and babies were included as believers in Christ in the New Testament, advocates of adult (believer's) baptism claim that children were not baptized in the New Testament. This claim did not arise until 15 centuries after Christ. To be sure, the New Testament does not describe the baptism of infants by themselves, but it does have many passages about the baptism of adults and groups of people, whole families or households. The question, then, is whether infants were **excluded** from baptism in all these passages, an exclusion never mentioned in the Bible nor by any Church father.

Acts 16:15 And when she was baptized, and her household, she besought *us*, saying, If ye have judged me to be faithful to the Lord, come into my house, and abide *there*. And she constrained us.

Acts 16:33 And he took them the same hour of the night, and washed *their* stripes; and was baptized, he and all his, straightway.

St. Luke, who wrote Acts, was a careful chronicler of history, as recent archeological finds have shown, and not one to mix things up. If children were excluded from the household being baptized in one passage, and he remained silent, it might be passed off as irrelevant to the context. However, three separate failures to inform the Church would be simply inexcusable. As a result, it is utterly consistent to conclude that children were never excluded from Holy Baptism until soon after the Zwinglians decided that baptism was only an ordinance. Then some of Zwingli's followers took his doctrine to its logical conclusion and made faith a requirement for an ordinance that did not matter, their rebellion leading some to be drowned in the tragic persecution following the break.

Advocates of adult or believer's baptism do not want early Church history to be invoked in favor of infant baptism, reckoning that the Church soon became apostate (or Roman Catholic) after the Apostolic Age. Some have theorized that when the Christian Church became part of society, requirements for membership were softened and children were baptized as part of a societal appropriation of Christianity. If theories must be proposed, then the data of history should reflect the truth of the explanation. In *The History of Infant Baptism*, Dr. W. Wall (1675-1775) copied the patristic texts in Greek and Latin, translated them, and discussed their support of infant baptism.[61] He found infant baptism taught by such Church fathers as: Justine Martyr (100-166), Irenaeus (ca. 115-177), Cyprian (200-258), St. Ambrose (340-397), Chrysostom (ca. 345-407), and many others, including Tertullian (ca. 150-ca.220), whose peculiar views included the idea that baptism should be delayed until a later age. Far from making a case against infant baptism, Tertullian's notion proves that it was the norm at his time to baptize infants. The extensive group of witnesses to infant baptism, their leadership at the beginning of the Church, and the amount of their writing on the subject may explain why Protestants do not want patristic evidence cited in favor of infant baptism. Considering the uproar caused by the many schisms and heresies within the early Church, it is odd to conclude that the Christ-taught apostles baptized only adults and that their followers at some point began a new practice and changed this Sacrament without a whisper of protest in the voluminous documents of the early Church, which we may study today in Latin, Greek, and English.

---

[61] Pieper, *Christian Dogmatics*, III, p. 163. "But according to the teaching of Calvinism this 'inner illumination' is not brought about through the Means of Grace; it is worked immediately by the Holy Ghost. Modern Reformed, too, teach this very emphatically. Hodge, for example, says: 'In the work of regeneration all second causes are excluded...Nothing intervenes between the volition of the Spirit and the regeneration of the soul...The infusion of a new life into the soul is the immediate work of the Sprit...The truth (in the case of adults) [that is, the setting forth of the truth of the Gospel through the external Word] attends the work of regeneration, but is not the means by which it is effected." [Hodge, *Systematic Theology*, II, 634f. Pieper, *Christian Dogmatics*, III, p. 120

By subjecting the Sacraments to rationalistic analysis, which balks at the mysterious work of God, the Protestants remove the assurance that is given through them, the declaration of forgiveness and the certainty of salvation.

> Thus Calvin, as we saw, cautions against seeking to discern one's election from the universal call, that is, from the Word of the Gospel (Institutes, III, 24, 8). Likewise the Consensus Tigurinus (c. 20) warns against the thought that the 'visible sign [the Sacraments], in the same moment when it is being offered, brings with it the grace of God' (Niemeyer, p. 195). The Geneva Catechism, too, enjoins ['De Sacramentis'], that salvation must not be sought in the visible signs.[62]

In contrast, Luther exalted the Sacrament of Holy Baptism:

> Thus we see what a very splendid thing Baptism is. It snatches us from the jaws of the devil, makes us God's own, restrains and removes sin, and then daily strengthens the new man within us. It is and remains ever efficacious until we pass from this state of misery to eternal glory. For this reason everyone should consider his Baptism as his daily dress, to be worn constantly. Every day he should be found in the faith and its fruits, suppressing the old man, and growing up in the new; for if we want to be Christians, we must practice the work whereby we are Christians. But if anyone falls from baptismal grace, let him return to it. For as Christ, the Mercy Seat, does not withdraw from us or forbid us to

---

[62] Francis Pieper, *Christian Dogmatics*, III, p. 145.

come to Him again even though we sin, so all His treasures and gifts also remain with us.[63]

Instead of doubting infant baptism, Luther praised the Sacrament as more trustworthy than adult baptism:

> I still maintain, as I have maintained in the *Postil* (SL 11, 496f.) that the surest Baptism is infant Baptism. For an old person may deceive, may come to Christ as a Judas and permit himself to be baptized. But a child cannot deceive. It comes to Christ in Baptism as John came to Him and as the little children were brought to Him, that His Word and work may come over them, touch them, and thus make them holy. For His Word and work cannot pass by without effect; and in Baptism they are directed at the child alone. If they were to fail of success here, they would have to be entire failures and useless means, which is impossible.[64]

A common objection of Protestants is that Lutherans think baptism alone is sufficient for salvation, making Lutherans lax in worship and the Christian life. No one can appeal to Luther to support such a mechanistic view of Holy Baptism, for he challenged it:

> To be sure, Baptism is so great that if you turn from sins and appeal to the covenant of Baptism, your sins are forgiven. Only see to it--if you sin in this wicked and wanton manner by presuming on God's grace--that the judgment does not lay hold of you and forestall your turning back. And even if you then wanted to believe and trust in your Baptism, your trial might by God's decree, be so great that faith could not stand the strain. If they scarcely remain in the faith who do no sin or who fall because of sheer weakness, where will your brazen wickedness remain, which has challenged and mocked God's grace? Let us, therefore, walk with care and fear that we may hold fast the riches of God's grace with a firm faith and joyfully give thanks to His mercy forever and ever. Amen.[65]

---

[63] *What Luther Says*, I, p. 61. Article on baptism, 1529.

[64] *Ibid.* Letter to two ministers, 1528

[65] *Ibid.* p. 57. Treatise on Baptism, 1519

Consequently, we must look to the power of God in the Word to accomplish His will, planting faith in the infant's heart, blessing the child just as surely as if the minister were Christ, who held small children tenderly in His arms, blessed them, and said – "To such children belong the Kingdom of Heaven." The pastor speaks for Christ and acts on His behalf. We should not dig in our heels and object that small children lack reason, since reason is not a component of faith—better translated as trust—and since reason actively rebels against faith.[66]

After mustering their best arguments to explain away the clear doctrine of the Bible ("Baptism now saves you," 1 Peter 3:21), and after ignoring the testimony of the Church fathers and 15 centuries of practice, the opponents of infant baptism defeat their own case by the widespread dedication of infants at their own worship services. In these dedication ceremonies, prayers are offered, Scriptures are read, and the parents promise to bring their children to church and teach them the Word of God. One proponent of infant dedication, Carl F. Henry, claimed in *Christianity Today* that it stayed with children all their lives.[67] Although Baptists avoid water, which is the visible sign of baptism, and do not want to claim infant dedication as baptism, those who dedicate infants are undoubtedly imitating the Sacrament of Holy Baptism.

---

[66] *Ibid.*, p. 51.

[67] *Christianity Today*, ca 1986.

The Lord's Supper

The Sacrament of Holy Communion is another area of division between Protestants and Lutherans. When altar fellowship (inter-communion) is discussed among liberal Lutherans and the Reformed, it is always on the basis of Lutherans retreating from their historic position, as shown by the ELCA-Reformed talks.[68] Protestants teach that the Lord's Supper is symbolic, an ordinance, which does not offer forgiveness or the Body and Blood of Christ. Those who follow the doctrines of John Calvin will allow for the spiritual presence of Christ, as the Episcopalians and Methodists do, but they do not accept the Word of Christ, "This is My Body." Their objection to the Real Presence of the Body and Blood of Christ is derived from a philosophical opinion of Calvin, called the *extra calvinisticum.*

Finitum non capax infiniti – the finite cannot contain the Infinite.[69]

Protestant objections to the Real Presence are rationalistic and relate to their problems with the relationship between the Two Natures of Christ.

---

[68] *Christian News*, "Lutherans, Reformed Propose Full Communion," March 23, 1992, p. 1. The American Lutheran Church voted for inter-communion with Reformed before the 1987 merger that created the Evangelical Lutheran Church in America. Faculty of the ALC seminary in Dubuque, Iowa held a joint communion service with the faculty of the local Reformed seminary.

[69] Herman Sasse, *This Is My Body, Luther's Contention for the Real Presence in the Sacrament of the Altar,* Adelaide: Lutheran Publishing House, 1959, p. 122. Hereafter cited as Sasse, *This Is My Body.*

Furthermore, consider this: All doctrines of the Bible are connected with one another; they form a unit. One error draws others in after it. Zwingli's first error was the denial of the presence of Christ's body and blood in the Lord's Supper. In order to support this error, he had to invent a false doctrine of Christ's Person, of heaven, of the right hand of God, etc.[70]

The Protestant objections to the Real Presence are:

1. How can Christ's Body and Blood be present in the elements of Holy Communion when Christ is seated in heaven?

2. How can Christ offer His Body to the world for ages to come?

3. How can forgiveness be received through the Lord's Supper?

Real Presence

Lutherans use the term Real Presence to distinguish between the actual promise of Christ and the Protestant view, which limits Him to a spiritual presence only. Some people would claim a difference between the crude rationalism of Zwingli and the eloquent rationalism of Calvin, but the fundamental issues remain the same, as Pieper stated:

> In fact, there is no basis for a real disagreement between Zwingli and Calvin. The situation here is analogous to the one that obtains in the doctrine of Christ's Person and Word and the doctrine of the Lord's Supper. In these doctrines Zwingli and Calvin and all Reformed will agree as long as they all teach that Christ's body can possess only a local and visible mode of subsistence or presence. Similarly, Zwingli and Calvin cannot differ materially in their teaching on the means of grace because they agree, first, that Christ's merit and saving grace do not apply to all who use the means of grace; secondly, that saving grace is not bound to the means of grace.[71]

---

[70] Francis Pieper, *The Difference between Orthodox and Heterodox Churches, and Supplement*, Coos Bay, Oregon: St. Paul's Lutheran Church, 1981, p. 41.

[71] Pieper, *Christian Dogmatics*, III, p. 163.

The final result of a rationalistic treatment of the Sacraments is a minister, a denomination, and a country turning from the truth of the Bible to Unitarianism, or to use the Reformation term, Socinianism. Krauth wrote about the effect of rationalism:

> ...It is exceedingly difficult to prevent this low view from running out into Socinianism, as, indeed, it actually has run in Calvinistic lands, so that it became a proverb, often met with in the older theological writers—"A young Calvinist, an old Socinian." This peril is confessed and mourned over by great Calvinistic divines. New England is an illustration of it on an immense scale, in our own land.[72]

The problem that Krauth complained about comes from the use of reason with the Word, instead of making reason subordinate to the Word.

> When intent upon establishing their peculiar tenets, Calvin and Zwingli likewise preferred rational argumentation to the plain proofs of Holy Writ. Their interpretation of the words of the Sacrament is but one glaring instance; but there are many more. The schools and the denominations which they founded became infected with this same disease of theology.[73]

If one stumbles at Christ in the elements of bread of wine, one will also ultimately reject God becoming man, which is another case of the finite containing the infinite, in defiance of the *extra calvinisticum*.

---

[72] Charles P. Krauth, *The Conservative Reformation and Its Theology*, Philadelphia: The United Lutheran Publication House, 1871, p. 489.

[73] Martin S. Sommer, *Concordia Pulpit for 1932*, Martin S. Sommer, St. Louis: Concordia Publishing House, 1931, p. iii.

Biblical Testimonies

The Lord's Supper was instituted by Christ on the night in which He was betrayed.

> Matthew 26:26 And as they were eating, Jesus took bread, and blessed *it*, and brake *it*, and gave *it* to the disciples, and said, Take, eat; this is my body. (Parallels – Mark 14:22; Luke 22:19)

The Lord's Supper was handed down to St. Paul, who showed how important the Sacrament was by repeating the Words of Institution and by recalling how he received it from Christ:

> 1 Corinthians 11:23 For I have received of the Lord that which also I delivered unto you, That the Lord Jesus the *same* night in which he was betrayed took bread: 24 And when he had given thanks, he brake *it*, and said, Take, eat: this is my body, which is broken for you: this do in remembrance of me. 25 After the same manner also *he took* the cup, when he had supped, saying, This cup is the new testament in my blood: this do ye, as oft as ye drink *it*, in remembrance of me. 26 For as often as ye eat this bread, and drink this cup, ye do shew the Lord's death till he come. 27 Wherefore whosoever shall eat this bread, and drink *this* cup of the Lord, unworthily, shall be guilty of the body and blood of the Lord.

St. Paul's description answers a number of significant questions. Holy Communion, like Holy Baptism, which the Apostle mentions often in his letters, is a major emphasis of the Church. Both reveal the power of the Holy Spirit working through the Word. The context of Paul's lesson is the abuse of the Agape feast among the Corinthians, which led to the improper and impious use of the Sacrament. Therefore, St. Paul contrasted their gluttony and drunkenness with what he received from Christ (whether through direct revelation or through the Apostles), showing how significant their sins were in this regard. The Lord's Supper could not have been merely symbolic or it would have mattered little that some who were poor came to the meal and did not receive the Lord's Supper. Those who equate coffee and doughnuts at church with Holy

Communion would miss the point here. Eating food with someone is not the same as receiving the Body of Christ.

Although each passage about Holy Communion destroys the notion that the Body and Blood are symbolic, St. Paul especially emphasizes in 1 Corinthians 11:27 that unworthy eating and drinking is a sin against the Body and Blood of Christ. The language employed by the Scriptures teaches us what Holy Communion means. Jesus and St. Paul both speak of the loaf and eating the Body, the cup and drinking the Blood. As a result, the two elements of bread and wine do not stop being what they are, but the Body and Blood of Christ are also present through the power of the Word in the consecration. Briefly, Lutherans teach that the two (bread and wine) become four (bread and wine along with the Body and Blood). Protestants teach that the two (bread and wine) remain two. Roman Catholics teach that the two (bread and wine) become two (Body and Blood). For Roman Catholics, the substance of the bread and wine change forever into the Body and Blood of Christ, although the appearance remains the same.

In another passage, 1 Corinthians 10:16, St. Paul teaches clearly that the earthly elements of wine and bread are the means by which we commune with Christ.

> 1 Corinthians 10:16 The cup of blessing which we bless, is it not the communion of the blood of Christ? The bread which we break, is it not the communion of the body of Christ?[74] (Lenski translation)

The Greek word of communion in this passage is *koinonia*, which has been debased in English to represent social groups and cell groups. The original use is exactly what people mean when they speak of communing with nature that is, becoming one with nature and receiving the blessings of that experience. Lenski calls *koinonia*

> ...an actual and a real participation in the blood of Christ, i.e., the blood shed on the cross for the remission of our sins. If either

---

[74] R. C. H. Lenski, *The Interpretation of St. Paul's First and Second Epistles to the Corinthians*, Columbus: Lutheran Book Concern, 1937, p. 407.

the wine of the cup or the blood of Christ is unreal, then a "communion" between them is also unreal, i.e., none exists.[75]

The *Stealthy Is* Argument

Another rationalism related to this issue concerns Christ speaking the words, "This is My Body." Some claim He used Aramaic, which does not have a word for *is* and therefore might have meant, "This symbolizes My Body." The concrete facts are at war with this speculation, since we have the original text in Greek, not Aramaic. We have no evidence that Christ instituted the Lord's Supper in Aramaic, only to have the Words of Institution mistranslated in Greek, a decided lapse by the Holy Spirit. Thus the *stealthy is* argument rests on an unwarranted assumption, that the Holy Spirit revealed a version of the Last Supper in Greek that differed from the actual event.

The Two Natures

If we only had these passages about Holy Communion to rely on, we could still be certain that the consecrated bread and wine also contain the Body and Blood of Christ. Other passages confirm that the Real Presence is truly part of God's plan. When Christ appeared in a locked room before His disciples, and showed them His glorified body, He revealed again that His divine nature could not be limited by His human nature. He was present bodily, with wounds that could be touched (John 20:19-30). Previously, He escaped miraculously through crowds surrounding Him and meaning to do Him harm: Luke 4:28-30, John 8:58-59. The empty tomb—revealed to the frightened soldiers—showed them that the Son of God rose from the dead and left the sealed stone tomb without needing someone to roll the stone away. The angel removed the stone to show that the grave could not contain the body of the crucified Messiah (Matthew 28:2-5).

We think of tangible objects as being limited, since we live with physical limitations, so the ceaseless offering of the Body and Blood of Christ seems impossible to human reason, although nothing is impossible with God. The Feeding of the Five Thousand (Mark 6:30ff.) proves that God can take tangible objects and multiply them beyond our reason's

---

[75] *Ibid.*, p. 409.

ability to comprehend, to provide such a miraculous abundance that the leftovers are far greater than the original offering of food. The miraculous feeding has been explained away by many rationalists, who cannot abide the miracles of God, but must turn them into easily understood quirks, showing once again man's ability to transform the clearest truth into the foulest error. The Feeding of the Five Thousand comforts us with the knowledge that God can do what He promises. We see how He challenges us beyond the limits of our reason, so that we trust in Him the way a small child trusts that his father is both loving and strong. If a young boy can put so much trust in his earthly father, who has so many failings, how much more can we trust in our Heavenly Father, Who is perfect, omniscient, and steadfast in His love for each one of us?

Forgiveness

The Sacramental nature of Holy Communion is revealed in the words "given and shed for you, for the remission of sins." Forgiveness can only come from God through the Blood of Christ Jesus. Man, obeying an ordinance, does not earn forgiveness, but God, through this Sacrament, offers it to those who are able to discern the Body and receive it in faith. Thus Luther taught in his Small Catechism that outward preparation for communion may be beneficial, but the most important preparation is having a heart that believes the words "given for you for the forgiveness of sins." Ignatius, an early Church father, called the Eucharist:

> ...a medicine of immortality, an antidote, that we may not die but live in God through Jesus Christ, a cleansing remedy through warding off and driving out evils.[76]

St. Bernard (1090-1153) said:

> The body of Christ is to the sick a medicine, to pilgrims a way; it strengthens the weak, delights the strong, heals weariness, preserves health. Through it man becomes more gentle under

---

[76] *Examination*, II, p. 234.

reproof, more patient under labor, more ardent for love, wiser for caution, more ready to obey, more devoted to giving of thanks.[77]

Chrysostom did not doubt the value of Holy Communion or its divine effects, but wrote:

> If those who touched the hem of His garment were properly healed, how much more shall we be strengthened if we have Him in us whole? He will quiet in us the savage law of our members, He will quench the perturbations of the mind, drive out all sicknesses, raise us up from every fall, and, when the power of the enemy has been overcome, He will incite us to true piety and indeed will transform us into His own image.[78]

Indeed, almost unlimited are the citations from the Church fathers to support the Real Presence of Christ's Body and Blood, the forgiveness of sin offered in Holy Communion. Even if that were not so, the truth of God's work through the Sacraments would be established by His Word:

> The devil is always plaguing the world by keeping people from distinguishing between the work of God and the work of men....But you should know that though no human being believed Baptism and the Gospel, the Gospel and Baptism would still be right; for both are not mine but God's Word and work.[79]

The Swiss Reformation was a departure from a consistent history of Church teaching about the Sacraments. Although many errors arose in regard to the Sacraments during the Medieval Age, people still regarded them as God's activity rather than man's. Zwingli, a self-taught theologian, could not comprehend the orthodox teaching of the Two Natures of Christ. He separated the Two Natures, due to his inherent rationalism, and therefore could not believe in Christ's presence in the

---

[77] *Ibid.*

[78] *Ibid.*

[79] *What Luther Says*, II, p. 705. November 24, 1537. John 1:30-34.

earthly elements. Because he associated the liturgy and Holy Communion with all the errors of Rome, he thought that by removing them he would get rid of the papal errors. According to Sasse:

> The Mass was not definitely abolished in Zurich until Easter 1525, when the Lord's Supper was celebrated with a new liturgy. The altar was replaced by a movable table covered with a white tablecloth. Cans, wooden cups, and wooden plates with unleavened bread were placed on the table. Deacons carried the gifts to the assembled congregation, and everyone broke for himself a small piece from the bread and drank from the cup...Impressive as the liturgy of Zurich may have been, it was no longer the old Sacrament of the Altar, but a new rite, "a memorial of thanksgiving and joy, not the *mysterium tremendum* of the Lutherans," as W. Koehler puts it. [80]

The people of Zurich must have felt they were losing the Sacrament, since they crowded the church, before the change took place, to receive the Body and Blood of Christ for the last time. In fact, Zwingli himself was troubled by a dream, which took place just before the new memorial meal was instituted. In the dream, a messenger called his attention to Exodus 12:11 ("It is the Lord's Passover.") proving the case for "This is My Body" being literal and not symbolic. [81]

The Sacraments in Roman Catholicism

In Protestantism, there are no Sacraments, only ordinances, while in Roman Catholicism; seven Sacraments are called the Means of Grace. Episcopalians loiter midway between the two, teaching two major Sacraments (Holy Baptism and Holy Communion) and five minor Sacraments, but also limiting Christ's presence in the Lord's Supper to a spiritual presence. Episcopalian worship and doctrine can range between low-church Baptist expressions and crypto-Romanism. As mentioned before, the term Sacrament is not a Biblical word itself but serves as shorthand for those passages that deal with the way in which God's

---

[80] Sasse, *This Is My Body*, p. 105.

[81] *Ibid.*

divine grace is communicated to people through earthly elements. "For Scripture never calls either Baptism or the Lord's Supper mysteries or Sacraments. Therefore this is an unwritten (*agraphos*) appellation."[82] Although Lutherans speak of two Sacraments, the Apology of the Augsburg Confession includes absolution as the third Sacrament:

> The genuine Sacraments, therefore, are Baptism, the Lord's Supper, and absolution (which is the Sacrament of penitence), for these rites have the commandment of God and the promise of grace, which is the heart of the New Testament.[83]

Today, Lutherans consider absolution included under the Sacrament of Holy Communion, but this does not remove from absolution the power of God's grace and the necessity of contrition and forgiveness as the daily practice of the Office of the Keys. Binding and loosing, forgiving and not forgiving sins – both belong to all Christians and are administered in the congregation by the pastor and congregation working together.

The Apology of the Augsburg Confession points out agreement between the confessors and the Roman party about the nature of the Sacraments, through which God moves hearts to believe, but disagreement about the number of Sacraments. The Roman position was hardened at the Council of Trent:

> If anyone says that the sacraments of the New Law were not all instituted by our Lord Jesus Christ, or that there are either more or fewer than seven, namely, baptism, confirmation, the Eucharist, penance, extreme unction, ordination, and marriage, or also that some of these seven are not truly and properly sacraments, let him be anathema [damned to Hell].[84]

The definition of a sacrament was still fluid for Lutherans during the Reformation. We have this beautiful statement from the Apology to the Augsburg Confession:

---

[82] *Examination*, II, p. 29.

[83] Apology of the Augsburg Confession, Article XIII, Number and Use of the Sacraments, Tappert, p. 211.

[84] [Session VII, Canon I] *Examination*, II, p. 21.

But if ordination be understood as applying to the ministry of the Word, we are not unwilling to call ordination a sacrament. For the ministry of the Word has God's command and glorious promises. Romans 1:16 The Gospel is the power of God unto salvation to every one that believeth. Likewise, Isaiah 55:11: So shall My Word be that goeth forth out of My mouth; it shall not return unto Me void, but it shall accomplish that which I please...And it is of advantage, so far as can be done, to adorn the ministry of the Word with every kind of praise against fanatical men, who dream that the Holy Ghost is given not through the Word, but because of certain preparations of their own.... [85]

Pronouncing an anathema upon those who disagree about the number of Sacraments seems extreme. Lutherans consider marriage part of God's created order, a ceremony that should be celebrated as a worship service, but it was instituted for all people before Christ. Lutheran pastors comfort the dying and offer them Holy Communion, but this is not considered a separate Sacrament. Confirmation is more important to Lutherans than any similar rite in most denominations, but it is really a preparation for adult membership in the Church and the reception of the Sacrament of Holy Communion. Ordination does not confer an indelible character (a Roman Catholic opinion). A man is not pastor unless he is called into Word and Sacrament ministry, normally by a congregation. Therefore, neither the title nor the office confers a special power in the Roman sense. Lutherans understand faithfulness to the Word of God as the essential foundation of a pastor's work. Melanchthon expressed this well when he wrote:

But if ordination be understood as applying to the ministry of the Word, we are not unwilling to call ordination a sacrament. For the ministry of the Word has God's command and glorious promises. Romans 1:16 The Gospel is the power of God unto salvation to every one that believeth. Likewise, Isaiah 55:11: So shall My Word be that goeth forth out of My mouth; it shall not return unto Me void, but it shall accomplish that which I please...And it is of advantage, so far as can be done, to adorn the ministry of the Word with every kind of praise against fanatical

---

[85] Apology Augsburg Confession, XIII. #11. Number/Use Sacraments, *Triglotta*, p. 311. Tappert, p. 212. Romans 1:16; Isaiah 55:11

men, who dream that the Holy Ghost is given not through the Word, but because of certain preparations of their own....[86]

The Sacrament of Penance in the Roman Catholic Church corresponds to absolution among the Lutherans, but differs in what is taught about complete forgiveness of sin and payment for sin. The issue is what we are teaching through the Sacraments, not whether this or that is called a Sacrament. In addition, the concept of the visibility of the Roman Catholic Church is very important when trying to understand the Mass:

> Pope Leo XIII in his important encyclical letter on the Church, *Satis Cognitum* (1896), clearly taught the visibility of the Church: "If we consider the chief end of his Church and the proximate efficient causes of salvation, it is undoubtedly spiritual; but in regard to these spiritual gifts, it is external and necessarily visible (no. 3)." There is a triple bond that united the members of the Church to each other and makes them recognizable as Catholics: profession of the same faith throughout the world, use of the same seven sacraments, and subordination to the same papal authority.[87]

The Roman Catholic Church is sacramental, even if preaching is weak or absent altogether. Nothing is clearer to Catholics, Lutherans, or Protestants than the sacramental emphasis in Catholicism. American Lutheranism has suffered from such a fear of succumbing to Roman doctrine that many positive, historic aspects of liturgical worship and practice have been avoided or abandoned in favor of Zwinglian rationalism, Evangelical revivals, and Pentecostal praise festivals replete with staged healings and calculated emotionalism. At a Roman Catholic university like Notre Dame, the frequency of Mass and its importance are overwhelming.

Lutherans disagree with Roman Catholics about the nature of the Sacraments of Holy Baptism and Holy Communion, not about the activity of God through these visible signs of His grace. Because Roman

---

[86] Apology Augsburg Confession, XIII. #11. Number/Use Sacraments, *Triglotta*, p. 311. Tappert, p. 212. Romans 1:16; Isaiah 55:11.

[87] Baker, *Fundamentals*, III, p. 139.

Catholics believe God is acting through the Sacraments, it is easier for them to understand Lutheran objections to certain doctrines than to discuss the Sacraments with Protestants, who have never been taught that baptismal water washes through the Word or that the Body and Blood of Christ offer forgiveness through the Holy Spirit.

Worthiness of the Minister

One of the earliest conflicts within the Church concerned the worthiness of the minister, or more precisely, the validity of the Sacraments performed by an unworthy minister. The difficulties arose when pastors gave in to persecutions or became false teachers, making people anxious about the acts that the ministers had performed in the Name of Christ. In this area, the Lutherans did not disagree with the Roman Catholics, since the Sacraments belong to God and obtain their power from the Word. Quenstedt, an orthodox Lutheran theologian, wrote:

> The Sacraments do not belong to the man who dispenses them, but to God, in whose name they are dispensed, and therefore the gracious efficacy and operation of the Sacrament depend on God alone, 1 Corinthians 3:5, and not on the character or quality of the minister.[88]

This divine effectiveness through the Word needs to be constantly emphasized.

The Lutherans objected to *ex opera operato*, the Roman doctrine that the Sacraments confer grace on the one who places no hindrances in the way, even though there was no good impulse in the recipient.

> They [our opponents, the Romanists] imagine that the Sacraments bestow the Holy Spirit *ex opera operato* without the proper attitude in the recipient, as though the gift of the Holy Spirit were a minor matter.[89]

---

[88] Baker, *Fundamentals* III, p. 139.

[89] Apology of the Augsburg Confession, Article IV, Justification, Tappert, p. 115.

According to the Lutheran Church, the parents bring their child to be baptized in faith, and the congregation witnesses the baptism in faith. Unfortunately, some Lutheran parents typify the common complaint made about infant baptism, by bringing their children to church only for baptism, confirmation, and marriage. The communicant receives the Body and Blood of Christ in faith because a heart that trusts in God's forgiveness is best prepared for the Eucharist. Roman Catholic doctrine exchanges the holy, gracious work of God, for a mechanical, mindless work of man. Therefore, the Augsburg Confession states:

> It is taught among us that the Sacraments were instituted not only to be signs by which people might be identified outwardly as Christians, but that they are signs and testimonies of God's will toward us for the purpose of wakening and strengthening our faith. For this reason they require faith, and they are rightly used when they are received in faith and for the purpose of strengthening the faith.[90]

Roman Catholic Errors about Holy Communion

Ever since the Council of Trent, the Roman Catholic Church has defended a number of errors concerning the Lord's Supper. Briefly stated, they are:

1. Transubstantiation – the substance of the bread and wine are changed into the Body and Blood of Christ when consecrated by the priest, so that their outward appearance remains the same but their real nature is changed permanently.

2. Reservation of the host – the consecrated bread is kept and worshiped in a special enclosed altar called a monstrance.

3. Corpus Christi – the consecrated bread is elevated and paraded through town in a special procession.

4. Withholding the cup – only the Body of Christ is given. This is no longer true in most Catholic parishes.

---

[90] *Ibid.*, Article XIII, The Use of the Sacraments, p. 35f.

5. Bloodless sacrifice – The Mass is the act of a priest sacrificing Christ, without blood, for sin. A Mass can be purchased to benefit the donor, the recipients, and the suffering souls in Purgatory.

These are Medieval errors that attached themselves to Christianity and became institutionalized at the Council of Trent. Reaction to the Medieval errors has led many, including Roman Catholics, away from the truth and the blessings inherent in the Sacraments. Doubt in the Mass as a sacrifice performed by a priest for the souls in Purgatory can lead to doubt in the Real Presence.

Transubstantiation

The doctrine of transubstantiation, the permanent change of bread and wine into the Body of Blood of Christ, is clearly refuted by Scripture, since St. Paul speaks several times of the consecrated element both as bread and as the Body of Christ (1 Corinthians 10:16-17; 11:26-27).[91] In rejecting the Real Presence of Christ's Body and Blood, the Protestants deny the Gospel promises offered in Holy Communion. In promoting transubstantiation, Roman Catholics have created a doctrine that is not Biblical and leads to extremes by the faithful. The *Book of Concord* states:

> As for transubstantiation, we have no regard for the subtle sophistry of those who teach that bread and wine surrender or lose their natural substance and retain only the appearance and shape of bread without any longer being real bread, for that bread is and remains there agrees better with the Scriptures, as St. Paul himself states, "The bread which we break (1 Corinthians 10:16), and again, "Let a man eat of the bread," (1 Corinthians 11:28).[92]

The plain words of the Apostle prevent confusion.

---

[91] *Examination*, II, p. 263.

[92] Smalcald Articles, Part III, Article VI, The Sacrament of the Altar, Tappert, p. 311.

In the past, some kept the host (consecrated bread) as a lucky charm, which led to the placing of the host directly in the mouth of the communicant. Others disputed about mice receiving Christ if they found a host reserved for adoration, a matter for mockery in James Joyce's *Portrait of the Artist as a Young Man*. In all such cases of abuse, the worst offense is taking away the Scriptural emphasis upon the faith of the recipient and the blessings of God's Word made visible in the Sacrament, replacing sound practice with superstition and magic, ending in apostasy and rationalism. Zwingli, who began as a poorly taught Roman Catholic priest, is one such example.

Reservation of the Host

> If anyone says that it is not permitted to reserve the holy Eucharist in a sacred place, but that it must of necessity be distributed immediately after the consecration to those who are present, or that it is not permitted to be carried to the sick in an honorable manner, let him be anathema [damned to Hell].

Lutherans teach that the elements of Holy Communion should not be reserved, since the adoration of the host leads to practices that many consider idolatry. The late Jaroslav Pelikan has described Roman Catholic novenas at the end of the day, where the lights were dimmed, "putting Jesus to bed," while singing a lullaby, "Good night, Sweet Jesus."[93]

Bloodless Sacrifice

The differences in pastoral ministry among Catholics, Lutherans, and Protestants are defined by the meaning attached to Holy Communion. For Protestants, the minister is a layman who does full-time what laymen do in their free time. Because the Protestant minister does not administer the Sacraments in the ancient sense, much of his work is seen as teaching and organizing. Many Protestant ministers respond to an inner call and create their own congregations. For Lutheran ministers, pastoral work has always been preaching, teaching

---

[93] Seventh Session, Council of Trent, Chapter IV, Canon VII, *Examination*, II, p. 293. *The Riddle of Roman Catholicism*, New York: Abingdon Press, 1959, p. 119.

and administering the Sacraments, with an emphasis upon sound doctrine:

> To obtain such faith God instituted the office of the ministry that is, provided the Gospel and the Sacraments. Through these, as through means, He gives the Holy Spirit, Who works faith, when and where He pleases, in those who hear the Gospel. And the Gospel teaches that we have a gracious God, not by our own merits but by the merit of Christ, when we believe this. Condemned are the Anabaptists and others who teach that the Holy Spirit comes to us through our own preparations, thoughts, and works without the external Word of the Gospel.[94]

A Lutheran may be trained at a seminary and yet never become a pastor, if he does not receive a divine call through a congregation. A Roman Catholic priest is given a cup when he is ordained, to symbolize his power to consecrate the elements of the Mass. His work is largely Sacramental and he remains a priest (indelible character) even if he performs only secular work. He is assigned his work by his bishop or religious superior, so his vocation is not dependent upon a congregation's call. He may belong to a religious order with special rights and obligations.

These distinctions in ministry all relate to Holy Communion. In the Roman Catholic Church, the Eucharist is directly linked with other disputed doctrines:

- Mary, who is portrayed as Co-Redemptrix, offering her Son on Calvary, like the priest offering Mass;

- Purgatory, where the multitudes suffer torment and find partial relief through the Mass, good works done on their behalf, and the intercession of Mary;

- Indulgences, which grant release from Purgatory for certain payments or obligations;

---

[94] Augsburg Confession, Article V, The Office of the Ministry, Tappert, p. 31.

- Papal infallibility, which ensures that the doctrines are received from the Holy Spirit through the pope;

- Justification, which allows for the forgiveness of sin but not the complete payment for sin, hence Purgatory, where full payment is made.

The Council Trent declared:

> And since in this divine sacrifice, which is accomplished in the Mass, that same Christ is contained and bloodlessly sacrificed who once, on the altar of the cross, offered Himself a bloody sacrifice, the holy synod teaches that this sacrifice is truly propitiatory and that through it comes to pass that, if we approach God with a true heart and right faith, with fear and reverence, contrite and penitent, we obtain mercy and find grace in timely help.[95]

This was echoed by the Second Vatican Council:

> As often as the sacrifice of the cross in which "Christ, our passover, has been sacrificed" (1 Corinthians 5:7) is celebrated on an altar, the work of our redemption is carried on.[96]

> Taking part in the Eucharistic Sacrifice, which is the fount and apex of the whole Christian life, they offer the divine Victim to God, and offer themselves along with It."[97]

Because some people argue that the Roman Catholic Church changed at the Second Vatican Council or changed the spirit of what followed, it is important to quote the conservative textbook of a Roman Catholic, which echoes the language of Trent, as does Vatican II.

---

[95] [Sixth Session, Chapter II] *Examination* , II, p. 440.

[96] *Lumen Gentium*, Dogmatic Constitution of the Church, I, 3, *Vatican II*, p. 16. 1 Corinthians 5:7.

[97] *Ibid.*, I, 11, p. 28.

The Mass is a re-presentation now, in an unbloody manner, of the bloody sacrifice of the Cross over nineteen hundred years ago. Since it is a re-offering of Jesus on Calvary, the Mass is rightly referred to as "the holy Sacrifice of the Mass," although we do not hear this expression much today.[98]

Martin Chemnitz objected to this doctrine when it was endorsed by the Council of Trent:

The papalist Mass, as we have described it in the beginning, militates against the one propitiatory sacrifice of Christ in many ways and is an affront to it. For there is only one propitiatory sacrifice that expiates and renders satisfaction for sins--the offering of Christ made on the cross (Hebrews 7:27; 9:12, 26; 10:12).[99]

The essential problem with portraying Holy Communion as a sacrifice is that it becomes man's work for God, not a reception of God's work for man.[100]

One result of the Roman view is the idea that people should pay for a Mass being said. This is called a votive or stipendiary Mass, which was condemned by the Augsburg Confession:

---

[98] Baker, *Fundamentals*, I, p. 142f.

[99] *Examination* , II, p. 494. After describing the elaborate and theatrical gestures used by priests during the consecration, Chemnitz observed: "They imagine that by means of these actions, motions, gestures, and ceremonies, with certain words added about sacrifice, oblation, and victim, they are sacrificing and offering the body and blood of Christ, yes, Christ, the Son of God Himself, anew to God the Father through such a theatrical representation (which is either a comedy or a tragedy) of Christ's passion." *Examination*, II, p. 446.

[100] "For a sacrifice, according to Augustine, *Contra adversarium legis et prophetarum*, Bk. 1, and De civitate Dei, Bk. 10, is a work which we offer, render, and dedicate to God in order that we may dwell in Him in holy fellowship. A sacrament, however, is a holy sign through which God freely offers, conveys, applies, and seals His gratuitous benefits to us. It is therefore an extraordinary perversion of the Lord's Supper to make a sacrifice out of a sacrament, in the way the papalists speak of the sacrifice of their Mass, namely, that the representatory action of the priest procures for us the application of the benefits of Christ and that anyone who causes a Mass to be celebrated in his behalf by this work procures grace and whatever other things are ascribed to the Mass." *Examination* , II, p. 498.

Then when our [Evangelical] preachers preached about these things and the priests were reminded of the terrible responsibility which should properly concern every Christian (namely, that whoever uses the Sacrament unworthily is guilty of the Body and Blood of Christ), such mercenary Masses and private Masses, which had hitherto been held under compulsion for the sake of revenue and stipends, were discontinued in our churches.[101]

Father Jugie defended votive Masses for the souls in Purgatory:

The most excellent and most efficacious of all the suffrages for the dead, is the Holy Mass...It is certain that every soul in Purgatory receives some diminution of its debt by the celebration of any Mass, even though we cannot measure that diminution precisely. This is very consoling for us all.[102]

After Vatican II, Father Baker wrote:

When a stipend is offered for a Mass to be celebrated for a particular intention, the priest must offer that Mass as a first intention. The practice of offering Mass for definite persons can be traced back to the third century. Thirdly, it is commonly held by theologians that there is a personal fruit of the Mass which the Lord grants to the celebrating priest and to all the faithful who are actually present at each Mass.[103]

A Lutheran would counter by saying that the greatest good we do for others is to teach them these truths of the Scriptures:

1. God does not desire the death of a single sinner.

---

[101] Augsburg Confession, Article XXIV, The Mass. Tappert, p. 57.

[102] Jugie, *Purgatory*, p. 96.

[103] Baker, *Fundamentals*, III, p. 273.

2. Christ has died for the sins of the world.

3. Contrite sinners receive complete pardon for all their sins (Psalm 103) through Christ.

4. Holy Baptism offers the indwelling of the Holy Spirit, the removal of the power of original sin, and forgiveness.

5. Holy Communion grants the gift of forgiveness, promised by the Gospel and received in faith.

6. Eternal life is given to all those who die trusting in Christ alone as their Savior.

These truths would be far more comforting and beneficial than all the Masses offered with the best of intentions. Therefore, Chemnitz stated:

> To institute a form of worship beside and without the Word of God, and indeed one to which is ascribed propitiation for sins, appeasement of the wrath of God, is a vain thing; it cannot please God; yes, it is idolatry. For "in vain they worship Me with doctrines and commandments of men." Likewise: 'Without faith it is impossible that a thing should please God.' Faith, however, "comes by hearing, and hearing by the revealed Word of God."[104]

---

[104] *Examination*, II, p. 493.

Comparison: The Means of Grace

Protestant – The Holy Spirit works independently of the Word, Baptism, and Communion (Zwingli and Calvin), showing the sovereign will of God. Baptism and Communion are usually called ordinances, testimonies to man's faith, which do not confer God's grace. The bread and wine are symbols or representations and remain bread and wine. The Lord's Supper is not considered communion with the Body and Blood of Christ but a memorial meal – "Do this in remembrance of Me." Salvation is confirmed by an inner illumination, commonly called being born again. Baptists and Pentecostals reject infant baptism, though infant dedication is widely practiced.

Lutheran – The Holy Spirit always works through the Word of God and never apart from the Word. The Holy Spirit works through the external (revealed) Word or through the visible Word in the Sacraments of Holy Baptism and Holy Communion. Through the appointed Means of Grace, God offers forgiveness. The will is passive, so the person contributes nothing (worthiness, a proper decision, or good works) to salvation, but receives God's grace in faith. During Holy Communion, Christ's Body and Blood are truly present with the bread and wine, not just spiritually present. Salvation is based upon the objective Word of God.

> I believe that I cannot by my own reason or strength believe in Jesus Christ, my Lord, or come to Him; but the Holy Ghost has called me by the Gospel, enlightened me with His gifts, sanctified and kept me in the truth faith; even as He calls, gathers, enlightens, and sanctifies the whole Christian Church on earth and keeps it with Jesus Christ in the one true faith...[105]

---

[105] Martin Luther, The Small Catechism, Explanation of the Third Article of the Creed. *Triglotta*, p. 545.

Roman Catholic – The visibility of the Roman Catholic Church (one doctrine, one infallible pope) assures members that the seven Sacraments are conferred by God. The five Sacraments not accepted by Lutherans as such are:

1. Confirmation
2. Marriage
3. Ordination
4. Penance
5. Extreme unction

The Sacraments work *ex opera operato*, apart from the faith of the recipient, provided no obstacle is placed in the way. The individual cooperates with the work that God begins in him, offering love, good works, and sacrifices to make himself worthy. However, he is never sure of salvation and will probably spend many years in Purgatory. Salvation is based upon but not absolutely limited to membership in the Roman Catholic Church.

Part Three: Complete Disagreement

Chapter Three: Justification by Faith

Justification is the term commonly used by theologians to describe the forgiveness of sins earned by Christ on the cross and received by man through faith. God uses the Law to make us humble and contrite through the work of the Holy Spirit, deeply aware of our sin and crushed by the terrors we face before Almighty God, Creator of heaven and earth. Hearts hardened by sin cannot receive the Gospel any more than a concrete parking lot can become a garden. First the Law is proclaimed, so that the Holy Spirit can work repentance that acknowledges the need for a Savior and also grasps the promises of the Gospel of Jesus Christ.

Romans 10:12 For there is no difference between the Jew and the Greek: for the same Lord over all is rich unto all that call upon him. 13 For whosoever shall call upon the name of the Lord shall be saved. 14 How then shall they call on him in whom they have not believed? and how shall they believe in him of whom they have not heard? and how shall they hear without a preacher? 15 And how shall they preach, except they be sent? as it is written, How beautiful are the feet of them that preach the gospel of peace, and bring glad tidings of good things!

Repentance means both sorrow for sin as well as faith in the Gospel of Christ Jesus.

> It is taught among us that those who sin after Baptism receive forgiveness of sin whenever they come to repentance, and absolution should not be denied them by the church. Properly speaking, true repentance is nothing else than to have contrition and sorrow or terror, on account of sin, and yet at the same time to believe the Gospel and absolution (namely, that sin has been forgiven and grace has been obtained through Christ), and this faith will comfort the heart and again set it at rest. Amendment of life and the forsaking of sin should then follow, for these must be the fruits of repentance, as John says, "Bear fruit that befits repentance."[106]

The Roman Catholic Church has a different doctrine of justification, which is summarized by Monsignor O'Hare:

> In her Council of Trent (1545-1563) she condemned, as was her right, the new-fangled teaching of Luther and warned her subjects against its entanglements and dangers. Then she proclaimed anew, for the enlightenment of all, the heavenly teaching committed to her keeping from the beginning and insisted that whilst faith is necessary to dispose the sinner to receive grace, it alone is not sufficient for justification.[107]

---

[106] Augsburg Confession, Article XII, Repentance, Tappert, p. 34f. *Triglotta*, p. 49. Two common errors are: 1) repentance is limited to feeling sorrow for sin; 2) sin is removed by acts of contrition rather than faith in the forgiveness offered by Christ.

[107] Msgr. Patrick F. O'Hare, *The Facts About Luther*, Rockford, Illinois: TAN Books and Publishers, 1987, p. 103. The introduction is dated 1916.

Since justification is "the article by which the Church stands or falls," careful attention must be paid to the way in which justification is taught by Catholics, Lutherans, and Protestants.

> The article of justification is the master and prince, the lord, the ruler, and the judge over all kinds of doctrines; it preserves and governs all church doctrine and raises up our conscience before God. Without this article the world is utter death and darkness. No error is so mean, so clumsy, and so outworn as not to be supremely pleasing to human reason and to seduce us if we are without the knowledge and the contemplation of this article.[108]

> By the one solid rock which we call the doctrine (*locum*) of justification we mean that we are redeemed from sin, death, and the devil and are made partakers of life eternal, not by ourselves...but by help from without (*alienum auxilium*), by the only-begotten Son of God, Jesus Christ.[109]

One of the classic Biblical passages for supporting this view of justification is Romans 1:17.

> Romans 1:17 For therein is the righteousness of God revealed from faith to faith: as it is written, The just shall live by faith.

Justification means the salvation of souls, eternal life, so all other doctrines are centered on this topic. What would the Virgin Birth mean without the work of our Savior who was born of the Virgin Mary? Christ came to save a world already condemned by sin, to justify the lost. Because justification is central, this doctrine caused the Reformation and subdivided the various Protestant groups.

The entire Bible relates to the doctrine of justification. The Scriptures were given to us so that Christ's work would be proclaimed in the clearest, plainest, and most efficacious manner. The creation of Adam and Eve foreshadowed the coming of the Second Adam, Christ, Who would restore to man the paradise lost by Adam's sin. God's

---

[108] *What Luther Says*, II, p. 703.

[109] *Ibid.*, II, p. 701.

condemnation of the serpent carried with it the first promise of a Savior, called the Protoevangelium or First Gospel.

> Genesis 3:14 And the LORD God said unto the serpent, Because thou hast done this, thou *art* cursed above all cattle, and above every beast of the field; upon thy belly shalt thou go, and dust shalt thou eat all the days of thy life: 15 And I will put enmity between thee and the woman, and between thy seed and her seed; it shall bruise thy head, and thou shalt bruise his heel.

Although God expelled Adam and Eve from the Garden of Eden, He nevertheless promised a Savior who would crush the head of Satan, and defeat sin and death, by being crucified. When God commanded Abraham to sacrifice his son, his only son, whom he loved, on Mt. Moriah, He gave mankind a personal portrait of what it meant for the Father to give His only Son for the sins of the world. Then, when God provided a ram as a substitute for the sacrifice, He also taught us that Jesus would be our substitute, becoming sin in our place, enduring the cross, and exchanging His righteousness for our sin (2 Corinthians 5:21).

Whenever the Jewish people prepared animal sacrifices for the atonement of sins, they were foreshadowing the atoning sacrifice of Christ. Whenever they selected the spotless Passover lamb in celebration of the Exodus, they were preparing for the day when John the Baptist would say, "Look, the Lamb of God, who takes away the sins of the world." (John 1:29) Whenever they read Isaiah 53, they were preparing for the day when the chapter would be part of the New Testament, a multitude of unusual prophecies fulfilled by Christ:

Isaiah 53:4 Surely he hath borne our griefs,

and carried our sorrows:

yet we did esteem him stricken, smitten of God, and afflicted.

5 But he *was* wounded for our transgressions,

he was bruised for our iniquities:

the chastisement of our peace *was* upon him;

and with his stripes we are healed.

6 All we like sheep have gone astray;

we have turned every one to his own way;

and the LORD hath laid on him the iniquity of us all.

In the fullness of time, God fulfilled all the prophecies of the Old Testament. Mary, a virginal young girl, was told by the angel Gabriel that she would bear the Son of God, Who would be miraculously conceived through the Holy Spirit. In faith, Mary replied to Gabriel, "I am the Lord's servant," and "May it be to me as you have said." (Luke 2:38)

Christ was born in the humblest of circumstances, honored by poor shepherds and by the wise men, but unknown to most, except for Herod, who wanted Him killed. At the proper time, Jesus was baptized by John in the Jordan River, tempted by Satan in the burning desert, and revealed to the world through His miracles. Although Jesus healed many people and performed miracles which only He could do, His work as the promised Messiah centered on the cross and His teaching about His work.

Mark 10:45 For even the Son of man came not to be ministered unto, but to minister, and to give his life a ransom for many.

When Christ was crucified, the world thought His enemies had won. The disciples cowered behind locked doors, in spite of His promise to rise from the dead. The risen Christ, Who could point to His scars, taught His disciples and on the Day of Pentecost, gave them the Holy Spirit as their Advocate, to speak the truth of God's saving work (Acts 2).

The Bible Is Clear: How We Are Justified

Romans 5:1 Therefore being justified by faith, we have peace with God through our Lord Jesus Christ: 2 By whom also we have access by faith into this grace wherein we stand, and rejoice in hope of the glory of God.

Romans 8:1 *There is* therefore now no condemnation to them which are in Christ Jesus, who walk not after the flesh, but after the Spirit.

Colossians 2:13 And you, being dead in your sins and the uncircumcision of your flesh, hath he quickened together with him, having forgiven you all trespasses;

1 John 1:7 But if we walk in the light, as he is in the light, we have fellowship one with another, and the blood of Jesus Christ his Son cleanseth us from all sin.

The doctrine of justification is central to a correct understanding of the Virgin Mary, Purgatory, Holy Communion, and all other doctrines of Christianity. For this reason, justification by the grace of God (freely given, as a gift), received through faith, ignited the Reformation and remained central to all future discussions and divisions. Luther's Reformation was based upon Biblical doctrine, not traditions. Rather than trying to remove everything that seemed Roman, such as statues and the Mass in Latin, Luther only sought to displace the false doctrines of the Medieval Age with the sound teaching of the Bible. As Charles P. Krauth wrote, Luther's was a conservative Reformation.[110] In contrast, Zwingli, the first Protestant reformer, sought to eliminate the trappings of Catholicism. Luther kept the historic liturgy, while Zwingli threw it out as representing Roman superstition. For this reason, most Protestants employ a non-liturgical worship service and remain relatively loose in their doctrinal definitions. Episcopalians are Catholic in worship, but in doctrine they may long for reunion with Rome or sit on the stage for a Billy Graham Crusade. Confessional Lutherans honor the biblical traditions of the liturgy and retain a love for doctrinal clarity.

In 1517, when Luther nailed the 95 Theses (debate topics written in Latin) onto the chapel door at Wittenberg, the pope did not take the unknown German monk seriously. The theses were translated into German and mass-produced on the newly invented Gutenberg printing press. Soon Luther's writings swept through Europe, attacking the theological and financial foundations of the papacy. The initial question of the 95 Theses concerned the sale of indulgences by the agents of the pope, especially one John Tetzel, whose zealous sales methods drove

---

[110] Charles P. Krauth, *The Conservative Reformation and Its Theology*, Philadelphia: United Lutheran Publication House, 1913.

Luther to question the doctrines behind the bizarre but successful methods.

The Reformation closed with the Council of Trent, the pope's answer to all the questions raised by Luther and other reformers. The Council of Trent met from 1545, a year before Luther died, to 1563, around the time of Melanchthon's death. The Roman Catholic Church did not call another council until Vatican I, 1869-1870. The Vatican I and Vatican II councils based their decrees upon Trent, so the decisions at Trent have been crucial for all Roman Catholic teaching since then. Trent decided upon its doctrine of justification at the last session. The Council of Trent rejected justification by faith alone, apart from the works of the law, which is the doctrine of the Bible, the early Church, and Martin Luther. Instead, the Council of Trent defended the Medieval, scholastic tradition of faith plus works (*fides formata*).

Council of Trent

> If anyone says that justifying faith is nothing else than trust in divine mercy, which remits sins for Christ's sake, or that it is this trust alone by which we are justified, let him be anathema [damned to Hell].[111]

> If anyone says that a man is absolved from sins and justified because of this that he confidently believes that he is absolved and justified, or that no one is truly justified except he who believes that he is justified, and that through this faith alone absolution and justification is affected, let him be anathema [damned to Hell].[112]

The language of Trent needs to be considered carefully. "Let him be anathema" means "let him be damned to Hell" or "cursed by God." The term *anathema* is taken from St. Paul writing to the Galatians where he used the term twice:

---

[111] *Examination*, I, p. 460.

[112] *Ibid.*, I, p. 551.

Galatians 1:8 But though we, or an angel from heaven, preach any other gospel unto you than that which we have preached unto you, let him be accursed [anathema]. 9 As we said before, so say I now again, If any *man* preach any other gospel unto you than that ye have received, let him be accursed [anathema].

The Apostle commanded them not to trust him or even an angel from God above the pure Word of God. The Council of Trent used Paul's language (anathema) but not his doctrine.

The word for faith in the New Testament can mean the Christian Faith, a body of doctrine (the shield of The Faith, Ephesians 6:16) but generally the term means trust, the inclination of the heart. Justification by faith alone signifies the work that God does, apart from any merit or good work in man. All Christians have problems with this, because our fallen nature wants to add some requirement, merit, or work in order to earn salvation. In addition, the world rewards people for work accomplished, for merit and virtue, so we are used to earning everything in some way. Still, the Scriptures clearly teach that Christ Himself paid the price for our sins, once for all people, so that no one can boast of anything except the cross of Jesus, God's own Son.

Atonement and Justification

The first edition of this book used the term objective justification as a synonym for the Atonement, to express the truth that Christ paid for the sins of the world. Many Lutherans think of objective justification as another way of speaking about the atoning death of Christ. However, this term has been used with some variation (general, objective, universal, and even universal objective justification) to express a concept alien to the Scriptures, the *Book of Concord*, and the Christian faith. Erring writers have claimed that God declared the entire world free of sin, without guilt, the moment Christ died on the cross, or alternately, the moment He rose from the dead. This universal absolution is declared to be true without any Scriptural text, Church father citation, or *Book of Concord* passage to support a concept of grace without the Means of Grace, forgiveness without faith. The sainted Robert Preus once taught this opinion, during

the heyday of Church Growth at Concordia Seminary, Ft. Wayne.[113]
Three influences may have impacted the 1981 essay:

1. Walther's promotion of the Easter absolution,

2. Missouri's debt to Pietism, and

3. The Norwegian Lutherans' historic fondness for this opinion.

However, Preus clarified the true meaning of justification in his final
book, *Justification and Rome*, which was published posthumously. Preus
wrote this definitive comment:

> But the imputation of Christ's righteousness to the sinner takes
> place when the Holy Spirit brings him to faith through Baptism
> and the Word of the Gospel. Our sins were imputed to Christ at
> His suffering and death, imputed objectively after He, by His
> active and passive obedience, fulfilled and *procured* all
> righteousness for us. But the imputation of His righteousness to
> us takes place when we are brought to faith.[114]

Preus immediately followed the statement above with a quotation from
Quenstedt, one of his favorite orthodox Lutheran authors:

> It is not just the same thing to say, "Christ's righteousness is
> imputed to us" and to say "Christ is our righteousness." For the
> imputation did not take place when Christ became our

---

[113] Concordia Seminary, Ft. Wayne, *Newsletter.* 1981 Quoted reverently at
http://www.reclaimingwalther.org/articles/jmc00225.htm

"In an initial burst of enthusiasm reflecting Preus' concern for missions, the Fort Wayne faculty
had petitioned the 1977 convention of the Missouri Synod to have each of its subdivisions or
districts "make a thorough study of the Church Growth materials." What is more, the districts
were to be urged to "organize, equip, and place into action all of the Church Growth principles as
needed in the evangelization of our nation and the world under the norms of the Scriptures and
the Lutheran Confessions." By the time of the 1986 synodical convention, however, the same
faculty, while appreciating the 'valuable lessons of common sense' to be learned from Church
Growth, asked that "the Synod warn against the Arminian and charismatic nature of the church-
growth movement." Kurt E. Marquart, "Robert D. Preus," *Handbook of Evangelical Theologians*, ed.,
Walter A. Elwell, Grand Rapids: Baker Book House, 1995, pp. 353-65. Reprinted in *Christian
News*, 6-26-95, p. 21.

[114] Robert D. Preus, *Justification and Rome*, St. Louis: Concordia Academic Press 1997, p. 72.
[emphasis in original]

righteousness. The righteousness of Christ is the effect of His office. The imputation is the application of the effect of His office. The one, however, does not do away with the other. Christ is our righteousness effectively when He justifies us. His righteousness is ours objectively because our faith rests in Him. His righteousness is ours formally in that His righteousness is imputed to us.[115]

Preus also quoted Abraham Calov with approval:

Although Christ has acquired for us the remission of sins, justification, and sonship, God just the same does not justify us prior to our faith. Nor do we become God's children in Christ in such a way that justification in the mind of God takes place before we believe.[116]

Justification by faith, in the original sense, was taught in the official catechism of the Missouri Synod, and then was gradually changed:

#305 Why do you say in this article: I believe in the Forgiveness of Sins? Because I hold with certainty that by my own powers or through my own works I cannot be justified before God, but that the forgiveness of sins is given me out of grace through faith in Jesus Christ. For where there is forgiveness of sins, there is also

---

[115] *Ibid.*, p. 73. The citation reads "*Systema*, Par. III, Cap. 8. S. 2, q. 5. *Observatio* 19 (II, 787)." Preus told a class I attended at Ft. Wayne that he wanted to name a son Quenstedt, but was vetoed by his sensible wife.

[116] [*Apodixis Articulorum Fide*, Lueneburg, 1684] Robert D. Preus *Justification and Rome*, St. Louis: Concordia Academic Press 1997, p. 131n. The Missouri Synod, the Wisconsin Synod, and the Evangelical Lutheran Synod chose to follow Walther's notion of an Easter absolution for the entire world, a declaration that everyone is forgiven. "For God has already forgiven you your sins 1800 years ago when He in Christ absolved all men by raising Him after He first had gone into bitter death for them. Only one thing remains on your part so that you also possess the gift. This one thing is--faith. And this brings me to the second part of today's Easter message, in which I now would show you that every man who wants to be saved must accept by faith the general absolution, pronounced 1800 years ago, as an absolution spoken individually to him." C. F. W. Walther, *The Word of His Grace, Sermon Selections*, "Christ's Resurrection--The World's Absolution" Lake Mills: Graphic Publishing Company, 1978 p. 233. *Brosamen*, p. 138. Mark 16:1-8.

true justification. Psalm 130:3-4; Psalm 143:2; Isaiah 64:6; Job 25:4-6 (Q. 124).[117]

A proper study of the chief article of the Christian Church will restore the meaning and terminology of the Scriptures, the Church fathers, Luther, the *Book of Concord*, and the orthodox Lutheran theologians.[118]

Original Sin

Two doctrines of the Bible argue against the notion that God has absolved the entire world and declared everyone innocent, free of sin, without any regard to faith. The first doctrine is Original Sin. The second is the Means of Grace, previously discussed. Since the Scriptures are consistent throughout, presenting a unified and harmonious teaching, something must be wrong when one article of faith clashes with another.

Original sin means that all humans have inherited the sin of Adam, who lost the image of God when he consciously rebelled against God's command in eating the forbidden fruit. Lutherans teach that our nature is permanently changed by original sin. Unless God works upon us, we are unable to accomplish anything pleasing in His eyes. We cannot even come to Him or believe in Him without the work of the Spirit through the Gospel promises. Lutherans have a realistic view of human sinfulness based upon Biblical teaching. Man is not inherently good.

> And first, it is true that Christians should regard and recognize as sin not only the actual transgression of God's commandments; but also that the horrible, dreadful hereditary malady by which the entire nature is corrupted should above all things be regarded and recognized as sin indeed, yea, as the chief sin, which is a root and fountainhead of all actual sins. And by Dr. Luther it is called a nature-sin or person-sin, thereby to indicate that, even though a person would think, speak, or do nothing evil (which, however, is impossible in this life, since the fall of our first parents), his

---

[117] *Kleiner Katechismus*, trans. Pastor Vernon Harley, LCMS, St. Louis: Concordia Publishing House, 1901, p. 164ff.

[118] Far more material, including verbatim quotations from all the pertinent sources, can be found in *Thy Strong Word*, by the author, to be re-published soon.

nature and person are nevertheless sinful, that is, thoroughly and utterly infected and corrupted before God by original sin, as by a spiritual leprosy; and on account of this corruption and because of the fall of the first man the nature or person is accused or condemned by God's Law, so that we are by nature the children of wrath, death, and damnation, unless we are delivered therefrom by the merit of Christ.[119]

Holy Baptism removes the guilt of original sin, although the material, as they call it, of the sin, i.e., concupiscence, remains. He [Luther] also added in reference to the material that the Holy Ghost, given through Baptism, begins to mortify the concupiscence, and creates new movements [a new light, a new sense and spirit] in man.[120]

Concupiscence is evil desire, meaning that we never get over our tendency to be envious, contentious, greedy, self-centered, ill-tempered, and impatient.

Roman Catholics teach a subtle but watered down version of original sin. They do not oppose the concept, so basic to St. Augustine's theology. Nevertheless, as contradictory as this seems, the Church of Rome teaches that people merit or earn grace, a topic considered below under condign and congruous grace. Another aspect of their teaching about original sin is man's cooperation in salvation, *fides formata*, faith formed by love, or justification by faith and works. Finally, Roman theology is very much concerned with asserting that the Virgin Mary was born without original sin (the Immaculate Conception) and never committed an actual sin in her life.

The Law and Original Sin

John Bunyan, who read Luther's *Commentary on Galatians* "second only to the Bible," portrayed the work of God's Law eloquently in his story about the Interpreter in *Pilgrim's Progress*. One person came into the room and swept it so that clouds of dust choked everyone. Then another person arrived and sprinkled oil so the dust settled. One represented the

---

[119] Formula of Concord, SD I. #5. Original Sin. *Triglotta*, p. 861. Tappert, p. 509.

[120] Apology Augsburg Confession, II. #35. Original Sin. *Triglotta*, p. 115. Tappert, p. 104f.

Law, stirring up our sinful nature but never making it better. The other represented the Gospel, removing the problems of sin.

> But the chief office or force of the Law is that it reveal original sin with all its fruits, and show man how very low his nature has fallen, and has become [fundamentally and] utterly corrupted; as the Law must tell man that he has no God nor regards [cares for] God, and worships other gods, a matter which before and without the Law he would not have believed. In this way he becomes terrified, is humbled, desponds, despairs, and anxiously desires aid, but sees no escape; he begins to be an enemy of [enraged at] God, and to murmur, etc. This is what Paul says, Romans 4:15: "The Law worketh wrath." And Romans 5:20: Sin is increased by the Law. ["The Law entered that the offense might abound."][121]

Because of original sin, the wrath of God remains on all unbelievers.

> John 3:35 The Father loveth the Son, and hath given all things into his hand. 36 He that believeth on the Son hath everlasting life: and he that believeth not the Son shall not see life; but the wrath of God abideth on him.

The ministry of the Word means to preach the Law in all its severity and the Gospel in all its sweetness. The Holy Spirit stirs up the dramatic contrast between the perfection of God's Law and man's weakened state. Just as hardened soil is broken up and prepared before planting, the heart is softened by the hammer of the Law, so the Gospel will find an opportunity to take root.

> Jeremiah 23:29 Is not my word like as a fire? saith the LORD; and like a hammer that breaketh the rock in pieces?

---

[121] Smalcald Articles, Third Part, II. #3. The Law. *Triglotta*, p. 479. Tappert, p.303. Romans 5:20; Romans 4:15.

The forgiven sinner rejoices in the Gospel promises, the remission of sin, and the promise of eternal life, for heaven springs up wherever Christ is proclaimed. The sinful nature remains and needs the continued ministry of the Word. As Luther said, "You can tie a hog to a tree, but you cannot keep him from squealing."[122]

Atonement and Redemption

Christians should never tire of speaking about the Atonement of Christ, the Redemption of the world. Everyone is better served when terms from the Bible and the *Book of Concord* are used.

> Christ did indeed suffer for the whole world; but how many are there who believe and cherish this fact? Therefore, although the work of redemption itself has been accomplished, it still cannot help and benefit a man unless he believes it and experiences its saving power in his heart.[123]

Our English language is impoverished compared to New Testament Greek, which has two words for redemption. One form emphasizes the purchase made by Christ, paying for us, redeeming us with His innocent blood.

Redemption as Purchase

1 Corinthians 6:20 For ye are bought with a price: therefore glorify God in your body, and in your spirit, which are God's.

2 Peter 2:1 But there were false prophets also among the people, even as there shall be false teachers among you, who privily shall bring in damnable heresies, even denying the Lord that bought them, and bring upon themselves swift destruction.

Redemption as Release

---

[122] Luther, *Sermons*, II, p. 243.

[123] *What Luther Says*, II, p. 705f.

Romans 3:24 Being justified freely by his grace through the redemption that is in Christ Jesus:

Hebrews 9:12 Neither by the blood of goats and calves, but by his own blood he entered in once into the holy place, having obtained eternal redemption *for us.*

The Bible has many images and terms for the work of Christ, to show that all has been accomplished in Him, for all people, for all time. This redemption, atonement, propitiation, or reconciliation is the Gospel message. Christians long to hear this message repeatedly because they are aware of their failings, their weaknesses, and their rebellion against God's Word. If the Gospel message is not universal in scope, each person is tempted to question his own merit or to brag about his worthiness.

The Roman Catholic View

Some are inclined to teach that the division between Luther and Medieval scholasticism has been healed by ecumenical talks, potluck dinners, and mutual understanding. In fact, many Roman Catholic theologians openly or covertly support what Luther taught, but their agreement with the Reformer is not expressed by the official doctrine of the Church of Rome. A modern, traditional Roman Catholic teacher wrote:

> But what did the Council [of Trent] mean by "faith"? It certainly rejected the Lutheran notion of "fiducial faith," which is a confident trust in God through the saving merits of Jesus Christ. In Luther's view, that was all that was required. In the Catholic view, faith, in addition to being an act of trust in God, also has a dogmatic content that the mind must give assent to. Thus, for Catholics faith consists in the firm acceptance of the divine truths of revelation on the authority of God who has revealed them. And Trent declared that fiducial faith alone is not sufficient to justify the sinner.[124]

[124] Baker, *Fundamentals*, III, p. 61.

Martin Chemnitz, the chief editor and theologian of the *Book of Concord*, a former student of Luther, wrote:

> Faith means to give assent to the whole Word of God that is set before us, and in it to the promise of the gratuitous reconciliation bestowed for the sake of Christ the Mediator.[125]

The Roman Catholic view of salvation through faith can be quite perplexing at this point. Faith plus agreement with dogmatic content suggests that one is saved only in the Roman Catholic Church. The anathemas of the Council of Trent rule out all of Protestantism, but the current emphasis of the Vatican is not upon excluding Protestants from the Kingdom of God, but maintaining the doctrine of *fides formata* (Latin, faith formed by love).

> Another error of the sixteenth-century Reformers was that fiducial faith alone is sufficient for justification and eternal salvation. The Catholic Church in the Council of Trent rejected that position. The Church teaches that even though faith (properly understood) is indispensable, still other virtuous acts are required for justification. The other needed dispositions of soul are spelled out by Trent: fear of divine justice, hope in the mercy of God, beginning to love God, hatred for sin and the intention to receive Baptism. This is very much in accord with the Bible which requires other acts of preparation for the coming of God's grace: the fear of God (Proverbs 14:27), hope (Sirach 2:9), love of God (Luke 7:27), sorrow for sin and penance (Acts 2:38; 3:19). So faith is absolutely essential, but it must be accompanied by other acts, such as hope and love.[126]

The Medieval view, which Trent endorsed, held that God began the work of salvation, which was supplemented and aided by man, infusing grace into the soul (*gratia infusa*), to complete and make pleasing God's initial

---

[125] *Examination*, I, p. 567.

[126] Baker, *Fundamentals*, III, p. 61f.

work. Although this doctrine had been condemned earlier by the Church as semi-Pelagianism, the papal party endorsed and defended it, using the recent tradition of Medieval scholasticism to reinterpret the Scriptures. Although God does in fact require contrition, or sorrow for sin, this is the work of the Holy Spirit through the Law, not an effort of man. Good works certainly follow from salvation, just as a smile comes from a happy person, but good works do not contribute to salvation any more than forcing a smile can make an unhappy person glad. Francis Pieper, one of the early leaders of the Lutheran Church-Missouri Synod, wrote about this:

> If we held that the work of Christ did not fully reconcile God but needs to be supplemented by the "infused grace," the keeping of the commandments of God and the Church, as Rome teaches [note-*Tridentinum*, Sess. VI, canon 11, 12, 20], or by "the reshaping of man's life into its divine form," as the modern Protestants teach, we should thereby divest the Christian religion of its specific character and reduce it to the level of the religions of the Law; and the assurance of grace and of the sonship with God would be replaced by the *monstrum incertitudinis* [monster of uncertainty].[127]

The question is whether faith alone is sufficient for justification and salvation or whether one must also fulfill certain requirements to satisfy God.

One is tempted to merge the Lutheran and Roman views, by saying it is a matter of semantics, how one discusses the place of good works in the Christian life. Much more is at stake. To understand the Roman Catholic view completely, we must consider the doctrine of Purgatory. Briefly, Purgatory is presented as a place where most Christians go after death to pay for their sins, aided by visits to Purgatory from the Virgin Mary, with the time decreased in Purgatory for all the

---

[127] Pieper, *Christian Dogmatics*, I, p. 36. Father Baker stated: "Calvin taught that it is impossible for the justified to lose the state of grace; Luther said that it can be lost only by the sin of unbelief. In opposition to those erroneous views, the Council of Trent said that the state of grace is lost by every mortal sin, and not just by the sin of unbelief...." Baker, *Fundamentals*, III, p. 76. Jugie noted: "These good souls," says St. Francis de Sales of those who sang his praises, "with all their glorifying me, will make me languish in Purgatory, for they will imagine that I have no need of prayer. Behold what such reputation will profit me." Jugie, *Purgatory*, p. 54.

good works done in the name of that person or performed in advance by that person. The non-Biblical doctrine of Purgatory, borrowed from the pagans, is explained with the statement that sins are forgiven through the cross of Christ but not yet paid for by the individual. Thus, for the Roman Catholic, the Christian life is one where the terrors of Hell are offered to the believer in the form of Purgatory. Purgatory is a warning that one can never do enough to earn God's favor, to appease His wrath. One illustration of this is from a Marian catechism:

> Reparation is one of the four kinds of prayer. Reparation is making satisfaction or atonement to God for sins committed against God by ourselves and others. Every sin is an offense against God and justice demands that we make satisfaction to God. Reparation is repairing the damage done to God...Each time we say an Act of Contrition we are making reparation to God.[128]

Faith and Good Works

The Scriptures speak of the glory of God and the depravity of man. The purpose of the revealed Word of God is to impart trust in God, so that we serve Him thankfully and joyfully, our good works energized by the Holy Spirit working through the Gospel, not offered up to placate an angry God. Job recalled the power of God revealed in the Creation and concluded:

> Job 26:7 He stretcheth out the north over the empty place,
>
> *and* hangeth the earth upon nothing.
>
> 8 He bindeth up the waters in his thick clouds;
>
> and the cloud is not rent under them.
>
> 9 He holdeth back the face of his throne,

---

[128] Father Robert J. Fox, *The Marian Catechism*, AMI Press, 1983, p. 105f. Reparatrix is another title of Mary, used officially by the papacy but unfamiliar to most people. Pope Pius X declared: "From this community of will and suffering between Christ and Mary she merited to become most worthily the Reparatrix of the lost world." Encyclical, *Ad diem illum*, February 2, 1904. *Mary, Mother of the Church*, p. 55.

and spreadeth his cloud upon it.

10 He hath compassed the waters with bounds,

until the day and night come to an end.

11 The pillars of heaven tremble

and are astonished at his reproof.

12 He divideth the sea with his power,

and by his understanding he smiteth through the proud.

13 By his spirit he hath garnished the heavens;

his hand hath formed the crooked serpent.

14 Lo, these *are* parts of his ways:

but how little a portion is heard of him?

but the thunder of his power who can understand?

One of the clearest signs of false doctrine is taking away from the glory of God by ascribing His power to man. This happens whenever man is credited with some role in his own salvation, in the performance of certain acts or reaching the proper frame of mind. Because God demands perfection (Matthew 5:48 Be ye therefore perfect, even as your Father which is in heaven is perfect.) no one can possibly fulfill the Law. The Law demands perfect obedience because God is righteous, but only the Gospel can give us the perfect obedience that Christ exchanged for our sinfulness. That is why the Gospel can have no Law requirement. God demands contrition and He gives us meek and contrite hearts through the proclamation of the Law. God demands faith, and He plants faith in our hearts through the imperishable seed of the Gospel. This distinction between Law and Gospel was first made by Luther, then continued by the *Book of Concord*, the orthodox theologians, and C. F. W. Walther in *The Proper Distinction between Law and Gospel.*

In John 6:28 people came to Jesus and asked, "What must we do to do the works God requires?" Jesus answered – the singular work of God is that "You believe in the One He sent." In the poetic phrases of the Little Gospel, no Law requirement can be found. –

John 3:16 For God so loved the world,

that he gave his only begotten Son,

> that whosoever believeth in him
>
> should not perish, but have everlasting life.

The relationship between faith as a gift of God and good works that proceed from salvation can be seen in Ephesians:

> Ephesians 2:8 For by grace are ye saved through faith; and that not of yourselves: *it is* the gift of God: 9 Not of works, lest any man should boast. 10 For we are his workmanship, created in Christ Jesus unto good works, which God hath before ordained that we should walk in them.

St. Paul used the example of Abraham to show that works do not contribute to our salvation, since Abraham believed before he fulfilled the Law by being circumcised.

> Romans 4:1 What shall we say then that Abraham our father, as pertaining to the flesh, hath found? 2 For if Abraham were justified by works, he hath *whereof* to glory; but not before God. 3 For what saith the scripture? Abraham believed God, and it was counted unto him for righteousness. 4 Now to him that worketh is the reward not reckoned of grace, but of debt. 5 But to him that worketh not, but believeth on him that justifieth the ungodly, his faith is counted for righteousness. 6 Even as David also describeth the blessedness of the man, unto whom God imputeth righteousness without works, 7 *Saying*, Blessed *are* they whose iniquities are forgiven, and whose sins are covered. 8 Blessed *is* the man to whom the Lord will not impute sin.

The Apostle also wrote:

> Romans 11:5 Even so then at this present time also there is a remnant according to the election of grace. 6 And if by grace, then *is it* no more of works: otherwise grace is no more grace. But if *it be* of works, then is it no more grace: otherwise work is no more work.

The message of the Apostle's letter to the Galatians is the same: If one single Law requirement, such as circumcision, is added to the Gospel, the Gospel becomes the Law. Luther concluded, "In justification, faith and works exclude each other entirely."[129]

Merit or Worthiness of the Christian

Lutherans claim for themselves only the merit of Christ for salvation, but the scholastics invented a two-fold system of merit that is still taught today in the Church of Rome. Chemnitz argued against it:

> And, in short, the *meritum condigni* is the Helen for which the Tridentine [Council of Trent = Tridentine] chapter concerning the growth of justification contends. For they imagine that the quality, or habit, of love is infused not that we may possess salvation to life eternal through this first grace but that, assisted by that grace, we may be able to merit eternal life for ourselves by our own good works. For concerning the *meritum condigni* Gabriel speaks thus: "The soul shaped by grace worthily (*de condigno*) merits eternal life."[130]

Father Baker illustrates the strength of the Council of Trent tradition in his defense of condign and congruous merit, centuries after the Council:

> If it is a strict right in justice, then Catholic theology calls it *de condigno* merit (the English word is "condign," which means "deserved". If it is a question simply of appropriateness or liberality on the part of the one giving the reward, it is called *de congruo* merit (the English word is "congruous" or "suitable"...The teaching of the Catholic Church is that, by his good works, the

---

[129] *What Luther Says*, II, p. 712.

[130] *Examination*, I, p. 541. Translator's note – "Scholastics taught that the good works of the unregenerate had only *meritum congrui*; the good works of the regenerate rewarded as *meritum condigni*, merit worthy of being rewarded with eternal life." See Baker, *Fundamentals*, III, p. 78.

person in the state of sanctifying grace really merits a supernatural reward from God.[131]

Adolph Hoenecke, the sainted Wisconsin Synod seminary professor, wrote a fine dogmatics text.[132] He summarized doctrinal comparisons with great precision.

Identical with papal teaching, that faith is not a means of grace and does not alone justify, is the other papal doctrine that works justify.[133]

Hoenecke expressed with clarity the heart of the difficulty that Lutherans and Protestants have with the Roman Catholic doctrine of salvation.

The Monster of Uncertainty

While the notion of meriting grace seems appealing at first glance, the final result of an emphasis upon human merit is uncertainty, for who is really sure of being worthy before God? Therefore, the Roman Catholic system not only creates uncertainty, but also criticizes the peace that comes from the objective reality of justification through the merits of Christ alone, Who makes the unworthy worthy of eternal life. Uncertainty about salvation, according to Father Baker, is the hallmark of Roman Catholicism.

For example, the Reformers said that the justified have an absolute certainty about their justification that excludes all

---

[131] Baker, *Fundamentals* , III, p. 78. (See *Examination*, I, p. 463.) "The justified person can merit congruously for others what he can merit for himself, for example, actual graces. So we can offer good works for others and also pray for them. St. James offers us good advice on this point: 'Pray for one another, and this will cure you; the heartfelt prayer of a good man works very powerfully' (James 5:16)." *Baker*, III, p. 86. Thus, Pope Pius X declared that Mary... "merits *de congruo* what Christ merits *de condigno*, and is the principal minister in the distribution of grace." Encyclical, *Ad diem illum*, 1904. *Mary, Mother of the Church*, p. 54.

[132] Two of the Hoenecke volumes are now available in English from Northwestern Publishing House in Milwaukee.

[133] *Evangelische-Lutherische Dogmatik*, 4 vols., Milwaukee: Northwestern Publishing House, 1912, III, p. 386. Note - Council of Trent, Session VI, XXXII.

possible doubt. The point here is the degree of certainty that we can attain about whether or not we are in the state of grace. Luther and Calvin said that we have absolute certainty. That does not square with the clear teaching of Holy Scripture on the subject. For St. Paul says: "Work out your salvation in fear and trembling" (Philippians 2:12) and, "My conscience does not reproach me at all, but that does not prove that I am acquitted: the Lord alone is my judge" (1 Corinthians. 4:4).[134]

Francis Pieper, who began his ministry as a Wisconsin Synod pastor, wrote:

> The *monstrum incertitudinis* exists only where faith is made to deal, not with the Gospel alone, but with the Gospel and the Law or the entire Scripture, or where faith is held to be not only the product of God alone, but also a moral achievement. It must be admitted that doubts do arise in the believer's heart, but such doubt, which originates in the flesh, must not be treated as something commendable, as is done by the Papists and synergists, but must be denounced as wickedness.[135]

The uncertainty bred by merit was highlighted in an article by a Roman Catholic layman in the conservative Roman Catholic *Twin Circle* newspaper:

> Recently I heard a homily that began: "Have you ever wondered whether you are doing enough to be saved?"... "Am I doing enough?" I kept asking myself...The theology of most Protestant sects (especially the fundamentalists) rests on the belief that we are saved by faith alone, and that good works do nothing toward helping us get to heaven. Once one has "accepted Jesus Christ as his Savior," he or she is saved. Period. This contrasts starkly with

---

[134] *Fundamentals*, III, p. 75f.

[135] Pieper, *Christian Dogmatics*, II, p. 445.

Catholic teaching, which holds that both faith and works are necessary for salvation.[136]

Another aspect of the Roman Catholic emphasis upon works and the Law is the portrayal of Christ. The Council of Trent declared:

> If anyone says that Christ Jesus was given to men by God as a redeemer in whom they should believe, and not also as a lawgiver whom they should obey, let him be anathema [damned to Hell].[137]

However, in the Gospel of John (1:17), we read that the Law came through Moses, grace and truth through Jesus Christ. In mixing the Law and the Gospel, especially in the work of the Redeemer, the Roman Catholic Church turns the Gospel into Law. They turn Christ into Moses and Moses into the Savior, as Luther once remarked. Instead of delivering sinners from the Law, the Medieval scholastic view handed them over to a new law, exemplified by the invention of Purgatory for the posthumous fulfillment of the Law's demands, even by the most faithful.

> The elite are assembled in the cloister to earn salvation for themselves by observing the *consilia evangelica*, devised by man, and to obtain a surplus of good works (*opera supererogationis*) for the benefit of others. However, since this process does not give full assurance (*Trid., Sess.* IV, canon 14, 9), they look to purgatory to complete their "sanctification" (*Trid., Sess.* VI, canon 30).[138]

James and Good Works

Much has been written, most of it misleading, about Luther's criticism of the Epistle of James. After suffering from the burden of

---

[136] William M. Vatavuk, *Catholic Twin Circle*, December 3, 1989, *Christian News*, December 18, 1989.

[137] *Examination*, I, p. 617.

[138] *Christian Dogmatics*, III, p. 64. (Pieper footnote – "See Luther on the 'blasphemous fraud of Purgatory, by which treacherous deception they have made fools of all the world.' St. Louis edition, XVI:1653f."

works-righteousness (salvation by fulfilling the Law) for years in the monastery, Luther did not want the Gospel of Christ twisted into Law. Liberals have quoted Luther out of context to portray an alleged attack on the Bible, which is as fanciful as James' supposed argument with St. Paul about the relationship between faith and works. James was used during the Reformation, as the book is now, to buttress the claims of the Roman party. The Lutherans responded in the Augsburg Confession, 1530:

> They [our opponents] do not teach now that we become righteous before God by our works alone, but they add faith in Christ and say faith and works make us righteous before God. This teaching may offer a little more comfort than the teaching that we are to rely solely on our works...We begin by teaching that our works cannot reconcile us with God or obtain grace for us, for this happens only through faith, that is, when we believe that our sins are forgiven for Christ's sake, who alone is the mediator who reconciles the Father. Whoever imagines that he can accomplish this by works, or that he can merit grace, despises Christ and seeks his own way to God, contrary to the Gospel...It must be done, not that we are to rely on them to earn grace but that we may do God's will and glorify Him. It is always faith alone that apprehends grace and forgiveness of sin.[139]

These key verses in James are used to question Lutheran doctrine:

- James 2:26 For as the body without the spirit is dead, so faith without works is dead also.

- "James 2:24 Ye see then how that by works a man is justified, and not by faith only.

---

[139] Augsburg Confession, Article XX, Good Works, German trans. Tappert, p. 41f. *Triglotta*, p. 53. Robert Sungenis wrote *Not by Faith Alone: The Biblical Evidence for the Catholic Doctrine of Justification*, Santa Barbara: Queenship Publishing, 1997.

Luther might have written verse 26 as "Faith without works is not faith at all." Following James, the Reformer always trusted that salvation produced fruit. If someone claimed he was a believer but did not help his neighbor, that individual needed to question whether he was truly repentant. James argument is against those who say they believe and yet do not act upon their beliefs, making faith a form of intellectual agreement, not a living trust in Christ. This passage, like many others in the New Testament (Parable of the Last Judgment, Matthew 25) addresses carnal security, the attitude of a person who attends church but remains unrepentant, thinking that membership bestows salvation and forgiveness without sorrow for sin and trust in the Gospel promises. The Apology of the Augsburg Confession states:

> James did not hold that by our good works we merit grace and the forgiveness of sins. He is talking about the works of the justified, who have already been reconciled and accepted and have obtained the forgiveness of sins.[140]

In contrast, the Roman Catholic Church has connected works with merit, using James.

> In this declaration of false security, we have the beginning of Luther's new gospel, which, needless to say, is directly and openly opposed to the Gospel of Jesus Christ. As a theologian, he should have realized that his notion of the absolute assurance of salvation imparted by faith was as false as it was unsound, and as a professor of Scripture, he should have realized that faith alone is barren and lifeless apart from the meritorious works which are necessarily connected with and founded on it.[141]

Since Abraham is the father of faith in the Bible, James used his example (as St. Paul did in Romans 4; see Hebrews 11) to emphasize the close relationship between genuine faith and works. The carnal security passages of the Bible challenge us to see anew that God created us to do

---

[140] Apology, IV, Justification, Tappert, p. 143.

[141] O'Hare, *The Facts About Luther*, p. 98.

good works, which do not merit salvation but grow as fruits of the Gospel. Works do not justify us in the eyes of God, because that would disparage the loving gift of the Son by the Father, and the loving gift of the Son for all of us sinners. Lutherans are not opposed to good works. The Augsburg Confession states:

> It is also taught among us that such faith should produce good fruits and good works and that we must do all such good works as God has commanded, but we should do them for God's sake and not place our trust in them as if thereby to merit favor before God.[142]

Jesus taught in John 15:1-8 that Gospel fruits come from remaining with Him, just as branches of the grapevine produce fruit from remaining on the vine. The Law produces contrition for our sins and the Gospel announces our forgiveness as a gift from God, a gift paid for by Christ Jesus. The best kind of motivation is Gospel motivation, that is, when a person does a good work moved by the Holy Spirit to show thankfulness to God, not out of fear, nor in the expectation of thanks or a reward. When the Law motivates us, we either become self-righteous, counting ourselves better than others, or hypocritical, pretending to be holy through our outward obedience. Luther wrote:

> If the article of justification is lost, all Christian doctrine is lost at the same time. And all the people in the world who do not hold to this justification are either Jews or Turks or papists or heretics; for there is no middle ground between these two righteousnesses: the active one of the Law and the passive one which comes from Christ. Therefore the man who strays from Christian righteousness must relapse into the active one, that is, since he has lost Christ, he must put his confidence in his own works.[143]

The truth of the Gospel is not based upon its popularity, nor upon the power of those who believe, nor upon its apparent effects at any given

---

[142] Augsburg Confession, Article VI, The New Obedience, Tappert, p. 31f.

143 *What Luther Says*, II, p. 703. Galatians lectures, 1531.

time. God's Word will endure, even when heaven and earth have passed away, as Luther noted:

> The devil is always plaguing the world by keeping people from distinguishing between the work of God and the work of men....But you should know that though no human being believed Baptism and the Gospel, the Gospel and Baptism would still be right; for both are not mine but God's Word and work.[144]

Another temptation is to think of faith as historical knowledge of the Scriptures, which any skeptic may have. An unbeliever may know the factual content of the Bible better than a believer who is new to the Christian faith. One of the most Scriptural novels ever written is *Moby Dick*, by Herman Melville, yet it contains no Gospel and often mocks orthodox Christianity. When Protestants try to argue people into the Kingdom of God, by proving Creation or other aspects of Biblical history, they are inadvertently offering faith as historical knowledge, rather than using the Word to create trust in God's mercy.[145] The Lutheran Confessions address this problem.

Paul clearly shows that faith does not simply mean historical knowledge but is a firm acceptance of God's promise:

> Romans 4:16 Therefore *it is* of faith, that *it might be* by grace; to the end the promise might be sure to all the seed; not to that only which is of the law, but to that also which is of the faith of Abraham; who is the father of us all,

The Book of Concord adds:

> For he says that only faith can accept the promise. He therefore correlates promise and faith. It will be easy to determine what

---

144 *Ibid.*, p. 705. November 24, 1537. John 1:30-34.

145 One popular technique is to offer the listener one of three choices. Jesus was either the Lord, a liar, or a lunatic. The Holy Spirit works through the Gospel, not through logical tricks.

faith is if we pay attention to the article of the Creed on the forgiveness of sins.[146]

Protestant Problems

Disagreement between Lutherans and Protestants about justification center on the role of the human will in salvation and the relationship between Law and Gospel. Concerning the will of man, the extremes are marked by the doctrine of the Pelagians and the true Calvinists. Pelagius (4th century A.D.), a contemporary of St. Augustine, taught that man was capable of perfection, that he was not depraved (the fallen nature inherited from Adam) and had the power to save himself. Modern day Pelagians are those who teach the Power of Positive Thinking, such as the late Norman Vincent Peale and his pupil Robert Schuller. In "Star Wars," Obi-Wan Kenobe represents Pelagianism and its close relationship with the occult when he says, "Use the Force, Luke. The Force is within you, within all of us. It surrounds us." Pelagians cannot be considered Christian because their doctrine is man-centered. Therefore, they are either Universalists like Peale (no Hell, everyone goes to Heaven) or occultists like Obi-Wan and Paul Y. Cho, or indifferent to doctrine, like Schuller, who exemplifies irony in featuring the testimony of unbelievers on his television show, The Hour of Power.

In contrast, during the Reformation, Calvin taught the predestination of a few to eternal life and the predestination of the majority to eternal damnation, double predestination. Calvinists also emphasize the total depravity of man and a limited atonement by Christ. Limited atonement means that Christ died only for the elect, not for the sins of the world, contrary to these passages:

2 Corinthians 5:14 For the love of Christ constraineth us; because we thus judge, that if one died for all, then were all dead: 15 And *that* he died for all, that they which live should not henceforth live unto themselves, but unto him which died for them, and rose again.

---

146 Apology of the Augsburg Confession, Article IV, Justification, Tappert, p. 114.

1 Peter 3:18 For Christ also hath once suffered for sins, the just for the unjust, that he might bring us to God, being put to death in the flesh, but quickened by the Spirit:

Calvinism and TULIP

Calvinism is commonly summarized by the acronym TULIP:

Total depravity,

Unconditional election,

Limited atonement,

Irresistible grace,

Perseverance of the saints.

Calvin's position was soon under attack and quickly lost ground to Arminianism, named for the Dutch theologian Jacob Arminius (1560-1609) who disagreed about the freedom of the will, limited atonement, and man's ability to resist the grace of God. The teaching of man's cooperation in his salvation influenced John and Charles Wesley, founders of the Methodist movement. Double predestination was not accepted by the Lutherans and Roman Catholics, nor by the majority of Protestants.

The lack of a confessional foundation has always plagued Protestants, who have splintered as a result. However, this lack of a confession has been a point of pride, with the Baptists saying, "No creed but the Bible," and the Presbyterians calling themselves the "church with the open Book." Protestantism can be subdivided into denominational groups, but actual agreement on all doctrines among these groups is rare. For instance, one can find Seventh Day Baptists, Calvinist Baptists, Free Will Baptists, and Regular Baptists. Most Protestants accept a form of synergism (man's cooperation with God in salvation) when they teach justification by faith. A common term for this is decision theology, coined from the frequent references to making a decision for Christ. Billy Graham's magazine is *Decision* and his radio show was called the Hour of Decision. Those Protestants who teach synergism also teach people to pray that "Jesus will come into your heart." Thus prayer displaces the Word and Sacraments as the Means of Grace. Decision theology also suggests that a person spiritually dead to Christ can pray to Jesus to come into his heart. Faith is the result of salvation, not the cause of salvation.

Lutheran criticism of prayer seems contradictory, for the Bible clearly urges us to pray. However, the difference involves the role of man's will. In the Bible, the will is passive in salvation, rather than active or cooperating. Synergism does not create certainty based upon the objective Word of God, but intensifies uncertainty. The Protestants emphasize the certainty of salvation through feeling saved, rather than the certainty of salvation through the Gospel promises found in the Scriptures. One might compare this to being rich by feeling rich or feeling rich by knowing it is true. This is not playing with words. The Protestant rejection of the Sacraments takes away the certainty that God grants us through His visible signs. For instance, when a handicapped girl of six dies without being able to speak, how does anyone know that the child is with Christ in heaven? The Protestant says, "The child is not accountable for sin because she is under the age of seven." This disturbing bit of rationalism is not comforting when the next child dies of the same condition at the age of seven plus.

In contrast, a Lutheran says, "This child was baptized. God placed faith into her heart through the Gospel promises combined with the earthly element of water. Not water, but the Holy Spirit working through the Word, saved her, as promised in John 3:5." The value of Holy Baptism has been unwittingly vindicated by the many church bodies that oppose infant baptism but practice the dedication of infants, using a service that is almost identical to Holy Baptism, except for the lack of water.

In dealing with justification, the main difference between Protestants and Lutherans may be summarized as the Lutheran emphasis upon the Word and Sacraments as the Means of Grace, contrasted to the Protestant doctrine of the independent work of the Holy Spirit, without means and yet almost always through prayer. Simply put, this shows that Lutherans trust the Word of God to convert people and to nurture them in the faith. Protestants add human reason to the Scriptures to make God's Word relevant, reasonable, germane, alive, or appealing. Unless passages are explained in a pleasing way in today's terms, Protestants think the Bible is a "dead letter," to use Calvin's term. Sadly, one example used to cast doubt on the efficacy of the Word is this claim – the Word is like a statue in a garden - that points the way to salvation but has no power to confer faith or forgiveness. This accounts for the great difference between Protestant and Lutheran worship. Protestants view Lutheran worship as too Catholic: staid, formal, lacking in spirit—or rather—the Holy Spirit. Lutherans who visit Protestant churches find the worship service influenced by the entertainment industry and popular music, with an emphasis on creating a mood rather than teaching the objective truth of God.

Many observers have noted that Roman Catholics and Protestants view the Christian life (sanctification) in similar ways, even though they are supposed to be doctrinal opponents. For instance, a strict Baptist will define the Christian life as one in which alcoholic beverages are given up entirely. The Roman Catholic, in a similar fashion, will give up meat on certain days of obligation, without considering abstinence from alcohol. Thinking of the Christian life in terms of laws and requirements is typical of both Roman Catholics and Protestants. One Lutheran movement, Pietism, is similar in practice and effect.

In fact, the greatest influence upon Protestants in America is Pietism, a movement that began at Halle University to bring life back into Christianity. Pietism emphasized prayer groups or cell groups and disparaged the Means of Grace, ordained clergy, and orthodox Lutheran doctrine. In other words, Pietism taught people to look for the fruits of the faith, the Christian life, rather than to start with the pure seed of the Word of God. In countries where the state church was deeply involved in the social ills of the day and the clergy were indifferent both to faith and good works, Pietism seemed to be an effective antidote to dead church life and lukewarm Christianity. Methodism, which was Pietistic in spirit, offered many people an alternative to the social ills of the day, especially alcoholism. Methodistic revivals called on people to take the pledge against alcohol. In subsequent years, the Methodist Church found a new form of Pietism in the Social Gospel movement, which tried to make the Christian Church a political change agent. The Social Gospel movement wanted the Church to address the social ills of the nation—labor laws, pure food and drug regulations, social security for the elderly—rather than the personal sins of the individual, which were addressed by the earlier Pietism leaders: alcoholism, gambling, sexual immorality. Thus Pietism began with noble goals and ended with a politicized and polarized church, measured not by sound doctrine, but by the outward effects of the Gospel, measured subjectively and differently by each generation. Hoenecke's critique of this confusion is clear and compelling:

At first glance, the total difference seems absolutely paltry, but in truth the dangerous direction of Pietism is made apparent: life over doctrine, sanctification over justification, and piety not as a consequence but declared as a stipulation of enlightenment, leading to a kind of synergism and Pelagianism.[147]

Law and Gospel

Lutherans alone emphasize the division of the entire Bible into Law and Gospel, the proper distinction between the threats of the Law and the comfort of the Gospel. The Law has three uses, often summarized as:

1. **Curb** – placing restrictions on what we do;

2. **Mirror** – showing us our true nature;

3. **Guide** – a map for the daily life of Christians.

First Use of the Law

The First Use of the Law is recognized across the world by the civil law set up in all countries. Civil law reflects the principles set up in God's Creation, even when the government is atheistic. This is called natural law and is the basis for the Constitution of the United States. These universal principles assume a Creator whose design is evident and whose laws must be obeyed. Every law passed by government, however flawed the regulation may be, reflects the Second Table of the Ten Commandments:

- Honor your father and mother.

- Do not murder.

- Do not commit adultery.

- Do not steal.

- Do not bear false witness.

- Do not covet.

Speed limits reflect the prohibition against murder, since reckless driving can kill. The issuing of marriage licenses by the government recognizes the institution of marriage, established by God as the proper channel for sexual desire and the way to raise children.

---

[147] Hoenecke, *Evangelische-Lutherische Dogmatik*, III, p. 253.

Second Use of the Law

The Second Use of the Law holds a mirror up to our natures, to show us what we really look like in the eyes of God. In this way, the Holy Spirit works through the Word to bring about genuine contrition, or sorrow for sin. The Law-as-a-mirror passages include more than the Ten Commandments. Any passage in the Bible that condemns or terrifies the conscience is a Law passage, whether in the Old or New Testament. The Law demands perfection, because God is perfect and just, but the Law cannot create perfection in us. An x-ray will reveal a broken bone but another x-ray will not heal the break. Many Christians will define sin with the Law and then insist, in various ways, "These are the works you must do to remove the sin, the obligations you must meet." More Law will not heal the wound but increase the torment of the conscience since the Law always condemns. Only the Gospel can bring healing.

The Bible condemns adultery but also lust; murder, but also murderous words; unbelief, but also hypocrisy and self-righteousness. The Law is necessary, because it crushes proud, unbelieving hearts, so that we recognize our sin and cry out, "What must we do to be saved?" The Second Use of the Law is good for believers because Christians need to repent of their sins daily, lest they harden their hearts and reject the Gospel.

Third Use of the Law

The Third Use of the Law serves as a guide for the Christian. Luther's explanation of the Ten Commandments is an excellent illustration of the Third Use. Each explanation combines what we should not do (Second Use) with what a Christian will do in love (Third Use). The following is from Luther's Small Catechism, *The Book of Concord*:

Honor your father and mother.

We should fear and love God that we may not despise nor anger our parents and masters, but give them honor, serve, obey, and hold them in love and esteem.

You shall not murder.

We should fear and love God that we may not hurt nor harm our neighbor in his body, but help and befriend him in every bodily need.

You shall not commit adultery.

We should fear and love God that we may lead a chaste and decent life in words and deeds, and each love and honor his spouse.

You shall not steal.

We should fear and love God that we may not take our neighbor's money or property, nor get them by false ware or dealing, but help him to improve and protect his property and business that his means are preserved and his condition is improved.

You shall not give false testimony against your neighbor.

We should fear and love God that we may not deceitfully belie, betray, slander, or defame our neighbor, but defend him, think and speak well of him, and put the best construction on everything.

You shall not covet your neighbor's house.

We should fear and love God that we may not craftily seek to get our neighbor's inheritance or house, and obtain it by a show of justice and right, etc., but help and be of service to him in keeping it.

You shall not covet your neighbor's wife, not his servants, nor his animals, nor anything that is his.

We should fear and love God that we may not estrange, force, or entice away our neighbor's wife, servants, or cattle, but urge them to stay and diligently do their duty.[148]

The Gospel includes any passage that promises God's love, mercy, and forgiveness. Many passages in the Old Testament are Gospel, such as Psalm 23, Psalm 103, Isaiah 40-66, all the prophecies of the Messiah, and so forth. The Gospel creates the faith in our hearts necessary for forgiveness, salvation, and eternal life. Thus the stricken,

---

[148] *Triglotta*, Small Catechism, The Ten Commandments, p. 541.

contrite sinner, who knows his need for a Savior, can be assured that Christ has died for his sins and has paid the complete penalty for them. The repentant sinner can be comforted with the Good News that this forgiveness, earned by Christ alone, is completely free and unconditional, without any Law requirements.

The Old Adam in us rebels against the nature of the gift. We want to attach a price or a condition, but the only requirement is faith, which God Himself provides through His invisible Word (preaching and teaching) and His visible Word (the Sacraments of Holy Baptism and Holy Communion). Faith is not a virtue for which man strives; nor is faith a quality that we can improve by our efforts. The Gospel message of the Bible is that Christ exchanged His perfect righteousness for our guilt, accepting the full wrath of God on the cross, serving as a substitute for us, fulfilling the First Gospel promise of Genesis 3:15 by crushing the head of Satan and being wounded in return. The atoning death of Christ revealed the true meaning of the foreshadowing events and prophesies that preceded Calvary: the substitution of the ram for Abraham's only son at Mt. Moriah (Genesis 22:1-18), the sacrifice of the spotless lamb at the Passover meal (Exodus 12:5), the Suffering Servant songs of Isaiah (42:1ff.; 52:13ff.; 53).

The Gospel not only declares our innocence and the gift of eternal life, but also motivates us so that all good works are done in thanksgiving to God, not as an obligation or penance for sin. If we need to do only one thing to deserve forgiveness, then forgiveness is not free. If any sin is not paid in full by Christ on the cross, then the atoning work of God's Son is incomplete and faulty.

Confusing Law and Gospel

Law can be confused with Gospel, and Gospel with Law. For instance, many would like to proclaim forgiveness to the unrepentant.[149] When this is done, the sinner becomes worse than ever, thinking of God as a heavenly Mr. Rogers who would never become upset over a mere mishap like adultery or murder. Liberalism is properly defined by H. Richard Niebuhr in *The Kingdom of God in America*, 1937, as..."a God

---

[149] Luther said that when the Gospel is offered to the unrepentant, the man will respond like a cow staring at a newly painted fence. Various forms of Universalism are popular today, regardless of their lack of Biblical support.

without wrath who brought men without sin into a kingdom without judgment through the ministrations of a Christ without a cross."[150] Removing sorrow for sin from God's plan of salvation is equal to eliminating the Gospel itself and substituting a feel-good religion that destroys souls.

Mingling Law with Gospel

When the Law is mingled with the Gospel, the Christian faith is also endangered, as indicated previously. St. Paul's encounter with the Judaizers in Galatians underlines the importance of justification by faith alone in the Bible. The Judaizers wanted to add circumcision as a requirement for salvation, while St. Paul argued that this was another Gospel for which the messenger should be anathema, damned to Hell (Galatians 1:8-9). The Apostle's anger was caused by his desire to keep the Gospel free of Law requirements that would destroy salvation as a gracious gift from God.

Sanctification in Roman Catholicism and in Protestantism is marked by the mingling of Law and Gospel. In the simplest words, it is defined by what a Christian does rather than what he believes. As Hoenecke observed (above), a common development is making sanctification a requirement for justification. For one group of Protestants, sanctification means never playing cards for any reason. For another, sanctification means never dancing, never watching anyone dance. For some, sanctification can include never wearing makeup or jewelry of any kind. Roman Catholics do not submit to the Methodist or holiness code of the Protestants, but they do speak of the Christian life as one of obligation, penance, and merits. For both groups, sanctification is confused with justification, and the Christian life is easily distorted into a life of action and deeds, with pure doctrine occupying a secondary place.

Those who have rebelled against Lutheran Pietism or the holiness code of Protestantism can easily list why they have rejected the traditions of their elders. One reason is the confusion of God's Law with man's law. Condemning any form of dancing is not the same as God's condemnation of lewd behavior. Rejecting all use of alcohol, including Communion wine, is contrary to Scripture, which prohibits drunkenness, not alcohol. The first generation of Protestants to adopt holiness rules

---

[150] Cited at http://libnt4.lib.tcu.edu/staff/bellinger/60003/lecture_on_hrn.htm.

(against dancing, gambling, drinking, cards, theaters) had the praiseworthy goal of avoiding the temptations of the world that choke the Word (Mark 4:19). Following generations have often rejected the whole message of the Christian faith along with the man-made rules imposed on them by the community of faith. Roman Catholics have also spurned the Christian faith for being one of obligation, duty, and an endless stream of good works, which are never enough.

Protestants and Roman Catholics together have criticized Lutherans for condemning good works, or at least for being weak on sanctification, as the critics like to say. The topic became such a source of contention for Lutherans that the Formula of Concord, 1580, had to address the issue. Two errors, which had been taught among the Lutherans, were condemned. The error taught by Major was that good works were necessary for salvation. Amsdorf mistakenly taught that good works were injurious to salvation. Both errors represented an extreme position not taught by the Scriptures or taught by the Church fathers. Luther wrote in his preface to the Commentary on Romans:

> Faith is a living, daring confidence in God's grace, so sure and certain that a man would stake his life on it a thousand times. This confidence in God's grace and knowledge of it makes men glad and bold and happy in dealing with God and all His creatures; and this is the work of the Holy Ghost in faith. Hence a man is ready and glad, without compulsion, to do good to everyone, to serve everyone, to suffer everything, in love and praise to God, Who has shown him this grace; and thus it is impossible to separate works from faith, quite as impossible as to separate heat and light from fires.[151]

Lutherans have been wary of making sanctification proof of justification, so the good works done in thanksgiving are often downplayed. Nevertheless, wherever the Gospel has been preached, Gospel fruits have been produced by the Word of God.

---

[151] Grand Rapids: Kregel Publications, 1976, p. xvii.

Justification Summary

Roman Catholic – Jesus Christ died on the cross for our sins, which are forgiven, but not paid for. The will is active in salvation. Good works complete the work begun by God in salvation and make the believer pleasing to Him. Salvation is not certain. This is completed by meritorious works performed and Masses said during life, by suffering in Purgatory after death, and by having Masses said after death.

Lutheran – God brings about sorrow for sin through the preaching of the Law. The Gospel creates and sustains faith, which is trust in God's mercy through Christ. The atoning death of Christ is universal, offering complete forgiveness and payment for sin. The will is passive in salvation, receiving in faith the Promises of God (the Gospel). The Holy Spirit works only through—and never apart from—the appointed Means of Grace: the Word and Sacraments of Holy Baptism and Holy Communion, to offer God's gift of pardon and peace, love and forgiveness. Good works are the fruit of faith, resulting from salvation, not creating worthiness for salvation, which is from Christ alone.

Protestant – The forgiveness won by Christ on the cross is complete and free. The Atonement is universal for Arminians (most Protestants), but limited to the elect among strict Calvinists. The Holy Spirit works apart from the Word, showing God's sovereignty. For most Protestants, the human will cooperates in salvation, making a decision to accept Christ as Savior. Prayer is a means of grace, providing the way by which Christ enters an individual's life, when He is invited into one's heart. Protestants often say, "God begins, but man completes the transaction." Sunday School and the prayer group are often more significant than the worship service. The Christian life may preclude alcohol, cards, movies, and other allures of the world in such systems as traditional Methodism and the Holiness movement. Christians are identified by their fruits, how they live, rather than by their doctrine, what they believe.

"#305. Why do you say in this article: I believe in the Forgiveness of Sins? Because I hold with certainty that by my own powers or through my own works I cannot be justified before God, but that the forgiveness of sins is given me out of grace through faith in Jesus Christ. For where there is forgiveness of sins, there is also true justification. Psalm 130:3-4; Psalm 143:2; Isaiah 64:6; Job 25:4-6 (Q. 124)."

Kleiner Katechismus, trans. Pastor Vernon Harley, LCMS, St. Louis: Concordia Publishing House, 1901, p. 164ff.

"#306. What is justification? Justification is that activity (Handlung) of God by which He out of pure grace and mercy for the sake of Christ's merits forgives the sins of a poor sinner who truly believes in Jesus Christ and receives him to everlasting life."

Kleiner Katechismus, trans. Pastor Vernon Harley, LCMS, St. Louis: Concordia Publishing House, 1901, p. 164ff.

Chapter Four: Purgatory

The doctrine of Purgatory is one of the clearest dividing lines between Roman Catholics on one side, who teach that sins must be cleansed after death, and Lutherans and Protestants on the other side who reject Purgatory as utterly without foundation in Scripture and completely foreign to the Gospel of Jesus Christ. Contradictory claims are made about the Eastern Orthodox rejecting Purgatory.

> The real history of Purgatory begins with a paradox, a twofold paradox. Those who have rightly been called the "founders" of the doctrine of Purgatory were Greek theologians. Although their ideas were not without impact on Greek Christianity, the Greek Church never developed the notion of Purgatory as such. Indeed, during the Middle Ages, Purgatory was one of the principal bones of contention between Greek Christians and Latin Christians.[152]

Although Purgatory does not receive the visibility it once did in the Roman Catholic Church, the doctrine remains central to the teachings, practice, and worship of the Church of Rome, closely connected with her understanding of salvation, Mary, papal authority, and the interpretation of Scripture. A mailing sent in 1991 from the Passionist Monastery, included this card printed for All Souls Day, illustrated with a picture of the Virgin Mary:

Prayer for the Souls in Purgatory

> O God, Creator and Redeemer of all the faithful, grant to the souls of our departed loved, the remission of all their sins, that by means of our pious supplications, they may obtain the joys of heaven, which they have ever earnestly desired. We ask this through Christ our Lord. Amen.

---

[152] Le Goff, *The Birth of Purgatory*, p. 52.

140

The card asked for the names of loved ones to be remembered and has this statement below the list:

> Yes, I want the above deceased remembered in daily Mass during the month of November. I am enclosing my donation to help the Passionist Priests and Brothers continue their Apostolic work.

This emphasis upon Purgatory is less visible in the typical Roman Catholic parish, but continues to be part of the official doctrine of the papacy.

Father Richard McBrien, a liberal Roman Catholic scholar, in his monumental work on Roman Catholicism, said this about Purgatory:

> The doctrine is reaffirmed in Pope Paul's Credo of the People of God (1968) and by the Congregation for the Doctrine of the Faith's "Letter on Certain Questions Concerning Eschatology" (1979) and is assumed by the Second Vatican Council's *Dogmatic Constitution on the Church*, n. 51. [153]

A modern historian of Purgatory wrote:

> In the area of dogma and theology, Purgatory was ultimately enshrined in the doctrine of the Catholic Church between the middle of the fifteenth and the beginning of the seventeenth century, first being affirmed against the Greeks at the Council of

---

[153] Richard P. McBrien, *Catholicism*, 2 vols., Minneapolis: Winston Press, 1980, II, p. 1144. Footnote 51. McBrien added: "The traditional doctrine is enunciated by the Second Council of Lyons (1274), Benedict XII's *Benedictus Deus* (1336), and especially in the Council of Florence's Decree for the Greeks (1439), which tried to strike a careful balance between the Western concept of satisfaction and expiation and the Eastern emphasis on purification." *Ibid.* Chemnitz wrote: "They say, indeed, that the sound doctrine of purgatory is taught in sacred councils. And the unlearned perhaps think that this had been done in the Nicene or other more ancient councils. But the council in question is the Council of Florence, held around A.D. 1439. Therefore they not imprudently decline the burden of proof in this matter and with bare but strong assertions strenuously try to blow up from the ashes and rekindle the fire of purgatory, which until now so splendidly warmed their kitchens." *Examination*, III, p. 227.

Florence (1439) and later against the Protestants at the Council of Trent (1562).[154]

The Dogmatic Constitution of the Second Vatican Council expressed the doctrine of Purgatory in the context of the communion of saints:

> This most sacred Synod accepts with great devotion the venerable faith of our ancestors regarding this vital fellowship with our brethren who are in heavenly glory or who are still being purified after death. It proposes again the decrees of the Second Council of Nicea, the Council of Florence, and the Council of Trent.[155]

Le Goff commented on the Council of Trent:

> Trent, an affair of theologians and rulers more than of pastors, established Purgatory in dogma once and for all but, like its thirteenth century predecessors, remained noncommittal as to Purgatory's imaginary content.[156]

Purgatory is not a popular topic for theologians, yet the doctrine cannot be separated from any other aspect of Roman Catholic teaching, worship, and practice. One Mariologist wrote: "Around the doctrine of Purgatory, many other doctrines necessarily gather."[157] Doctrines gather around Purgatory because the Christian faith is unitary rather than modular. What one believes about the Two Natures of Christ, for example, will determine what is confessed about the Lord's Supper. One

---

[154] *Birth of Purgatory*, p. 357.

[155] *Lumen Gentium*, Chapter VII, *Vatican II*, p. 84. A footnote by Abbott on the same page expressed more unity between the Eastern Orthodox and the Church of Rome about Purgatory than one finds in the history books: #249 "The Council of Nicea II (787) and Florence (1439) are ecumenically important because they express points of agreement between the Greek and Latin churches regarding the invocation of the saints, the veneration of sacred images, and suffrages for the souls in Purgatory. The Council of Trent (1549-1563) treated these questions once more in the context of the Protestant Reformation."

[156] *Birth of Purgatory*, p. 357.

[157] Jugie, *Purgatory*, p. 27.

error, which seems small at first, will lead to greater errors, and eventually, to apostasy.[158] Several of the doctrines that are peculiar to Roman Catholicism grew together, one reflective of the other. Mary's role as a comforter in Purgatory, confirmed by the authority of the infallible pope, is just one example of a confluence of doctrines. Among Lutherans, justification by faith alone is necessarily associated with the Means of Grace because God's grace comes to us solely through the Word and Sacraments. Among Protestants, certain doctrines of Christ are related directly to a symbolic interpretation of Holy Communion with the Real Presence of Christ set aside. Therefore, when a Roman Catholic considers sanctification, the Christian life (acts of contrition, good works, attendance at Mass) all actions and attitudes are centered in the doctrine of Purgatory, even if the topic itself has been de-emphasized.[159]

The Biblical Passages

The primary passages in Scripture which are used to defend the doctrine of Purgatory are discussed below. McBrien wrote:

> There is, for all practical purposes, no Biblical basis for the doctrine of Purgatory...On the other hand, there is no contradictory evidence in either Old or New Testaments.[160]

One of the most important passages for the Roman argument is 2 Maccabees 12:41-46. Second Maccabees is not found in most Bibles used by Lutherans and Protestants. The book is one of the thirteen called the Old Testament Apocrypha, which were never accepted as canonical by the Church. These apocryphal books include 1 and 2 Maccabees, which are historical books about the Jewish War of Independence, around 165 B.C. Lutherans consider the apocryphal books "useful and edifying" for the Church but not the revelation of God. They were included in

---

[158] "In philosophy an error that is small at the beginning becomes very great in the end. So a small error in theology overturns the whole body of doctrine...That is why we may not surrender or change even an iota (*apiculum*) of doctrine." *What Luther Says*, III, p. 1365. Galatians 5:9.

[159] The Church Growth Movement has influenced Roman Catholicism, too. Hiding doctrinal differences is key to the disciples of Fuller, so certain Roman parishes use the name Community Church, trying to appear as generic and non-threatening as possible.

[160] McBrien, *Catholicism*, II, p. 238.

Lutheran Bibles at first, but the decision of the Council of Trent to make them equal to the canonical Scriptures played a role in having them left out of Lutheran and Protestant Bibles from that time on. St. Jerome, who translated the Bible into Latin, (the Vulgate, since it was in the common or vulgar tongue of his time), did not want to translate or include the apocryphal books. St. Jerome wrote:

> The Church reads these for the edification of the common people, not however to confirm the authority of church dogmas, for their authority is judged less suitable for establishing things which have come into dispute.[161]

Therefore, this passage from 2 Maccabees cannot be considered on an equal basis with the Old Testament.

> All then bless the ways of the Lord, the just judge who brings hidden things to light, and gave themselves to prayer, begging that the sin committed [amulets of idols found on bodies of men] might be fully blotted out. Next, the valiant Judas urged the people to keep themselves free from all sin, having seen with their own eyes the effects of the sin of those who had fallen; after this he took a collection from them individually, amounting to nearly two thousand drachmae, and sent it to Jerusalem to have a sacrifice for sin offered, an altogether fine and noble action, in which he took full account of the resurrection. For if he had not expected the fallen to rise again it would have been superfluous and foolish to pray for the dead, whereas if he had in view the splendid recompense reserved for those who make a pious end, the thought was holy and devout. This is why he had this atonement sacrifice offered for the dead, so that they might be released from their sin.[162]

---

[161] *Examination*, III, p. 238.

[162] *The Jerusalem Bible*, New York: Doubleday and Company, 1966, p. 624. "Prayer for the souls of the faithful departed is as old as the Church. It was already a practice of the Jews, as is witnessed by the second book of the Maccabees (xii, 39-46)." Jugie, *Purgatory*, p. 12.

Chemnitz voiced the doubts of many scholars about the credibility of 2 Maccabees when he wrote: "And Josephus, although he diligently records the history of the Maccabees, makes no mention of this sacrifice for the dead."[163] Chemnitz also wondered about such a weak underpinning for the doctrine of Purgatory:

> Even if we allow for the accuracy of this anecdote, what does it prove? The passage shows that in this instance, without any command from God or the Scriptures, a Jewish leader borrowed from the customs of pagan neighbors and performed a sacrifice on behalf of the dead. Moreover, this is reported, if it happened at all, during a time when the nation was at low ebb.[164]

Thus, if the passage is read by itself and no further study is done, one might get the impression that performing some work for the dead had an ancient, Biblical basis upon which the Church built the realm of Purgatory. In fact, even with the speculation of a few Church fathers (influenced by pagan authors) Purgatory did not ignite until the 12th or 13th century after Christ.

The other key passage for the support of Purgatory is from the Apostle Paul and deserves to be read carefully.

> 1 Corinthians 3:10 According to the grace of God which is given unto me, as a wise masterbuilder, I have laid the foundation, and another buildeth thereon. But let every man take heed how he buildeth thereupon. 11 For other foundation can no man lay than that is laid, which is Jesus Christ. 12 Now if any man build upon this foundation gold, silver, precious stones, wood, hay, stubble; 13 Every man's work shall be made manifest: for the day shall declare it, because it shall be revealed by fire; and the fire shall try every man's work of what sort it is. 14 If any man's work abide which he hath built thereupon, he shall receive a reward. 15 If any man's work shall be burned, he shall suffer loss: but he himself shall be saved; yet so as by fire.

---

[163] *Examination*, III, p. 236.

[164] *Ibid.*, p. 235.

In this passage from 1 Corinthians, St. Paul emphasizes the foundation of the Christian Church—and all Christian teaching—to be Christ Jesus. He is the bedrock on which the Church is built, as He said to St. Peter in Matthew 16. Many types of teachers came along after Christ. The Apostles built the Church with gold, silver, and precious stones: the doctrines taught to them by Christ. Others, already in the Apostolic age, tried to buy the power of the Holy Spirit (Acts 8:18), added man-made doctrines to the Word of God (Judaizers in Galatians), and even taught as Scripture, doctrines clearly opposed by the Bible (1 John). In his farewell speech to the Ephesian elders, St. Paul warned them not only against wolves from the outside slaying the flock, but also false teachers from within the visible church:

> Acts 20:29 For I know this, that after my departing shall grievous wolves enter in among you, not sparing the flock. 30 Also of your own selves shall men arise, speaking perverse things, to draw away disciples after them.

This passage from 1 Corinthians 3 is used by Roman Catholics to support the doctrine of Purgatory, but in reality, God is warning all Christians that man-made structures will not endure the final test, the Day of Judgment. Some will believe in Christ as their Savior, in spite of false teachers who substitute rationalism, emotionalism, and superstition for the Christian faith. But every error contributes to weakness and uncertainty. The person who trusts in God and has a faith nurtured by the Word and Sacraments will be like a tree planted by water: he will not lose faith, as Psalm 1 promises. But where will the nominal Christian find comfort when he cannot find his way in a Bible, or remember its content, or mixes Christianity with occultism, magic, New Age philosophy, and get-rich-quick schemes? His faith is built of stubble, which does not even rate as a building material.

If we examine the 1 Corinthians 3 passage itself, the meaning is clear enough. Because the Church is nearing its second thousand years, one can pile up citations (out of context) to support almost any concept, which may gain credibility and authority with time. Working back to the Biblical text, after reading many examples of error, can easily influence the reader (already conditioned by the errors) to misunderstand the text or to overlook the actual meaning of the passage. All theologians make mistakes, as they confess, so the authority of one writer, even if he was orthodox in intent and practice, cannot be used to support a doctrine that cannot be found in the Scriptures. A little known writer, given the name Ambrosiaster, began the process of making this passage from 1 Corinthians foundational for the Medieval period by being the first person to describe it as supporting Purgatory. Ambrosiaster wrote:

> He [Paul] said: "yet so as by fire," because this salvation exists not without pain; for he did not say, 'he shall be saved by fire,' but when he says, "yet so as by fire," he wants to show that this salvation is to come, but that he must suffer the pains of fire; so that, purged by fire, he may be saved and not, like the infidels, tormented forever by eternal fire; if for a portion of his works he has some value, it is because he believed in Christ.[165]

Ambrosiaster applied the Platonic concept of a purging fire in the afterlife to this passage in St. Paul's letter, even though these verses make no mention of a post-mortem experience of cleansing from sin. However, the passage in question is more obscure, full of symbolic language that is easily distorted by the clever or poorly informed. We do not even know who this Ambrosiaster was. He seemed to have no knowledge of the original Greek text. The Christian Church has honored the rule that the dark or obscure passages of Scripture must be illuminated by the clear passages. This rule includes the warning that doctrines cannot be based upon difficult to understand Scriptures. According to Chemnitz, the statement of St. Paul (1 Corinthians 3:15) is difficult to understand and should be placed among the things that Peter says (2 Peter 3:16) are difficult, which should not be distorted by people.[166]

> 2 Peter 3:15 And account *that* the longsuffering of our Lord *is* salvation; even as our beloved brother Paul also according to the wisdom given unto him hath written unto you; 16 As also in all

---

[165] *Birth of Purgatory*, p. 61, (Migne, *PL*, 17:211). Ambrosiaster is simply a name assigned to this writing. No one knows who wrote it.

[166] *Examination*, III, p. 253. "The papalists labor with great zeal to gather wood, hay, and stubble from the rites of satisfaction of the ancient church to light their purgatory." *Ibid.*, p. 256. Luther called John a "book for heretics" since its symbolic picture-language is twisted by false teachers.

his epistles, speaking in them of these things; in which are some things hard to be understood, which they that are unlearned and unstable wrest, as *they do* also the other scriptures, unto their own destruction. 17 Ye therefore, beloved, seeing ye know *these things* before, beware lest ye also, being led away with the error of the wicked, fall from your own stedfastness. 18 But grow in grace, and *in* the knowledge of our Lord and Saviour Jesus Christ. To him *be* glory both now and for ever. Amen.

Lenski explained 1 Corinthians 3:10-15 in a way similar to St. Augustine's interpretation in *City of God*, Book 21, Chapter 25:

> Paul's word regarding fire is used by the Catholics as proof for their doctrine of purgatory. But this fire is restricted to the last day; it is not a fire of purgation but of final judgment; it is intended for the builders and only by a deduction for certain unwise Christians.[167]

Chemnitz wrote about St. Augustine's exegesis:

> He shows, moreover, that it is customary in Scripture to call temptation and tribulation in this life a fire. As the furnace tests the vessels of the potter, so also tribulation tests unjust people.[168]

History of the Doctrine of Purgatory

Purgatory was one of the last doctrines to develop in the Roman Catholic Church. Pope Innocent III (1198-1216) gave an historic sermon on All Saints Day:

> The three armies are the Church triumphant in Heaven, the Church militant on earth, and the Church "abiding in Purgatory."

---

[167] R. C. H. Lenski, *The Interpretation of First and Second Corinthians*, Columbus: Wartburg Press, 1946, p. 146. 1 Corinthians 3:15.

[168] *Examination*, III, p. 254.

The first acts through praise, the second through combat, and the third through fire.[169]

The official birthday of Purgatory, according to Le Goff, is March 6, 1254, just before Pope Innocent IV died. The pope sent a letter to the Greeks through his legate, asking that the Greek Orthodox accept the concept of Purgatory, which is defined by the pope as follows:

> For, in this temporary fire, sins, not of course crimes and capital errors, which could not previously have been forgiven through penance, but slight and minor sins, are purged; if they have not been forgiven during existence, they weigh down the soul after death.[170]

Le Goff claimed: "This letter is the birth certificate of Purgatory as a doctrinally defined place." The concept of Purgatory is from pagan philosophers, a faction mentioned by Chemnitz writing against Purgatory and also freely admitted by Martin Jugie in writing in favor of Purgatory. Chemnitz wrote:

> First I find papalist purgatory with Plato, who lived about 400 years before the Incarnation of Christ—exactly the same idea and in almost the same words as it is described by the papalists.[171]

Jugie confessed:

> That first ground of reason for the existence of the intermediate state between Heaven and Hell, was appreciated by the pagans themselves. The philosopher Plato speaks of it in truly remarkable words, in which the Catholic theologians need hardly

---

[169] *Birth of Purgatory*, p. 174.

[170] *Ibid.*, p. 283f. "The great century of creation, the twelfth, was also the century in which Purgatory was born, and this birth can only be understood when set against the context of the feudal system then being given its definitive shape." *Ibid.*, p. 13.

[171] *Examination*, II, p. 231.

make a change. "Immediately on separation from the body," he says, "the souls come before their judge to be attentively examined." Does he see a soul disfigured by sin? Heaped with ignominy he will send it to the dungeon where it will suffer the just chastisement of its crimes. But there are some who profit by the pains which they endure...(See the Georgias and the Phaedo)[172]

Justifying Purgatory through Plato's works may seem startling to most Lutherans and Protestants, but it illustrates what happened in the age of Augustine, when Latin and Greek classics were the foundation and the norm of culture, unlike today, when few study either of those languages and even fewer master the literature.

Seeds of Purgatory, Early Medieval Period

Increasingly, during the Medieval period (dated from the Sack of Rome in 410 AD to the Fall of Constantinople in 1453) the Christian faith was made to conform to the classics of Greek and Latin thought. This was partly because of St. Augustine's influence, who wrote his *City of God* as a way of explaining why the Sack of Rome did not mean the end of Christianity, which was already identified with Eternal Rome. Western Civilization was shocked and anxious over the events and the weakness leading to the humiliation of Rome. Christians equated the visible church with the failing Roman Empire. Using his gigantic intellect, his encyclopedic knowledge of classical literature, and his Biblical expertise, St. Augustine provided the Christian Church an enduring classic that has influenced every age of the Church. St. Augustine's ability to fuse his knowledge of classical literature with his love for the Scriptures was the foundation for centuries of imitators and admirers.[173] Although dwarfed by St. Augustine's influence, St. Ambrose and St. Jerome, contemporaries of the African bishop, were both classically trained and also had a great impact on the Church. For instance, St. Jerome's *Against Helvidius* was still a standard work during the Reformation, defending the perpetual

---

[172] Jugie, *Purgatory*, p. 21.

[173] Luther was an Augustinian monk who knew well the writings of the Bishop of Hippo. In addition, the Jansenists, who united with the Gallicans against the Ultramontanes, were devoted to the life and writings of St. Augustine. See the chapter on Infallibility.

virginity of Mary. Luther agreed with the essay, written around 1000 years before.

Before Augustine, two Greek fathers, Clement (d. before 215) and Origen (d. 253 or 254) allowed the Platonic concept of Purgatory to flow into their work. Origen wrote about John baptizing in the Jordan:

> As John stood near the Jordon...so will the lord Jesus Christ stand in a river of fire [*in igne flumine*] next to a flaming sword and baptize all those who should go to paradise after they die but who lack purgation [*purgatione indiget*], causing them to enter into the place they wish to go.[174]

Origen thought that all would pass through fire in the afterlife, but that believers would be protected, just as the Israelites were protected against the Red Sea.

Clement of Alexandria described two fires in the afterlife: one a punitive fire, the other a fire that "sanctifies" and "does not consume, like the fire of the forge...which penetrates the soul that passes through it."[175]

St. Augustine

Although St. Augustine did little to advance the doctrine of Purgatory, his authority has been used to argue for the orthodoxy and antiquity of the concept. In his *Confessions*, St. Augustine wrote about the death of his mother and his prayers for her. Although he indicated that he also wanted the readers to pray for his departed parents, St. Augustine made a clear Evangelical statement about the meaning of salvation and the atoning death of Christ:

> Let not the devil who is lion and serpent in one, bar her way by force or by guile. For she will not answer that she has no debt to pay, for fear that her cunning accuser should prove her wrong and win her for himself. Her reply will be that her debt has been

---

[174] Origen's Twenty Fourth Homily of the Commentary on Luke. *Birth of Purgatory*, p. 54.

[175] *Ibid.*

paid by Christ, to whom none can repay the price which he paid for us, though the debt was not His to pay.[176]

Chemnitz found this prayer a "glorious confession of faith."[177] Those who commend St. Augustine for supporting the doctrine of Purgatory enjoy quoting from the *City of God* and the *Enchiridion*. In the *City of God*, St. Augustine wrote: "...the fire of transitory tribulation which consumes the worldly venial sins here and therefore not there, I do not condemn it, because it is perhaps true."[178] He also wrote:

> And one can ask whether it is so, and it may either be found or remain a secret that some believers are saved through a certain purgatory, the more slowly or quickly according as they loved perishing goods more or less.[179]

Those who argue for Purgatory, using the Bishop of Hippo's expertise, do not quote, as Chemnitz did, St. Augustine's letter to Dulcitius about Purgatory and related issues:

> We have transcribed these things, however with the understanding that **no canonical authority is to be given them**.[180]

St. Augustine wrote in his Commentary on the Psalms that Purgatory was an obscure question, but he commented on Psalm 37 in the same book, which greatly influenced Medieval theologians.

---

[176] Augustine, *Confessions*, 9:13:34-37; cited in *Birth of Purgatory*, p. 65.

[177] *Examination*, III, p. 279.

[178] *Ibid.*, p. 255. A similar statement can be found in Augustine's *De fide et operibus*, (*On Faith and Works*) chapter 14: "Whether men suffer these things only in this life or whether some such judgments follow after this life, this understanding of Paul's statement, namely that it refers to the fire of trial or tribulation, is (*according to my judgment*) not averse to regard for the truth." *Ibid.*, emphasis in Chemnitz citation.

[179] *Enchiridion*, chapter 69.

[180] *Examination*, III, p. 255.

Although some will be saved by fire, this fire will be more terrible than anything that a man can suffer in this life.[181]

St. Augustine's clearest exposition about a cleansing in the afterlife and the beneficial value of Masses, prayers, and alms was written in the conclusion of his essay, *On the Care To Be Given to the Dead*:

> Since this is so, we should not think that any aid comes to the dead for whom we are providing care, except what we solemnly pray for in their behalf at the altars, either by sacrifices of prayers or of alms...It is better that there be a superabundance of aids for those to whom these works are neither a hindrance nor a help, than that there be a lack for those who are thus aided.[182]

Arguing against the newly defined doctrine of Purgatory (official in 1254), Chemnitz wrote about the emphasis of St. Augustine upon the Scriptures as the foundation, standard, rule, and authority for all doctrinal disputes:

> For beautiful is the statement of Cyprian, which Augustine declares to be the best without any doubt, showing what ought to be done when examples and customs are held up to us which do not have the authority of the canonical Scripture. "If," says he, "we return to the head and origin of the divine tradition, human error will cease. For if the channel of water, which before flowed copiously and purely, either fails or brings muddy water, then certainly one goes to the source in order to find out whether there is something wrong in the veins or in the source, or whether something got in midway." So also it is rightly, necessarily, and indeed safely done when things that happened in later times in matters of religion must be examined.[183]

---

[181] *Commentaries on the Psalms*, written ca. 400-414, Psalm 37. *Birth of Purgatory*, p. 68.

[182] Augustine, *On the Care to Be Given to the Dead*. Cited in *Birth of Purgatory*, p. 82.

[183] *Examination*, III, p. 237. "Back to the sources" is *ad fontes* in Latin. The author attended the Ad Fontes conference, aimed at ELCA clergy in the 1980's. Curiously, the author spoke with ELCA pastors Richard J. Neuhaus and Leonard Klein, both of whom joined the Church of Rome and became priests soon after the conference.

As strange as St. Augustine's comments about apparitions might be to us, how much stranger would it be for Augustine to discover the Church of Rome ignoring his words on the Scriptures as the only norm of faith while quoting his ambiguous opinions on the afterlife? Late in life, knowing what a great body of theological literature he was leaving behind, St. Augustine published his *Retractions*, showing that he was aware of his capability of error.

> Where, however, the dispute is about a very obscure matter, and the divine Scriptures do not help us with sure and clear documents, human presumption ought to restrain itself and not incline to one side. Rather, if any one proclaims anything about any matter which pertains to our faith and life as a sure and necessary dogma or article of faith, over and above what you have received in the Scripture of the Law and of the Gospel, let him be anathema! [damned to Hell][184]

St. Augustine's prestige and enduring impact upon the Church made it possible to build upon the ambiguous support he gave to Purgatory, while forgetting his clear statements about the absolute necessity of returning to the Scriptures when an issue is disputed, or overlooking Augustine's diplomatic efforts to steer others away from Origen's odd notions. Le Goff gave an accurate portrait of the part played by Augustine when he wrote:

> It was the role of Augustine, who left so deep an imprint on Christianity and who, in the Middle Ages, was regarded as probably the greatest of all the Christian "authorities," to have been the first to introduce a number of ingredients that later went to make up the doctrine of Purgatory.[185]

---

[184] Augustine, *Contra litteras Petiliani.* cited in *Examination*, III, p. 260f.

[185] *Birth of Purgatory*, p. 61.

Pope Gregory the Great

St. Augustine's ruminations about the afterlife might have remained harmless, had not his successors built, from his incidental remarks, a structure for Purgatory, embellished with tales from the crypt. Gregory the Great became pope in 590, with disasters everywhere: the Black Plague, the flooding of the Tiber River, and foreign invasions. Pope Gregory thought the world was coming rapidly to an end, a situation that he thought allowed the spiritual matters of the future age to shine through more clearly, not unlike the occult spirituality of today. He liked to use anecdotes about the dead returning to earth to urge that more be done for them. A priest went to the baths and spoke to an attendant, in reality a distressed soul who was forced to remain on earth because of his sins. The apparition asked the priest to intercede before God on his behalf.

> With these words he disappeared, thus revealing that he was really a spirit in the guise of a human being. For an entire week the priest cried for this man and every day offered the Host; when he returned to the baths, the fellow was nowhere to be found. This proves that sacred offerings can be useful to dead souls.[186]

Gregory's stories became models for the Medieval proponents of Purgatory, and thus we have a fairly substantial amount of literature that is based upon dreams and apparitions. Visions of Mary and apparitions of various dead people suffering in Purgatory are part of the fabric of Roman Catholic doctrine. Chemnitz made this droll comment:

> This continuation of the history of purgatory shows how, when ghosts had once been admitted to the teaching office of the church, fables of apparitions and visions without end and measure were heaped up. For John of Damascus tells stories which are so fabulous that not even the papalists are able to approve all of them.[187]

---

186 Gregory the Great, *Dialogi*, 4.57.1-7. *Birth of Purgatory*, p. 92.

187 *Examination*, III, p. 292. Jugie offered this encouraging insight: "Private revelations worthy of belief assure us that this hope is no deceptive will-o'-the-wisp--the revelation, for instance, of

The Medieval Scholastics

The greatest Medieval theologian in the tradition of St. Augustine was St. Thomas Aquinas, the Dominican who systematized the doctrine of Western Christianity in the style of Aristotle, using logical arguments to build up an intellectual structure that remains the framework for all Roman Catholic teaching today. The philosophical approach of Aquinas was not wrong in itself, but was vulnerable to the weight of extra-Biblical tradition. The glory of Greece and the grandeur of Rome can be used to communicate the Gospel, but one cannot necessarily harmonize pagan philosophical concepts with the revelation of God's Word.

Therefore, the Medieval period drew so much wisdom from pagan sources and gave so much authority to classical authors that non-Biblical doctrines found fertile soil in which to grow. Today in America, the same can be said about the growing ignorance of church members about the Scriptures, which is providing a breeding ground for occult religion, pseudo-Christian cults, and the merging of paganism with mainline and Pentecostal Christianity. Americans can find much material from the Medieval era that is no more magical or silly than what they buy in their own Christian book stores. For instance, Paul Y. Cho teaches his followers to make use of the divine power of the Fourth Dimension, the spirit world, to gather riches and goods for themselves by forming mental images of their desires and by writing out lists of demands for God to obey. Cho's book is found in many Christian bookstores, which believers read, without blushing:

Then I said, "Close your eyes. Can you see your husband now?"

"Yes, I can see him clearly."

"Okay. Let's order him how. Until you see your husband clearly in your imagination you can't order, because **God will never answer**. You must see him clearly before you begin to pray. God **never answers vague prayers**..."

Soeur Marie-Denise of the Order of the Visitation, who died at Annecy in 1653." [She and her order prayed for a powerful prince for nine years and learned that their efforts released him from a few hours of Purgatory, that he would remain in Purgatory until shortly before Judgment Day.] Jugie, *Purgatory* , p. 25.

They were happily married in that church, and on their marriage day her mother took that paper written with the ten points, and read it publicly before the people, then tore it up.[188]

The Medieval era was not as dark and ignorant as people imagine, but it was a period when education was limited to relatively few, travel and commerce were not very extensive, and the social structure was rigid, allowing for very little change in many centuries. Each generation built upon the wisdom of previous generations, especially in the Western church, where the use of Latin made each theological work universal and authoritative. One did not need to be French or speak the local language to teach at the University of Paris. In contrast, the modern theologian is limited by his knowledge of foreign languages. He may ignore a vast body of work, as Albert Schweitzer did with the English lives of Jesus, simply because he was unfamiliar with the language. The Latin of the Medieval theologians gave them a broader world view, but their love of pagan classics diminished the authority of the Bible.

The Roman Catholic Church teaches that doctrines develop, and Purgatory definitely emerged slowly from Medieval theology, enhanced by the poetic genius of Dante. His three volume epic poem on the afterlife included Hell, Heaven, and Purgatory. The *Purgatorio* was completed in 1319.

A little more than a hundred years after its inception, Purgatory benefited from an extraordinary stroke of luck: the poetic genius of Dante Alighieri, born in Florence in 1265, carved out for it an enduring place in human memory.[189]

---

[188] Paul Yonggi Cho, with a foreword by Dr. Robert Schuller, *The Fourth Dimension*, 2 vols., South Plainfield, NJ: Bridge Publishing, 1979, I, p. 20f. Cho's apostasy may be wormwood to most Christians, but he is loved by Church Growth ministers. "Since the spiritual world hugged the third dimension, incubating on the third dimension, it was by this incubation of the fourth dimension on the third dimension that the earth was recreated." *Ibid.*, I, p. 39.

[189] *Purgatorio* was completed in 1319. *Birth of Purgatory*, p. 334. Special editions of Dante's *Divine Comedy* are often given as gifts among prominent Roman Catholics. The University of Notre Dame has quite a collection of massive, ornately decorated editions.

The doctrine of Purgatory seemed logical. A person would pass through a cleansing experience immediately after death, which would make him worthy of Paradise. Father Healy, a Carmelite, wrote:

> The doctrine of Purgatory was clearly proclaimed in the Church at the Second Council of Lyons (1274), and in many official statements thereafter. The Council of Trent (1563) in reaction to the Reformers reaffirmed the Church's teaching on Purgatory, on the value of prayers for the dead and especially of the Sacrifice of the Mass. Again and again the Church has restated this doctrine down to our own time. It is clearly taught in the Second Vatican Council, and more recently the Congregation for the Doctrine of the Faith defended the practice of prayers, funeral rites and veneration of the dead.[190]

Purgatory was being taught in the Church of Rome at the time of Martin Luther, and indulgences were sold as a way of avoiding some or all of the entire penalty due.

> Here now the Holy See at Rome, coming to the aid of the poor Church, invented indulgences, whereby it forgave and remitted [expiation or] satisfaction, first, for a single instance, for seven years, for a hundred years, and distributed them among the cardinals and bishops, so that one could grant indulgence for a hundred years and another for a hundred days. But he reserved to himself alone the power to remit the entire satisfaction.[191]

---

[190] Kilian Healy, O.Carm., *The Assumption of Mary*, Wilmington, Delaware: Michael Glazier, 1982, p. 127.

[191] Smalcald Articles, Part III, Article III. #24. Repentance. *Concordia Triglotta*, p. 485. Tappert, p. 307. "There was a saying in the Middle Ages, based on Daniel 11:43, that the devil would show the Antichrist the hidden treasures of the earth in order that men might be seduced by them." *Ibid.*, "However, the *questors* [solicitors] of the Hospital of the Holy Spirit in the city of Rome undertook a reckoning, and found that the indulgences of all the stations in the city of Rome come to a total of more than a million years and more than 42 plenary indulgences [total forgiveness of the penalty of Purgatory], besides the souls which are liberated from purgatory!" *Examination*, IV, p. 232.

The gross exaggerations of John Tetzel in selling indulgences prompted Luther to post the 95 Theses on the castle church door at Wittenberg. Tetzel was a roguish salesman of indulgences, who promised in a German jingle at the time:

> As soon as the coin in the coffer rings,
>
> The soul from Purgatory springs.

The indulgence was offered as a way of sharing the pope's super-abundance of merits (supererogatory grace), which he controlled as the Vicar of Christ on earth. To help finance St. Peter's Basilica in Rome, one of the largest churches in the world, the pope sold church offices for large sums of money. The newly minted bishops and cardinals had to borrow money to pay for the office, so the pope gave them a license to sell indulgences to pay for the loans, which paid for the purchase of church offices, which paid for St. Peter's in Rome. The traffic in indulgences was an integral part of the economy.

The Elector Frederick had a vast collection of the relics of saints at the Wittenberg Castle Church, the official catalogue including:

1. Five particles of the milk of the Virgin Mary.
2. One piece of the tree where Mary nursed the Lord near the Garden of Balsam.
3. Four pieces of the hair of Mary.
4. Three pieces of the shirt of Mary.
5. Three pieces of one robe of Mary.
6. Eight pieces of other robes of Mary.
7. Four pieces of the belt of Mary.
8. Seven pieces of the veil of Mary.
9. Two pieces of the veil of Mary which was sprinkled with the blood of Christ under the Cross.
10. One piece of the city where Mary died.
11. One piece of the wax candle given to Our Lady when she died.
12. Six pieces of the grave of Mary.

13. One piece of the place where Mary ascended into heaven.[192]

The Council of Trent was called in 1545, to answer the doctrinal questions opened up by the Reformation. The Council met sporadically until 1563, due to many interruptions. The pope was reluctant to call the Council, since papal versus conciliar power was still being contested at that time. The Council of Trent affirmed the doctrine of Purgatory, but also warned vaguely about abuses of the doctrine.

> The Christian doctrine of Purgatory was not finally worked out until the sixteenth century by the Council of Trent. Rejected by Protestants, it was an exclusively Catholic doctrine. After Trent, Bellarmine and Suarez, who were responsible for Purgatory, put forth several Biblical references in support of the newly approved doctrine.[193]

Doctrines of Purgatory

In order to understand Roman Catholic piety, it is necessary to study the basic doctrines of Purgatory. Catharine of Genoa (1447-1510), who published her visions of Purgatory, said, "Purgatory—what a grand thing!"[194]

This material is not available to many people and will help explain the substance of Roman Catholic practice, even if the topic is downplayed today. The basic concepts are:

1. The nature and purpose of Purgatory.

2. Mary's role as Queen of Purgatory and the scapular.

3. The Mass.

---

[192] *The Reformation, A Narrative History Related by Contemporary Observers and Participants*, ed. Hans J. Hillerbrand, New York: Harper and Row 1964, p. 47.

[193] *Birth of Purgatory*, p. 41f. 1 Corinthians 3:11-15; Luke 16:19-26; 2 Maccabees 12:41-46; Matthew 12:31f.

[194] *Ibid.*, p. v. "With Gertrude the Great (d. 1301 or 1302) Purgatory entered the highest realms of mysticism, and later attained the pinnacle (or, if you prefer, the depths) of hysterical devotion with Saint Catharine of Genoa (1447-1510), the author of *A Treatise on Purgatory*." *Ibid.*, p. 356.

Nature and Purpose of Purgatory

Purgatory and justification by faith must be considered together, since one precludes the other. Human reason cannot grasp forgiveness of sins as a gift of God, paid by Christ's atoning death on the cross. The Holy Spirit must teach us through the Word. In contrast –

> The doctrine of Purgatory is so reasonable, that the disciples of Luther and Calvin have not hesitated to criticize on this point the teaching of their masters.[195]

The doctrine of Purgatory appeals to human reason, which says, "There must still be a price, even if sins are forgiven." The nature of Purgatory is to serve as a temporary Hell where sins are cleansed by the suffering of the dead person and paid through the prayers and Masses offered by the Church Militant on earth.

> In Church terminology prayers for the poor souls in purgatory are often called suffrages—a word derived from the Latin *suffragium* which means "supplication." The way suffrages work is that the satisfactory value of prayers and good works is offered to God in substitution for the temporal punishments for sins, which the poor souls still have to render. God accepts the offerings and because of them remits all or a portion of the temporal punishments due to sins...."[196]

Purgatory is an enormous debtors' prison (a Marshalsea, according to Jugie) where one remains until the penalties are paid in full.

In Roman Catholic theology, Holy Baptism frees the Christian from original sin, but penance cleanses him from the taint of actual sin. However, various sources portray baptism as making God angry because we continue to be sinners, taking away the comfort of Holy Baptism and proclaiming God's outraged love and avenging arm.

---

[195] Jugie, *Purgatory*, p. 21.

[196] Baker, *Fundamentals*, III, p. 156f.

That second stream [to wash us from our sins] is the Sacrament of Penance. But this time, the pardon will not be so generous as at Baptism. Outraged love will raise the arm of avenging justice. The soul is released from the sin and from the eternal punishment which was its due; but it must submit to a temporal chastisement proportionate to the gravity of its offence. There is no absconding from this chastisement. If the debt is not paid here below, it is carried forward to the next life. All this is clearly taught by the Council of Trent: "The fruit of Baptism differs from the fruit of Penance... By Baptism, we are clothed with Christ, we become in Him truly a new creature, for we receive the full and entire remission of our sins. By the Sacrament of Penance, it is impossible for us to come to that new and perfect life without great efforts and abundance of tears...." (Session XIV, Ch. II)[197]

Although Purgatory is portrayed as a place of torture and suffering, it is also viewed as a safety net that catches the multitude who are not worthy of Heaven when they die. Forgetting who lit the fires of Purgatory with their hay, wood, and stubble, Jugie stated:

It would be therefore unjust to accuse God of severity, when He hangs over our heads the threat of Purgatory. Rather is this a proof of His infinite goodness.[198]

There are three reasons for passing through Purgatory:

1. Venial (minor) sins not paid for while living;

2. Impurity of the soul;

3. Any remaining debt from mortal or venial sins.[199]

---

[197] Jugie, *Purgatory*, p. 7. "purgatory is no exception to the general law that God made all things for love." *Ibid.*, p. 22.

[198] Jugie, *Purgatory*, p. 23.

[199] *Ibid.*, p. 4.

Purgatory does not comprise a major portion of a Roman Catholic theological library. At the pontifical Josephinum Library in Columbus, Ohio, the section on Mary includes hundreds of books, while Purgatory is limited to a handful. Since Scripture is silent about Purgatory— which is the negation of the Gospel—the nature of Purgatory necessarily comes from visions like those of Catherine of Genoa and the feverish imagination of others. Although Jugie writes glowingly about the joy of Purgatory, his descriptions offer little comfort:

> Whole years of sorrow, of weariness, of poverty, of sickness are nothing in comparison with one hour of the Purgatorial fires.[200]

The nature of Purgatory is vulnerable to humor, when well-intentioned promoters suggest that, in the midst of terrible joyful suffering, one can form new friendships, meet relatives, and encounter one's former religious superior.

> In Purgatory, one is known and one makes new friends. How many contemporaries, citizens, neighbors, friends, relations, the newly arrived must find in Purgatory! A son finds himself again with his parents, a brother with his sister, a religious with his superior.[201]

Chemnitz, whose *Examination of the Council of Trent* is full of witticisms, could not resist having some fun with one claim about Purgatory.

> Also a certain monk who, in order to induce sleep, had at one time drunk unmixed wine had been dreadfully tormented in purgatory according to the same, [Bernardino of Sienna, Italian

---

[200] *Ibid.*, p. 25f. "Those who have written comprehensively of Purgatory, have spoken not only of its pains, but of its joys also." *Ibid.*, p. 73. The following example from this book illustrates why people turned to the Blessed Virgin Mother for comfort, love, and forgiveness: "When St. Margaret of Cortona had prayed much for her deceased father, Our Saviour gave her this revelation: 'Be not disquieted because of his past life, because the pains of Purgatory are of different kinds. He has suffered the most intense of these pains, because I will by purifying him in the most terrible fashion, to deliver him very soon.'" *Ibid.*, p. 53.

[201] *Purgatory*, p. 381.

Franciscan, 1380-1444] Sermon 160. O blessed therefore are the innkeepers who, while they adulterate the wine with water, save many souls from purgatory![202]

Mary and the Scapular Promise

One reason for the relative lack of books about Purgatory itself may be the Church of Rome's emphasis upon Mary and her role as the Queen of Purgatory. Devotion to the Blessed Virgin Mother presumes her role in aiding the souls suffering in Purgatory. Kilian Healy, a Carmelite, wrote: "This belief that Mary comes to the aid of the dead continued down through the centuries."[203] The purpose of Marian devotion is to implore her to aid the souls suffering in the cleansing fires. Father Schouppe, a Jesuit, wrote:

> In the first place, in order to obtain great purity of soul, and in consequence to have little reason to fear Purgatory, we must cherish a great devotion towards the Blessed Virgin Mary. This good Mother will so assist her dear children in cleansing their souls and in shortening their Purgatory that they may live in the greatest confidence.[204]

The scapular, which is described in greater detail in the chapter about Mary, is offered to Roman Catholic faithful as a Marian sacrament of sorts, protecting them again earthly danger and greatly reducing their time in Purgatory. Miraculous signs also attend non-believers who wear the scapular, extending *ex opera operato* to this practice. The scapular promise was supposedly revealed to St. Simon Stock, a Carmelite leader, by the Virgin Mary, in the 13th century, and endorsed soon after by Pope John XXII. The scapular is like the Temple Garments of the Latter Day Saints, not visible to most but still significant.

---

[202] *Examination*, III, p. 300.

[203] Healey, *The Assumption of Mary*, p. 129f.

[204] Rev. F. X. Schouppe, S.J., *Purgatory, Illustrated by the Lives and Legends of the Saints*, Rockford: TAN Books, 1973, p. 288. Thomas A. Nelson founded TAN books in 1967 to reproduce the old Catholic books no longer in print because of Roman publishers going out of business. The TAN books best illustrate the old Catholics polemics against Luther and the Protestants.

The great reward was a promise given by the Blessed Virgin to Pope John XXII [1300's] that those who wore the Brown Scapular, lived a life of chastity (purity) according to their state in life, and recited the Office of Our Lady, would through her intercession be released from purgatory on the first Saturday after death This is called the Sabbatine Privilege. Nine different Popes, besides Pope John XXII, have spoken of the Sabbatine Privilege and reconfirmed the teaching.[205]

The scapular promise offers almost immediate relief from Purgatory to those who die wearing the scapular.

The original scapular was a long, narrow piece of cloth with a hole in the middle for the head, worn over the shoulders so that half of the scapular hung in the front and the other half hung down in the back. Some orders sewed hoods onto the back of the scapular. The purpose of the scapular, like an apron, was to protect the cassock or habit from dirt and wear and tear.[206]

Confraternities

Another source of relief from Purgatorial suffering is membership in a confraternity of the rosary, in which members promise to aid their fellow members by their rosary devotions, which center around Mary and her intercessions with Christ on behalf of the faithful. Chemnitz noted:

They write in the *Speculum rosariorum* that a certain girl, who according to the sentence of the Judge ought to have been tormented for 700 years in purgatory, was freed after 15 days through the merits of participation in the brotherhood of the Rosary of Mary.[207]

---

[205] Father Robert J. Fox, *The Marian Catechism*, Washington, New Jersey: AMI Press, 1983, p. 85f.

[206] Carmelite sisters. Retrieved from http://www.carmelitedcj.org/saints/scapular.asp.

[207] *Examination*, III, p. 319.

Philip Melanchthon, who taught Chemnitz, addressed the issue of Mary helping souls after death in the Apology of the Augsburg Confession.

> Granting that the blessed Mary prays for the Church, does she receive souls in death, [the example of her faith and her humility]. But the subject itself declares that in public opinion the blessed Virgin has succeeded altogether to the place of Christ. Men have invoked her, have trusted in her mercy, through her have desired to appease Christ, as though He were not a Propitiator, but only a dreadful judge and avenger.[208]

The Augsburg Confession, which was conciliatory in nature, still harshly criticized the abuse of the Mass as a means for obtaining relief for souls in Purgatory.

> At the same time the abominable error was condemned according to which it was taught that our Lord Jesus Christ had by his death made satisfaction only for original sin, and had instituted the Mass as a sacrifice for other sins. This transformed the Mass into a sacrifice for the living and the dead, a sacrifice by means of which sin was taken away and God was reconciled. Thereupon followed a debate as to whether one Mass held for many people merited as much as a special Mass held for an individual. Out of this grew the countless multiplication of Masses, by the performance of which men expected to get everything they needed from God. Meanwhile faith in Christ and true service of God were forgotten.[209]

In the Augsburg Confession, the Lutheran signers laid to rest any concept of someone other than Christ serving as the Mediator between God and man.

---

[208] Apology of the Augsburg Confession, Article XXI, Invocation of Saints, *Triglotta*, p. 349f. Tappert, p. 232f.

[209] Augsburg Confession, The Mass, XXIV, #21, Tappert, p. 58.

However, it cannot be proved from the Scriptures that we are to invoke saints or seek help from them. "For there is one mediator between God and men, Christ Jesus (1 Timothy 2:5), who is the only saviour, the only high priest, advocate, and intercessor before God (Romans 8:34). He has promised to hear our prayers. Moreover, according to the Scriptures the highest form of divine service is sincerely to seek and call upon this same Jesus Christ in every time of need. "If anyone sins we have an advocate with the Father, Jesus Christ the righteous. (1 John 2:1)[210]

The Mass and Indulgences

Many Lutherans and Protestants do not understand the meaning of the Roman Catholic Mass and its relationship to Purgatory.

> We read in the *Life of St. Elizabeth of Portugal* that after the death of her daughter Constance she learned the pitiful state of the deceased in Purgatory and the price which God exacted for her ransom...that she was condemned to long and terrible suffering, but that she would be delivered if for the space of a year the Holy Sacrifice of the Mass was celebrated for her every day.[211]

In addition, many assume that indulgences disappeared after the Reformation. In both cases the doctrine of Purgatory is central to their meaning and use in the Church of Rome. The Roman Mass is central to the life of the faithful, since it offers relief from Purgatory for those who attend and for those who receive their benefit in the fiery debtors' prison. Lutherans and Protestants share in the supposed blessings, according to Jugie:

---

[210] Augsburg Confession, German translation. Article XXI, The Cult of Saints, Tappert, p. 47. "The veneration of the saints became more and more popular through the fifteenth century. Their number was legion, each with a special revelation to a certain region, town, trade, sickness or need, but all with imposing relevance for the Christian believer." Hillberbrand, *The Reformation*, p. 17.

[211] Schoupee, *Purgatory*, p. 158.

Since the coming of Christ, even those souls who come to Purgatory in schism, in heresy, in infidelity, have a share in the fruit of the Masses celebrated in the whole universe, in the numerous suffrages offered by the Church militant.[212]

If Jugie seems too dated to be taken seriously, one must also consider the recent statement of Father Baker:

When a stipend is offered for a Mass to be celebrated for a particular intention, the priest must offer that Mass as a first intention. The practice of offering Mass for definite persons can be traced back to the third century. Thirdly, it is commonly held by theologians that there is a personal fruit of the Mass which the Lord grants to the celebrating priest and to all the faithful who are actually present at each Mass.[213]

In defending the endowed Mass and a longer stay experiencing the joys of Purgatory, Jugie mentioned an important theologian of the Council of Trent, Peter Soto, who was the object of Chemnitz' scorn:

In approving of Masses in Perpetuity for the dead, the Church approves of such constant remembrance. In this, she shows herself in disagreement with that strange opinion of P. Dominic Soto, who played an important part in the Council of Trent. This theologian affirms that the sufferings of Purgatory are so terrible and the suffrages of the Church so efficacious, that a soul, no matter what its debt, cannot remain there more than ten years. That would be to give the lie to many private revelations.[214]

Thus it is extremely difficult to ascertain how long one must remain in Purgatory, since those who helped build the realm and describe it so vividly are contradicted by others.

---

[212] Jugie, *Purgatory*, p. 37.

[213] Baker, *Fundamentals*, III, p. 273.

[214] Jugie, *Purgatory*, p. 56f.

Avoiding Purgatory

Since Purgatory is always unpleasant, a mini-Hell for the semi-saved, Roman Catholic authors have determined a number of ways to avoid it. Some of them are:

1. Holy Baptism followed by immediate death;

2. Martyrdom;

3. Frequent confession;

4. Indulgences;

5. Frequent Masses, daily Mass being the ideal;

6. The sacrament of extreme unction;

7. Giving up the benefits of Communion and donating them to those who are living;

8. Becoming a nun or a priest.[215]

Jugie stated: "To sum up, then: in making every effort to avoid Purgatory, one will at least reach Purgatory; but in proposing the mere avoidance of Hell, one is already on the way to it."[216]

Biblical Response

No doctrine more clearly shows Roman Catholicism's uncertainty of salvation than that of Purgatory. The many visions which fill the books on Purgatory reveal that even the most saintly cloistered nun, strictly observing all the rules of her order will still suffer from a lengthy stay in Purgatory. The more the remedies for Purgatory increased (the rosary, the scapular, the indulgence) the more people's anxieties were intensified about their future lives and the suffering of their friends and relatives. Some Purgatory stories are amusing, but the overwhelming

---

[215] Jugie, *Purgatory*, p. 137. "There is one means of helping the Holy Souls which stand out from all the others as the 'heroic act.' It consists in offering to God, for the relief of the souls in Purgatory, all the satisfactory works done during one's life, and all the suffrages which shall be offered for one's soul after death. It is as thus understood, that the Church has recognized it and enriched it with indulgences." *Ibid.*, p. 181.

[216] *Ibid.*, p. 112. Mother Angelica, on EWTN TV, spoke about Purgatory when she was asked, "What if you end up in Purgatory." She replied with a smile, "I would say – I made it!"

effect of hearing them is sorrow for those who sought and still seek the comfort of the Gospel, only to receive reasons for more anxiety, fear, and uncertainty.

> In any case, the Church, in the ecclesiastical, clerical sense, drew considerable power from the new system of the hereafter. It administered or supervised prayers, alms, Masses, and offerings of all kinds made by the living on behalf of the dead and reaped the benefits thereof. Thanks to Purgatory the Church developed the system of indulgences, a source of great power and profit until it became a dangerous weapon that was ultimately turned back against the Church.[217]

The centuries of Roman Catholic tradition in favor of Purgatory still do not make up for the lack of support in the Scriptures, the early Church, and the early Medieval Church. Chemnitz wrote:

> No false dogma has ever been spread in the church which was not put forth with some plausible show, for sheep's clothing is the show of false religion (says Chrysostom). Indeed, the weaker and more ruinous the cause is, the more arguments it needs, sought everywhere and in every way possible, as though to cover it over with paint or to swathe it with medicine. For Pindar [famous Greek lyric poet, 518-438 B.C.] says, "For a just cause three words are sufficient." Therefore the papalists have gathered very many and varied arguments in order to establish purgatory.[218]

Chrysostom, following the example of the Church fathers, did not look for traditions that were extra-Biblical or new doctrines that rested upon a false understanding of Scripture:

> They say that we are to understand the things concerning Paradise not as they are written but in a different way. But when

---

[217] *Birth of Purgatory*, p. 249.

[218] *Examination*, III, p. 325.

Scripture wants to teach us something like that, it interprets itself and does not permit the hearer to err. I therefore beg and entreat that we close our ears to all these things and follow the canon of Holy Scripture exactly.[219]

An orthodox teacher of Christian doctrine is a sinner and may err, but he will always direct his students back to the Scriptures. The revealed Word of God is the sole source of our knowledge about God, His fatherly mercy, His redemption of our souls through His Son Jesus Christ, and the work of His Holy Spirit in Word and Sacrament.

---

[219] Chrysostom, Homily 13, on Genesis. *Examination*, I, p. 154.

Purgatory Summarized

Early Foundations

1. The pagan sources for Purgatory are Plato's Gorgias and Phaedo.

2. The texts used to defend the doctrine are 2 Maccabees 12:41-45 (Old Testament Apocrypha) and 1 Corinthians 3:10-15.

3. The early Church fathers whose comments are used to support Purgatory are: Ambrosiaster, Clement, Origen, and St. Augustine.

4. Purgatory was rejected by the Greek Orthodox at the Fifth General Synod in 500 AD.

Growing Roman Catholic Support for Purgatory

1. In 1263, St. Thomas Aquinas argued for Purgatory against the Greek Orthodox in *Contra Errores Graecorum*.

2. In 1274, The Second Council of Lyons accepted the doctrine of Purgatory for the first time.

3. In 1439, the Council of Florence voted against the Greek Orthodox position.

4. At the Council of Basel, the Greeks opposed Purgatory.

5. In 1563, the Council of Trent solidified all Medieval errors concerning Purgatory and damned to Hell all those holding a contrary position (Lutherans and Protestants).

6. In 1870, the First Vatican Council confirmed the decrees of Trent.

7. In 1968, Pope Paul's *Credo of the People of God* affirmed Purgatory.

8. In 1979, the "Letter on Certain Questions Concerning Eschatology" supported Purgatory.

9. The Second Vatican Council assumed the doctrine of Purgatory in its Dogmatic Constitution on the Church, *Lumen Gentium*, number 51.

Chapter Five: The Infallible Pope

The day on which the doctrine of papal infallibility was accepted by the Roman Catholic Church was notable:

> On Monday, July 18, [1870] in the fourth session of the council, the constitution *Pastor Aeternus* was accepted by 533 *placet* votes against two non-*placet* ones. (They were the votes of Bishop Fitzgerald of Little Rock and Bishop Riccio of Cajazzo.) At the same time the prorogation of the council was likewise decided. A violent thunderstorm raged while the session was in progress. The lightening flashed and the thunder pealed for a whole hour and a half. "A more effective scene I never witnessed," wrote Mozley, The *Times* correspondent. When the result of the vote was taken up to the Pope the darkness was such that a taper had to be brought, to enable him to read the text: "We define, with the assent of the holy council, all that has been read and confirm it in virtue of apostolic authority."[220]

The vote on *Pastor Aeternus* seems to have been overwhelmingly positive, but 106 men were absent, the opposition having decided to leave early in a group to avoid casting a negative vote. One of the dissenters, Archbishop Haynald of Hungary, when leaving Eternal Rome, confessed to another opponent of infallibility: "Monsignor, we have made a great mistake."[221] The outbreak of the Franco-Prussian War led to the adjournment of Vatican I and the withdrawal of the French garrison that kept Rome a papal city. In a few months, the Italian forces were successful in making Rome the capital of Italy rather than the center of the papal empire.

> The outbreak of the Franco-Prussian War led to the adjournment of the Council, the recall of the French garrison, and the consequent collapse of papal rule in Rome. From 1870 to 1929

---

220 Hubert Jedin, *Ecumenical Councils of the Catholic Church*, New York: Paulist Press, 1960, p. 168.

221 Henry T. Hudson, *Papal Power*, p. 87.

there was no Papal State and the pope sulked in the Vatican, refusing the settlements offered by the Italian State.[222]

Like other controversial doctrines, papal infallibility has had a long history in the church, with many significant figures lined up on both sides of the debate. Briefly, this doctrine holds that the pope is infallible in doctrine when teaching *ex cathedra* (Latin, from the chair, the bishop's chair that gives a cathedral its name). Bishops in the ancient church taught from a prominent chair in the front of the cathedral. More is involved than the infallibility of the pope. In *Unam Sanctam*, Pope Boniface VIII claimed "that to be subject to the Roman Pontiff is necessary for salvation."[223] The issue also includes the authority of Scriptures, tradition, and reason, the infallibility of the clergy, and the use of doctrine.

> The possessors of the infallibility of the Church are the Holy Father (when he speaks *ex cathedra*) and the whole body of Catholic bishops throughout the world when they teach in union with the pope on matters of faith and morals.[224]

One of the severest critics of infallibility, August Hasler, who served in the Vatican, considers the *ex cathedra* limitation an evasion, since the term can be applied to a pronouncement or encyclical or denied to an embarrassment from the past.

> Only *ex cathedra* pronouncements are to be infallible. Since this concept did not even exist before the sixteenth century, it cannot be said with certainty of any papal declaration from the first fifteen hundred years that it was made *ex cathedra*. This did away

---

[222] James Hastings Nichols, *History of Christianity*, 1650-1950, New York: The Ronald Press Company, 1956, p. 216.

[223] Hans Kueng, *Infallible? An Inquiry*, trans. Edward Quinn, Garden City: Doubleday, 1971, p. 117.

[224] Baker, *Fundamentals*, III, p. 136.

with all sorts of unpleasantness, such as the condemnation of Pope Honorius I as a heretic by three ecumenical councils.[225]

Many would like to know more about how the decisions of 1869-1870 Council were passed, but the Vatican has not released the documents.[226]

The Bible

The Scriptures do not offer anything resembling a papacy with universal authority over the Church. The apostles clearly held positions of authority in the early Church, and some were more prominent than others: Peter, James, John, and Paul. However, when doctrine was being disputed within the Church, a council was called, as we see in Acts 15. Present were apostles, elders, and the congregation in Jerusalem (Acts 15:12).

> Acts 15:1 And certain men which came down from Judaea taught the brethren, *and said*, Except ye be circumcised after the manner of Moses, ye cannot be saved. 2 When therefore Paul and Barnabas had no small dissension and disputation with them, they determined that Paul and Barnabas, and certain other of them, should go up to Jerusalem unto the apostles and elders about this question. 3 And being brought on their way by the church, they passed through Phoenicia and Samaria, declaring the conversion of the Gentiles: and they caused great joy unto all the brethren. 4 And when they were come to Jerusalem, they were

---

[225] August Bernhard Hasler, *How the Pope Became Infallible, Pius IX and the Politics of Persuasion*, Garden City: Doubleday, 1981, p. 183. Kueng's preface to this book in 1979 resurrected Roman Catholic anger over his *Infallible? An Inquiry*, and led in the same year to Kueng being removed as a theologian approved by the Roman Catholic Church. He continued to teach at the University of Tuebingen in Germany and saw his lecture audience increase from 100 to 1,000. Kueng wrote: "With what right do you lay claim to the infallibility of the Holy Spirit of God, which 'blows where it wills,' you who are men and not God? Doesn't 'to err is human' hold true for you? Or has God anywhere ascribed to you his own infallibility? If so, that would have to be attested to in the most unambiguous language. People in the Bible (and in the Church of the New Testament, beginning with Peter, the 'Rock') do not exactly convey an impression of infallibility...And thus, for many long decades nobody mentioned any infallibility of the bishop of Rome (nor, for the time being, of the ecumenical councils either)." "Introduction: The Infallibility Debate—Where Are We Now?" by Hans Kueng, Hasler, p. 2.

[226] *Ibid.*, p. 234.

received of the church, and *of* the apostles and elders, and they declared all things that God had done with them. 5 But there rose up certain of the sect of the Pharisees which believed, saying, That it was needful to circumcise them, and to command *them* to keep the law of Moses. 6 And the apostles and elders came together for to consider of this matter.

Peter, considered the first pope by the Roman Catholic Church, exhibited a definite leadership role:

Acts 15:7 And when there had been much disputing, Peter rose up, and said unto them, Men *and* brethren, ye know how that a good while ago God made choice among us, that the Gentiles by my mouth should hear the word of the gospel, and believe. 8 And God, which knoweth the hearts, bare them witness, giving them the Holy Ghost, even as *he did* unto us; 9 And put no difference between us and them, purifying their hearts by faith. 10 Now therefore why tempt ye God, to put a yoke upon the neck of the disciples, which neither our fathers nor we were able to bear? 11 But we believe that through the grace of the Lord Jesus Christ we shall be saved, even as they.

The context does not show Peter in a position superior to others, since James also speaks with authority:

Acts 15:12 Then all the multitude kept silence, and gave audience to Barnabas and Paul, declaring what miracles and wonders God had wrought among the Gentiles by them. 13 And after they had held their peace, James answered, saying, Men *and* brethren, hearken unto me: 14 Simeon hath declared how God at the first did visit the Gentiles, to take out of them a people for his name. 15 And to this agree the words of the prophets; as it is written, 16 After this I will return, and will build again the tabernacle of David, which is fallen down; and I will build again the ruins thereof, and I will set it up: 17 That the residue of men might seek after the Lord, and all the Gentiles, upon whom my name is called, saith the Lord, who doeth all these things. 18 Known unto God are all his works from the beginning of the world. 19

Wherefore my sentence is, that we trouble not them, which from among the Gentiles are turned to God: 20 But that we write unto them, that they abstain from pollutions of idols, and *from* fornication, and *from* things strangled, and *from* blood. 21 For Moses of old time hath in every city them that preach him, being read in the synagogues every Sabbath day.

Speaking against the doctrine of papal infallibility, Bishop Joseph Strossmayer said to the members of the First Vatican Council:

The more I examine, O venerable brethren, the more I am convinced that in the Scriptures the son of Jonas does not appear to be first.[227]

Although Peter spoke, James offered the judgment that was accepted and made the doctrine of the Council of Jerusalem. However, this conclusion was not offered as the doctrine of James or Peter, but the teaching of the whole Church:

Acts 15:22 Then pleased it the apostles and elders, with the whole church, to send chosen men of their own company to Antioch with Paul and Barnabas; *namely*, Judas surnamed Barsabas, and Silas, chief men among the brethren: 23 And they wrote *letters* by them after this manner; The apostles and elders and brethren *send* greeting unto the brethren which are of the Gentiles in Antioch and Syria and Cilicia: 24 Forasmuch as we have heard, that certain which went out from us have troubled you with words, subverting your souls, saying, Ye *must* be circumcised, and keep the law: to whom we gave no *such* commandment: 25 It seemed

---

[227] Hudson, *Papal Power*, p. 120. The speech is also reproduced in *Christian News*, July 4, 1988, p. 15. Strossmayer (1815-1905) never left the Church of Rome. For many years he refused to accept the doctrine of papal infallibility. Sounding like Luther, he said in 1871, "I'd rather die than go against my conscience and my convictions. Better to be exposed to every humiliation than to bend my knee to Baal, to arrogance incarnate." He was reconciled with Pope Pius IX in 1875 and accepted the doctrine in 1881 under Pope Leo XIII. At the end of his life he claimed that his opposition to infallibility was based only upon it being declared at an inopportune time. (Hasler, p. 224f.) Strossmayer's speech appeared in the February, 1889 *Lehre und Wehre*, published by the Lutheran Church-Missouri Synod. *Christian News Enclyclopedia*, p. 3922.

good unto us, being assembled with one accord, to send chosen men unto you with our beloved Barnabas and Paul, 26 Men that have hazarded their lives for the name of our Lord Jesus Christ. 27 We have sent therefore Judas and Silas, who shall also tell *you* the same things by mouth. 28 For it seemed good to the Holy Ghost, and to us, to lay upon you no greater burden than these necessary things; 29 That ye abstain from meats offered to idols, and from blood, and from things strangled, and from fornication: from which if ye keep yourselves, ye shall do well. Fare ye well.

R. C. H. Lenski, a conservative Lutheran professor in Biblical studies, wrote this about Acts 15:

The apostles are not a body substituting for Moses and decreeing laws similar to those Moses gave to Israel at God's command. The resolution that James offers is to be no papal bull.[228]

The early Church benefited from the teaching authority of the apostles, but this did not exempt the congregations from doctrinal conflict. Nor were the apostles always in perfect agreement, as St. Paul admitted in Galatians 2:11.

Galatians 2:11 But when Peter was come to Antioch, I withstood him to the face, because he was to be blamed.

St. Paul warned the Ephesian elders against fierce wolves (false teachers) from the outside and rising up from within the flock. (Acts 20:28ff.) Christ Himself warned His audience against wolves in sheep's clothing, false teachers who said, "Lord, Lord," and performed wonders to mislead the people, Matthew 7:21ff.[229] The Holy Spirit, speaking through

---

[228] R. C. H. Lenski, *The Interpretation of the Acts of the Apostles*, Columbus: Lutheran Book Concern, 1934, p. 608.

[229] "Who can number the secret gifts of grace which God has bestowed upon his church through the intercession of the Blessed Virgin throughout this period?...No sooner had Pius IX proclaimed as a dogma of the Catholic Faith the preservation of Mary from original stain, than the Virgin herself began in Lourdes those wonderful manifestations, followed by the vast and magnificent movements, which have resulted in those two temples dedicated to the Immaculate

the Apostle Paul, taught that sects and divisions were part of God's plan—allowed by God, not approved by Him—to prove what is true in the Christian Church.

> 1 Corinthians 11:18 For first of all, when ye come together in the church, I hear that there be divisions among you; and I partly believe it. 19 For there must be also heresies among you, that they which are approved may be made manifest among you.

The early Church struggled to maintain doctrinal unity through the Holy Spirit. The term *episkopos* (bishop) in the New Testament literally means supervisor. Other types of Word and Sacrament ministry existed in the New Testament, including apostles, prophets, evangelists, pastors, and teachers (Ephesians 4:11). The authority of the early Church was the revelation of God, which was given directly through the apostles, who handed down what they were taught by Christ (1 Corinthians 11 and 15). No one was given the authority to be creative with the doctrine of the Church, to introduce new teachings or to change what was taught by Christ and handed down through the apostles. Therefore, the genuine apostolic writings became the teaching authority of the Church, even before the apostles died.

The episcopal office, in which a single person exercised authority over a group of congregations, and where bishops united as a fraternity across the Church, emerged gradually over a period of time. The Bible does not provide a specific church order, and we know little about how the early Church was governed. We do know that the Scriptures focus on correct doctrine as primary rather than a particular style of government or leadership. Christians were told to "observe and avoid those who caused divisions and taught contrary to what was handed down" (Romans 16:16). Pastors were commanded to teach sound doctrine, continuing Christ's command to avoid wolves in sheep's clothing (Matthew 7:15; John 10:12; Acts 20:29). In 1 Timothy, St. Paul exhibited no patience or love for the false teacher, describing him perfectly as he would appear in many future generations of church life:

Mother, where the prodigies which still continue to take place through her intercession furnish splendid arguments against the incredulity of our days." Pope Pius X, Encyclical, *Ad diem illum*, February 2, 1904. Father Francis Ripley, *Mary, Mother of the Church*, p. 66.

1 Timothy 6:3 If any man teach otherwise, and consent not to wholesome words, *even* the words of our Lord Jesus Christ, and to the doctrine which is according to godliness; 4 He is proud, knowing nothing, but doting about questions and strifes of words, whereof cometh envy, strife, railings, evil surmisings,

The teaching office of the pastor was carefully described by St. Paul, who was taught the Gospel by Christ Himself (Galatians 1). He then taught Timothy exactly the same doctrine, without adding or subtracting. The Apostle did not change the Deposit of Faith, an important term used later by the Church of Rome to add new doctrines, such as Purgatory.

2 Timothy 1:13 Hold fast the form of sound words, which thou hast heard of me, in faith and love which is in Christ Jesus. 14 That good thing which was committed unto thee keep by the Holy Ghost which dwelleth in us.

Refusal to listen to orthodox Christian teaching is a sign of the end times, during which church leaders turn away from (apostasy—literally) the truth and teach anti-Christian doctrines in the name of Christ. Although this happened in the very beginning of the Church, the end-time is marked by the overwhelming popularity and success of charlatans and con-artists who tell nominal Christians exactly what they want to hear.

2 Timothy 4:3 For the time will come when they will not endure sound doctrine; but after their own lusts shall they heap to themselves teachers, having itching ears; 4 And they shall turn away *their* ears from the truth, and shall be turned unto fables.

Nevertheless, a pastor must be able to teach the Word of God and use the Word as a weapon against all false doctrines.

Titus 1:9 Holding fast the faithful word as he hath been taught, that he may be able by sound doctrine both to exhort and to convince the gainsayers.

The Apostle John wrote that those who came to the house-church should be questioned first and not even allowed inside the home if they were false (1 John 4:3). Clearly, pure doctrine was primary in the apostolic Church. Although the Bishop of Rome eventually claimed primacy over other bishops, this was a late development without Scriptural support. Nevertheless, certain passages in the New Testament are cited as the foundation for the papacy.

The primary Biblical passage used to buttress the papacy is Matthew 16:18-19:

> Matthew 16:18 And I say also unto thee, That thou art Peter (*petros*), and upon this rock (*petra*) I will build my church; and the gates of hell shall not prevail against it. 19 And I will give unto thee the keys of the kingdom of heaven: and whatsoever thou shalt bind on earth shall be bound in heaven: and whatsoever thou shalt loose on earth shall be loosed in heaven.

Jesus' words are a play upon the meaning of Peter, which means "a small rock" in Greek. However, the second word is not the same word, but similar to Peter (*petros*), in both sound in meaning. The word (*petra*) means "a rock ledge" in Greek. Therefore, Jesus' words might be translated more literally as "You are the Rock and on this Bedrock will I build My Church...And the gates of Hell will not prevail against it." Some emphasize the confession of faith in Christ as the bedrock, but that would make man's confession the foundation. Scripture offers a perfect parallel to this passage, shedding light on it, showing us that Christ Himself is the Bedrock.

> 1 Corinthians 10:3 And did all eat the same spiritual meat; 4 And did all drink the same spiritual drink: for they drank of that spiritual Rock (*petra*) that followed them: and that Rock was Christ.

The papal coat of arms features a pair of keys, indicating that Christ gave Peter the keys of binding and loosing, the keys that stand for offering forgiveness for the penitent and refusing forgiveness to the impenitent. Since Christ says "to you" (singular) are given the keys, the Church of Rome has explained this passage as the formation of the papacy by

Christ. If we compare the parallel passage in the Gospel of John, we see that the second person plural form is used for the verb:

> John 20:22 And when he had said this, he breathed on *them*, and saith unto them, Receive ye the Holy Ghost: 23 Whose soever sins ye remit, they are remitted unto them; *and* whose soever *sins* ye retain, they are retained.

A similar passage also uses the second person plural, not the singular form:

> Matthew 18:18 Verily I say unto you, Whatsoever ye [plural] shall bind on earth shall be bound in heaven: and whatsoever ye [plural] shall loose on earth shall be loosed in heaven.

Moreover, Jesus did not give the office of the keys to the apostles or to one apostle alone, but to the whole Church. Forgiving one another is an essential part of the Lord's Prayer and Jesus' explanation.

> Matthew 6:14 For if ye forgive men their trespasses, your heavenly Father will also forgive you:

The office of the keys, according to the Bible, belongs to all Christians. Lenski explained:

> The apostles, and after them the pastors, are only the ministers of the church. Through them the church speaks and acts.[230]

This is especially clear in Jesus' teaching about excommunication in Matthew 18:15-18, where the final authority is not vested in a person but in the congregation.[231]

---

[230] *Ibid.* See also Lenski's *The Interpretation of the Gospel of Matthew*, 1932, p. 611. However, this does not support the Fuller-Seminary-inspired *Everyone a Minister*, by Oscar Feucht.

[231] *Ibid.*, p. 683.

The concluding chapter of John is also used to defend the so-called New Testament origins of the papacy, as if Jesus meant to appoint Peter as the first Bishop of Rome.

> John 21:15 So when they had dined, Jesus saith to Simon Peter, Simon, *son* of Jonas, lovest thou me more than these? He saith unto him, Yea, Lord; thou knowest that I love thee. He saith unto him, Feed my lambs. 16 He saith to him again the second time, Simon, *son* of Jonas, lovest thou me? He saith unto him, Yea, Lord; thou knowest that I love thee. He saith unto him, Feed my sheep. 17 He saith unto him the third time, Simon, *son* of Jonas, lovest thou me? Peter was grieved because he said unto him the third time, Lovest thou me? And he said unto him, Lord, thou knowest all things; thou knowest that I love thee. Jesus saith unto him, Feed my sheep. 18 Verily, verily, I say unto thee, When thou wast young, thou girdedst thyself, and walkedst whither thou wouldest: but when thou shalt be old, thou shalt stretch forth thy hands, and another shall gird thee, and carry *thee* whither thou wouldest not.

This passage is directly related to Peter's threefold denial of Jesus during the trial of his Master. Peter denied Christ three times beside a charcoal warmer, and three times Christ probed the depth of Peter's love beside a charcoal fire (John 18:18; 21:9). No passage in the New Testament more vividly portrays the penitent sinner being forgiven by Christ. Jesus' command to Peter is not to be a ruler of the Church but to feed the sheep, by nurturing them with the Word. The Treatise on the Power and Primacy of the Pope in the *Book of Concord* states:

> As to the passages "Feed my sheep" (John 21:17) and "Do you love me more than these?" (John 21:15), it in no wise follows that they bestow a special superiority on Peter, for Christ bids Peter to pasture the sheep, that is, to preach the Word or govern the church with the Word. This commission Peter holds in common with the rest of the apostles.[232]

---

232 Tappert, p. 325, #30. *Triglotta*, p. 513.

Peter had been martyred for three decades when John's Gospel was written, but John did not record any successor to Peter, if Peter were indeed the first Bishop of Rome. About the Biblical and historical claims for the papal primacy and infallibility, Hans Kueng wrote:

> ...only from the fourth century onward was Matthew 16:18f. used (particularly by the Roman pontiffs, Damasus and Leo) to support a claim to primacy, and even then without any formal claim to infallibility. And finally, in all Eastern exegesis of Matthew 16:18 until into the eighth century and beyond, it was considered at best as a reference to Peter's personal primacy, without any serious thought of a Roman primacy. And, with reference to Matthew 16:18 or Luke 22:32, neither in East nor West is there ever a claim raised for the infallibility of the Roman pontiff.[233]

History of Infallibility

The doctrine of infallibility is relatively recent, raised anew by Cardinal Bellarmine, 1542-1621, and Cardinal Caesar Baronius, 1538-1607, after the Reformation. Its brief, earlier history was marked only by papal condemnation. St. Augustine, one of the most influential theologians of the Christian Church, considered one of the four Doctors of the Church of Rome, wrote:

> I neither can nor should deny that, as in my larger works, so also in so many of my smaller ones, there is so much which can be criticized with just judgment and without rashness.[234]

The Franciscan priest Peter Olivi, 1248-1298, was the first to attribute infallibility to the pope, but Pope John XXII denounced infallibility as Satanic in the bull *Qui quorundam*, 1324. Olivi wanted a decision on Franciscan poverty by a previous pope to be locked in by the concept of infallibility, but Pope John XXII had a different opinion about monkish

---

233 Kueng, *Infallible? An Inquiry*, p. 111. Matthew 16:18; Luke 22:32.

234 Augustine, *Ad Vincentium Victorem*, Book 2, *Examination*, I, p. 260, cited in *Examination*, I, p. 260.

poverty and therefore rejected this new declaration of papal infallibility. From an administrative point of view, infallibility binds the pope to the decisions of pontiffs before him and to his own decisions as well. What Olivi wanted to accomplish through infallibility was seen by the pope as an obstacle, not a boon. The debate, which has continued within Roman Catholicism since Vatican I, has proved that Pope John XXII was correct.

Pope Pius IX

The central figure in establishing infallibility is Pope Pius IX (1792-1881), who came to power in 1846 as a liberal but was shocked by the 1848 revolution that drove him into exile, forcing him to wear a disguise to escape the city of Rome. The Vatican of the 19th century struggled to maintain ownership of the papal states of Italy, which were the remnants of Rome's former· political power. The Vatican's Swiss guards today are the remnants of former papal military power. Pope Pius IX was rescued from exile by the troops of Louis Napoleon, who gave him back the Papal States and also supplied him with a garrison of troops to maintain control.[235] Some attribute Pius IX's ultra-conservatism to his revulsion at seeing so much social turmoil. Italian wits called him Pio Nono Secundo (The Second Pius the Ninth) for his drastic change of perspective. In exile in 1849 he assembled that coterie of advisers, chiefly the Jesuits of the periodical *Civilta Cattolica*, who mapped out his strategy, including the three chief ecclesiastical acts of his reign:

1. The Proclamation of the Immaculate Conception of Mary;

2. The formulation of a list of sociopolitical heresies;

3. The declaration of infallibility for the pope, separate from that of the Church of Rome.[236]

Hans Kueng wanted to make it clear that the issue was not solely ecclesiastical, but directly involved with the political power of the papacy.

Would the papal states, restored in 1849, but by the intervention of the Piedmontese government in 1860 restricted to Rome and its neighborhood—known everywhere for their monseignorial

---

[235] Nichols, *History of Christianity*, 1650-1950, p. 209.

[236] *Ibid.*, p. 210.

mismanagement and social backwardness—have to be given up or could they hold out in the long run, solely with French support, in the face of the Italian unity movement which meant to make Rome its capital. In the Vatican the situation was viewed with the utmost anxiety.[237]

Nevertheless, Pope Pius IX did not invent papal infallibility or work to establish it by himself. Pope Gregory XVI, who ruled just before Pius IX, from 1831 to 1846, encouraged the view. As a monk, before he became pope, the future Gregory XVI wrote *The Triumph of the Holy See and the Church over the Attacks of the Innovators.* "In it he defended the thesis that as a true monarch the pope was also necessarily infallible."[238]

Infallibility was considered an attribute of the Roman Catholic Church already, before a separate definition of papal infallibility became a movement.

> Passing over the immortality of the soul and the existence of a future life, both necessarily presupposed, Purgatory implies the infallibility of the Church, on the authority of which we accept that truth, which is indicated in Holy Scripture in but an obscure manner--a fact which explains its rejection or its modification by the dissident Churches.[239]

Pope Pius and the Ultramontanes were able to focus the doctrine on the doctrine of infallibility of the *pope* rather than that of the Church of Rome. This action gave the papacy more authority and the papal curia (Vatican advisers), cardinals, bishops, and ecumenical councils less authority. The Ultramontanes were those members of the Roman Catholic Church who wanted more power "beyond the mountains" (Rome is beyond the Alps), rather than in the state church. In France, those who favored national control of the Church of Rome were called Gallicans. They saw themselves as more progressive and nationalistic, not wanting control of their bishops and cardinals to come from beyond the mountains in Rome. The Gallican movement, named for the Four

---

[237] *Infallible? An Inquiry,* p. 91.

[238] Hasler, p. 42.

[239] Jugie, *Purgatory,* p. 27.

Articles drawn up by the French clergy, passed in 1682 by Louis XIV, and imposed on France, is summarized below by David John Sharrock:

1. Neither the Pope nor the Church has any power over temporal rules, and kings cannot be deposed by spiritual authorities, nor can subjects be released from their oath of allegiance.

2. As stated by the Council of Constance, papal power is limited by General Councils.

3. The exercise of papal power is limited by the customs of privileges of the Gallican Church.

4. Although the pope has the chief voice in questions of faith, yet his decision is not unalterable unless the consent of the church is given.[240]

Gallicanism united with Jansenism in France, but also spilled over into the various countries of Europe. The ultimate summary of the Gallican spirit within the Roman Catholic Church was published in 1763 under the pseudonym "Febronius" by Bishop Nicholas von Hontheim, 1701-1790, and became the basis for Liguori's reactionary defense of the papacy.[241] When Napoleon signed a Concordat in 1801 with Pope Pius VII, the Organic Articles, which Napoleon added, provided:

...for the teaching of the Four Gallican Articles in all seminaries, required government permission for all church meetings--diocesan, metropolitan, or national--and government approval of all papal letters, legates, or even decrees of ecumenical councils before promulgation in France.[242]

---

[240] David John Sharrock, C.SS.R., *The Theological Defense of Papal Power by St. Alphonsus de Liguori*, Washington D.C.: Catholic University of America Press, 1961, p. 12f. Hereafter cited as Sharrock, *Papal Power*.

[241] *Ibid.*, p. 26.

[242] Nichols, *History of Christianity*, p. 129. Pope Pius VII's predecessor had an ignominious end. The French army deposed Pope Pius VI in 1798, giving him 48 hours to leave Rome. "So the Pope left and a Te Deum was sung in St. Peter's over the deposition, at which some of the cardinals assisted...In the civil registry of the French Republic his death [1799, in exile at Valence] was noticed as follows: 'Citizen John Braschi. Trade: pontiff.'" *Ibid.*, p. 126.

Thus the issue of papal primacy and infallibility was directly involved in the long-standing European conflict of caesareo-papism (state control of the church) *versus* theocracy (church control of the state). The First Vatican Council was Pope Pius IX's answer to long-standing dissent within the Church of Rome concerning the authority of the papacy, but was also used to lay claim to the papacy's political control of Europe.

After witnessing the effects of the 1848 revolution, Pope Pius IX appointed Ultramontane leaders whenever possible. The Ultramontanes called Pius IX "King, Pope-King, Supreme Ruler of the World, King of Kings," and applied hymns of the breviary to him.

> Bishop Berteaud of Tulle described the pope as "the word (of God) made flesh, living on in our midst."[243]

The Jesuit periodical *Civilta Cattolica* claimed that "...the infallibility of the Pope is the infallibility of Jesus Christ Himself," and "When the Pope thinks, it is God who is thinking in him."[244] Louis Veuillot, a layman who was one of the most influential Ultramontanes asked at Vatican I:

> Does the Church believe, or does she not believe, that her Head is inspired directly by God, that is to say, infallible in his decisions regarding faith and morals?[245]

Mermillod, the auxiliary bishop of Geneva, spoke at Vatican I of "three incarnations of the Son of God," in the Virgin's womb, in the Eucharist, and in the old man in the Vatican.[246] Catholics, Lutherans, and Protestants acknowledge that the infallibilist movement was helped enormously by Pope Pius IX's declaration of the Immaculate Conception of Mary in the papal bull *Ineffabilis Deus* in 1854:

---

[243] Hasler, p. 47f.

[244] C. Butler, *The Vatican Council, 1869-1879*, London, 1962, p. 61; cited in *Infallible?*, p. 98.

[245] *Ibid.*

[246] R. Aubert, *Vatican I*, p. 33; cited in *Infallible? An Inquiry*, p. 99.

The way for papal infallibility had been prepared by the doctrine of the immaculate conception of Mary (1854) which the pope had raised to the status of dogma without the assent of a council.[247]

The encyclical letter, *Quanta cura* (1864) which included the Syllabus of Errors, condemned a host of revolutionary and progressive trends, including freedom of religion. The Syllabus of Errors continued the reactionary tendency of the papacy and furthered claims of infallibility by the exercise of papal power. Pope Pius convened the First Vatican Council on December 8, 1869, the Feast of the Immaculate Conception, emphasizing his 1854 act. He had already laid the groundwork for his solo promulgation of dogma in his first encyclical, *Nostis*, on December 8, 1849, by speaking of the irreformable magisterium.[248] Pope Pius proved that he was already *de facto* infallible by saying

> People want to credit me with infallibility. I don't need it at all. Am I not infallible already? Didn't I establish the dogma of the Virgin's Immaculate Conception all by myself several years ago?[249]

This is acknowledged by those who support papal infallibility:

> Clear examples of this are the definition by Pope Pius IX in 1854 of the Immaculate Conception of Mary, and the definition by Pope Pius XII in 1950 of Mary's glorious Assumption into heaven, body and soul.[250]

Clergy and laity sent petitions to the Vatican in support of papal infallibility. Theologians and leaders who supported papal infallibility in books and articles were thanked and rewarded by the pope.

---

[247] Otto W. Heick, *A History of Christian Thought*, 2 vols., Philadelphia: Fortress Press, 1966, II, p. 312.

[248] Hasler, p. 82.

[249] *Ibid.*, p. 82.

[250] Baker, *Fundamentals*, III, p. 117.

In 1870, the Vatican Council by its Constitution, *Pastor Aeternus* defined the nature of the power which the Roman Pontiff possesses. The very next year, Pope Pius IX declared St. Alphonsus de Liguori a Doctor of the Church and singled out Alphonsus' defense of the rights of the Apostolic See.[251]

John Bosco, who founded the Salesian religious order, had a vision in 1870 that urged the pope to declare infallibility. Bosco was made a saint in 1934.[252] Those who opposed papal infallibility were scolded and disciplined. After the Greek-Melkite patriarch, Gregor Yussef, gave a speech against papal infallibility, Pope Pius IX called him in for an audience. When the patriarch kissed the foot of the pope, a traditional gesture of homage, the pope placed his foot on the head or neck of the cleric and said, "Gregor, you hard head you." Pope Pius IX rubbed his foot on the patriarch's head a while longer. For this reason, the Greek-Melkite Church has filed petitions opposing Pius IX's canonization as a saint.[253]

The movement toward infallibility was not smooth, not without conflict. One of the prime opponents was Cardinal Guidi, reported in several dispatches by Polish Count Wladislaw Kulczycki to be the son of Pope Pius IX.[254] The German church historian Johann Joseph Ignaz von Doellinger published a series of five articles in the Augsburg *Allgemeine Zeitung* entitled "Der Papst und das Konzil," (The Pope and the Council) using the pen name "Janus."

> These articles not only refuted, on historical grounds, the undoubtedly exaggerated conception of papal infallibility advocated by Louis Veuillot and Dr. Ward and their followers, but they also attacked papal authority itself with a sharpness unknown since the days of Sarpi. In July the articles appeared in book form.[255]

---

[251] Sharrock, p. vii.

[252] Hasler, p. 111f.

[253] *Ibid.*, p. 89. More than one Lutheran can identify with this story. Marx was correct in saying that history repeats itself, the first time as a tragedy, later as a farce.

[254] *Ibid.*, p. 92.

[255] Hubert Jedin, *Ecumenical Councils of the Catholic Church*, New York: Paulist Press, 1960, p. 152. Sarpi is a church historian who dealt with the Council of Trent. Louis Veuillot, a layman and

Ward's position on papal infallibility is described by Kueng:

> For the protagonist of infallibility in England, W. G. Ward, convert and editor of the *Dublin Review*, "all direct doctrinal instructions of all encyclicals, of all letters to individual bishops and allocutions, published by the Popes, are *ex cathedra* pronouncements and *ipso facto* infallible."[256]

Doellinger's book was placed on the papal *Index of Forbidden Books*, not to be read by any Roman Catholic in any language. Doellinger was one of many distinguished professors who formed the Old Catholic Church in the wake of Vatican I. James Hastings Nichols observed:

> The "Old Catholic" group which refused to accept the decrees had a large number of distinguished scholars, but not one bishop from the minority had the courage of his convictions.[257]

LePage Renoug's *The Condemnation of Pope Honorius* was also placed on the *Index of Prohibited Books*. The bishops supporting papal infallibility could not find "a single pope before the sixteenth century who had clearly and unequivocally pleaded for the doctrine of infallibility."[258]

Bishop Strossmayer's Opposition to Infallibility

Some popes taught error, as Bishop Strossmayer told his audience at Vatican I:

---

editor of *Univers*, wrote: "Where we Catholics are in the minority, we demand freedom in the name of your principles, where we are in the majority, we deny it in the name of our principles." Nichols, *History of Christianity*, p. 210

[256] Kueng, p. 57. Quotation from Butler, *The Vatican Council*, p. 57.

[257] *History of Christianity*, p. 216. The Old Catholic group had great difficulties obtaining clergy, reached its peak strength of 50,000 in 1878, and entered relations with Eastern Orthodoxy and Anglicanism, 1874-1879, at the Bonn Conference. *Ibid.*, p. 224.

[258] Hasler, p. 162.

Pope Victor (192) first approved of Montanism, and then later condemned it. Marcellinus (296-303) was an idolater. He entered into the temple of Vesta and offered incense to the goddess...Liberius (358) consented to the condemnation of Athanasius, and made a profession of Arianism, that he might be recalled from his exile and reinstated in his see. Honorius (625) adhered to Monothelitism: Father Gratry has proved it to demonstration. Gregory I (785-90) calls anyone Antichrist who takes the name of Universal Bishop, and contrariwise Boniface III (607,8) made the parricide Emperor Phocas confer that title upon him. Paschal II (1088-99) and Eugenius III (1145-153) authorized dueling; Julius II (1509) and Pius IV (1560) forbade it...Sixtus V (1585-1590) published an edition of the Bible, and by a bull recommended it to be read; Pius VII condemned the reading of it. Clement XIV (1700-21) abolished the order of the Jesuits, permitted by Paul III, and Pius VII reestablished it.[259]

An acclaimed church historian, James Hastings Nichols, noted that Pope Honorius has been anathematized by three ecumenical councils and at least 55 popes and "...this anathema had been read once a year in the breviary by every priest in the Latin church for centuries."[260] When one church official opposed the doctrine of papal infallibility because of a lack of tradition in the Church of Rome to support it, Pope Pius IX uttered the famous words:

I am the Tradition.[261]

Vengeful Aftermath of Vatican I

The decree on papal infallibility was passed by Vatican I during that violent thunderstorm described at the beginning of this chapter. Pope Pius IX wore down his opponents during the council. The summer

---

[259] Hudson, *Papal Power, Its Origins and Development*, (Bishop Strossmayer's speech, 1870, part one on popes), p. 127f.

[260] *History of Christianity*, p. 215.

[261] Heick, II, p. 313.

heat and a siege of malaria weakened the elderly prelates. Civil disorder placed additional pressure on the Council, so that it was never formally ended but merely adjourned. In France, Bishop Flavian Hugonin of Bayeeux "had to go into hiding for months to escape the wrath of the Infallibilists in his diocese."[262] In America, the Jesuits "incited" clergy and laity against the opposing bishops after Vatican I.

> Before long, one of the key figures in the resistance movement, Archbishop Peter Richard Kenrick of St. Louis, succumbed to the pressure.[263]

Archbishop Kenrick submitted to the doctrine. Bishop Francois Lecourtier threw his documents into the Tiber River in Rome and left Vatican I early. The papers were pulled out of the river and turned over to the Vatican. Lecourtier was removed three years later as Bishop of Montpellier.[264] The Vatican court preacher was fired for his opposition to infallibility, even though he submitted.[265] The dean of the theology faculty at the Sorbonne, France, Henri Maret, was forced to withdraw his book, *The Council and Religious Peace.*[266]

Prelates and theologians remained opposed to infallibility. In Germany, 20 professors in theology and philosophy were excommunicated.

> Two thirds of all Catholic historians teaching at German universities left the Church.[267]

Vatican I also had profound political implications, which led to a period known as the *Kulturkampf,* or cultural struggle:

---

[262] Hasler, p. 204.

[263] Hasler, p. 205.

[264] *Ibid.,* p. 139.

[265] *Ibid.,* 197.

[266] *Ibid.,* p. 202.

[267] *Ibid.,* p. 227.

In the period after the Vatican Council, the Roman Church engaged in bitter struggle with several of the leading European states. The church's claim to the right to rule over the civil states, as expressed in the Syllabus and strengthened by the decrees of the Vatican Council, conflicted with the increasingly absolute claims of the modern state.[268]

Infallibility Explained and Expanded

Those who deny papal infallibility are anathema, damned to Hell, according to Vatican I. The decree of infallibility in the dogmatic constitution *Pastor Aeternus* states that:

> The Roman Pontiff, when he speaks *ex cathedra*, that is, when in discharge of the office of pastor and doctor of all Christians, by virtue of his supreme Apostolic authority, he defines a doctrine regarding faith or morals to be held by the universal Church, by the divine assistance promised to him in blessed Peter, is possessed of that infallibility with which the divine Redeemer willed that his Church should be endowed for defining doctrine regarding faith or morals; and that therefore such definitions of the Roman Pontiff are irreformable of themselves and not from the consent of the Church.[269]

After Vatican I, papal infallibility was supported or suggested by the following popes:

- Pope Leo XIII, in *Satis Cogitum*, 1896;

- Pope Pius X, in *Lamentabili*, 1907;

- Pope Pius XII, in *Mystici Corporis*, 1943, *Humani Generis*, 1950, and *Ineffabilis Deus*, 1950.[270]

---

[268] *History of Christianity*, p. 219.

[269] Schaff, *Creeds of Christendom*, II, 234ff. Cited in Heick, II, p. 313.

[270] Hudson, *Papal Power*, p. 91.

No one is clear about the limitations of papal infallibility, which may diminish with time, then increase again. Pope Pius XII applied infallibility to all papal encyclicals in *Humani generis*.

> With a single stroke Pius XII deprived the theologians of any possible excuse by adding that encyclicals had the same binding force as *ex cathedra* decisions and could resolve any doctrinal controversy with definitive authority.[271]

According to Kueng, Pope John XXIII provided a respite in the growth of papal infallibility claims:

> It was again John XXIII who had revealed a new ideal of an unpretentious, ecumenically and humanly disposed Petrine *ministry* to the brethren and attached so little importance to the infallibility attributed to him that he could say on one occasion with a smile: "I'm not infallible; I'm infallible only when I speak *ex cathedra*. But I'll never speak *ex cathedra*." And John XXIII never did speak *ex cathedra*.[272]

Active support for papal infallibility continued under Pope John Paul II. On May 15, 1980, the pope sent a letter to the German Bishops Conference praising the decision on papal infallibility of the Congregation of the Doctrine of the Faith.[273] Father Baker's explanation reveals an interesting repudiation of the Biblical example, the Council of Jerusalem, Acts 15:

> According to an ancient saying, "the First See is judged by no one." The reason is that there is no higher spiritual judge on earth than the pope. He has the right to decide all Church disputes. For the same reason, there is no right of appeal from a decision of the Holy Father to a higher court. No such court exists, not even a

---

[271] Hasler, p. 261.

[272] Kueng, p. 87.

[273] Hasler, p. 313.

General Council. These points were all clearly spelled out by the First Vatican Council in 1870.[274]

Although the Second Vatican Council has been portrayed as a liberal answer to the reactionary doctrines of the First Vatican Council, a careful reading of the documents reveals an expansion of infallibility, to include all clergy who teach in harmony with the pope.

> The bishops exercise their infallible teaching power in an extraordinary manner when, in conjunction with the pope, they gather together in an ecumenical council, as they did at Vatican Council II, 1962-1965. They also exercise their infallible teaching authority in an ordinary manner when, scattered in their dioceses and in moral unity with the pope, they unanimously promulgate the same teachings on faith and morals.[275]

Father Baker did not invent a new doctrine or dishonestly expand upon Vatican decisions that were really quite liberal and progressive, for the documents say:

> This infallibility with which the divine Redeemer willed His Church to be endowed in defining a doctrine of faith and morals extends as far as extends the deposit of divine revelation, which must be religiously guarded and faithfully expounded. [Note: cf. *Verbum Dei*, Article X] This is the infallibility which the Roman Pontiff, the head of the college of bishops, enjoys in virtue of his office, when, as the supreme shepherd and teacher of all the faithful, who confirms his brethren in their faith (cf. Luke 22:32),

---

274 Baker, *Fundamentals*, III, p. 116. Tappert noted: "Pope Gelasius had asserted, 'The pope is to be judged by no one,' as early as the end of the fifth century. The claims of the councils in the fifteenth century to superiority over the pope were condemned by Pope Leo X in 1516." Treatise on the Power and Primacy of the Pope, Tappert, p. 327. (2 Thessalonians 2:3-4)

275 Baker, *Fundamentals*, III, p. 137.

he proclaims by a definitive act some doctrine of faith or morals.[276]

Vatican II explicitly supported all the claims of Vatican I about the power, primacy, and infallibility of the papacy.

> And all this teaching about the institution, the perpetuity, the force and reason for the sacred primacy of the Roman pontiff and of his infallible teaching authority, this sacred synod again proposes to be firmly believed by the faithful.[277]

Kueng stated:

> The third chapter [of *Lumen Gentium*], on "the hierarchical structure of the Church, with special reference to the episcopate," is introduced with a massive confirmation of Vatican I and its statements on the primacy and infallibility of the pope (art. 18).[278]

Not mentioned in most of the literature is this forceful statement of Vatican I, which Vatican II endorsed:

> If anyone, therefore, shall say that blessed Peter the apostle was not appointed the prince of all the apostles and the visible head of the whole church militant; or that the same directly and immediately received from the same our Lord Jesus Christ a

---

[276] *Lumen Gentium*, Dogmatic Constitution of the Church, III, 25, *Vatican II*, p. 48f. The Abbott edition contains this note: "Cf. Vatican Council I, the dogmatic constitution Pastor Aeternus, Denzinger, 1839, (3074)."

[277] *Ibid.*, p. 38. Abbott note: "It [Vatican II] repeats the doctrine of Vatican I concerning the primacy of Peter among the apostles and reaffirms the primacy and infallibility of the Pope as Peter's successor." (Abbott, p. 37f.) "These two articles, the direct authority of the pope in every diocese, and the doctrine of the papal infallibility, completed together the conversion of the Roman Catholic Church into an absolute monarchy without constitutional restraints or responsibility." Nichols, *History of Christianity*, p. 214. Hudson, *Papal Power*, p. 93.

[278] Kueng, p. 69.

primacy of honour only, and not of true and proper jurisdiction--
let him be anathema [damned to Hell].[279]

In effect, the First Vatican Council, confirmed by the Second Vatican
Council, damned to Hell a vast body of previous Roman Catholic leaders
who never dreamed of such a doctrine, since it was late in origin and
slow in taking hold within the Church of Rome, damning also to Hell
those Roman Catholic thinkers who previously considered the doctrine
as loyal members of the church and rejected it. Bishop Strossmayer
declared:

> I have found nothing either near nor far which sanctions the
> opinion of the Ultramontanes. And still more, to my very great
> surprise, I find in the apostolic days no question of a pope,
> successor to St. Peter, and vicar of Jesus Christ, any more than of
> Mahomet who did not then exist...Now, having read the whole
> New Testament, I declare before God, with my hand raised to
> that great crucifix, that I have found no trace of the papacy as it
> exists at this moment.[280]

That is why Bishop Strossmayer concluded, amid cries of "It is not true;
it is not true!" –

> Now, unless you hold that the church of the apostles was
> heretical (which none of us would either desire or dare to say), we
> are obliged to confess that the church has never been more
> beautiful, more pure, or more holy, than in the days when there
> was no pope.[281]

---

[279] Hudson, *Papal Power*, p. 88. "If anyone, therefore, shall say that blessed Peter the apostle was
not appointed the prince of all the apostles and the visible head of the whole church militant; or
that he same directly and immediately received from the same our Lord Jesus Christ a primacy of
honour only, and not of true and proper jurisdiction—let him be anathema [damned to Hell]."
Dogmatic Constitution, Vatican I. Geddes MacGregor, *The Vatican Revolution*, London MacMillan,
1958, p. 169; cited in Hudson.

[280] Hudson, p. 118.

[281] *Ibid.*, p. 121.

Papal infallibility, in effect becomes circular reasoning:

> Our certainty about the reality and truth of Mary's Immaculate Conception comes from the fact that the infallible Church of Christ teaches it as a doctrine revealed by God.[282]

Doctrinal Answers to Infallibility

Although the papacy has asserted its power over the centuries, the claims of Vatican I and II are innovations. The modern papal leaders built upon an imperial tendency that once claimed all of Europe as property donated to the Church of Rome by Charlemagne, but the earlier popes never imagined claiming a god-like infallibility. Space does not permit a complete analysis of papal prerogatives, a list of who first asserted them, and another list of those who denied them. Roman Catholic experts have confessed that these attributes are not based upon Scripture but have developed out of a tradition claiming apostolic authority. One authority lists the foundation of all papal claims as three-fold:

1. Peter was appointed by Christ to be His successor as the head of the Church. The New Testament does not support this claim, as Bishop Strossmayer said.

2. Peter went to Rome and founded the bishopric there. Some early and reliable witnesses place Peter and Paul in Rome, but if Peter established the papacy there, his successors did not become aware of it for centuries.

3. Peter's successors inherited his prerogatives and authority. This is disputed by the Eastern Orthodox Church, which has a thorough knowledge of the early Church fathers, and by the Old Catholic Church, a church formed by Doellinger and others in the wake of Vatican I. Many churches have bishops without a pope and Episcopal authority without infallibility.[283]

---

[282] Baker, *Fundamentals*, II, p. 327.

[283] The three claims are found in John T. Shotwell and Louise Ropes Loomis, *The See of Peter*, New York: Columbia University Press, 1927, p. xxiii. "Jesus prayed that Peter should be strengthened in his faith and that he should strengthen the brethren: 'I have prayed for you, Simon, that your

Definition of the Church

The papacy itself has been divisive for Roman Catholics, Lutherans, and Protestants, but another issue, the definition of the Church, is also involved. Briefly speaking, Lutherans and Protestants view the true Church as invisible or hidden, while Roman Catholics emphasize the visibility of the Church. One cannot separate church government from the concept of the Church.

The Biblical View

In the Bible we have an emphasis upon membership in the Kingdom of God through faith in Christ, such as when St. Paul addressed his first letter to the Corinthian Christians in the following way:

> 1 Corinthians 1:2 Unto the church of God which is at Corinth, to them that are sanctified in Christ Jesus, called *to be* saints, with all that in every place call upon the name of Jesus Christ our Lord, both theirs and ours:

The Corinthians not only belonged to a particular congregation but were also united with all those who called on the name of our Lord Jesus Christ. The Scriptures teach us that only one genuine Church exists, but the Word of God does not identify the true Church with one particular denomination.

> Ephesians 4:4 *There is* one body, and one Spirit, even as ye are called in one hope of your calling; 5 One Lord, one faith, one baptism, 6 One God and Father of all, who *is* above all, and through all, and in you all.

---

faith may not fail, and once you have recovered, you in your turn must strengthen your brothers' (Luke 22:32). Dangers to the Faith exist at all times, so in order to fulfill this task properly, in matters of faith and morals the pope must be infallible." *Fundamentals*, III, p. 119.

This one Church is maintained by correct doctrine, not by a particular structure. The Bible tells us almost nothing about structure, but consistently stresses the pure teaching of God's Word.

> 1 John 4:1 Beloved, believe not every spirit, but try the spirits whether they are of God: because many false prophets are gone out into the world.

> John 8:31 Then said Jesus to those Jews which believed on him, If ye continue in my word, *then* are ye my disciples indeed;

Although neutrality about religion is considered a great virtue today, the Apostle Paul did not teach his followers to practice it. Instead, he warned:

> Romans 16:17 Now I beseech you, brethren, mark them which cause divisions and offences contrary to the doctrine which ye have learned; and avoid them. 18 For they that are such serve not our Lord Jesus Christ, but their own belly; and by good words and fair speeches deceive the hearts of the simple.

St. Paul compared false teaching to gangrene or cancer, a condition requiring surgery rather than neutrality in the name of love.

> 2 Timothy 2:17 And their word will eat as doth a canker: of whom is Hymenaeus and Philetus;

The doctrine described in the New Testament is what Christ taught the apostles, passed down to succeeding generations, at first orally and soon (before 100 A.D.) in writing. Roman Catholics teach that a vast body of information, the Deposit of Faith, was passed down by word of mouth through bishops and never recorded in the Scriptures.

> Peter Soto uses these words: "It is an infallible Catholic rule: Whatever the Roman Church believes, holds, and observes, even if it is not contained in the Scriptures, that was handed down by the apostles." Again: "Those customs whose beginning, author,

and origin are unknown or cannot be found have without any doubt been handed down by the apostles."[284]

Christians certainly do have a few traditions about the apostles that were not recorded in the New Testament, but were noted in the earliest Church fathers. These traditions are historical anecdotes and not new doctrines to be accepted. According to the papacy, Roman Catholics must accept: justification by faith-plus-works, Purgatory, the Immaculate Conception of Mary, the Assumption of Mary, and the infallibility of the pope—or be damned to Hell. New Testament Christians were warned to contend for the faith, because anything contrary to God's Word is ultimately man-centered and robs God of the glory due to Him alone. In Jude's letter we have a good example of The Faith being used as a body of teaching, a truth worth fighting for, since false teachers have slipped into the Church to destroy it.

> Jude 1:3 Beloved, when I gave all diligence to write unto you of the common salvation, it was needful for me to write unto you, and exhort *you* that ye should earnestly contend for the faith which was once delivered unto the saints. 4 For there are certain men crept in unawares, who were before of old ordained to this condemnation, ungodly men, turning the grace of our God into lasciviousness, and denying the only Lord God, and our Lord Jesus Christ.

We should follow Jesus' admonition:

> Matthew 7:15 Beware of false prophets, which come to you in sheep's clothing, but inwardly they are ravening wolves. 16 Ye shall know them by their fruits. Do men gather grapes of thorns, or figs of thistles? 17 Even so every good tree bringeth forth good fruit; but a corrupt tree bringeth forth evil fruit...

---

[284] *Examination*, I, p. 273.

St. Paul warned the Thessalonians to "Prove all things; hold fast that which is good. Abstain from all appearance of evil." (1 Thessalonians 5:21-22)

The power of the papacy is closely related to the visibility of the church:

> Pope Leo XIII in his important encyclical letter on the Church, *Satis Cognitum* (1896), clearly taught the visibility of the Church: "If we consider the chief end of his Church and the proximate efficient causes of salvation, it is undoubtedly spiritual; but in regard to these spiritual gifts, it is external and necessarily visible (no. 3)." There is a triple bond that united the members of the Church to each other and makes them recognizable as Catholics: profession of the same faith throughout the world, use of the same seven sacraments, and subordination to the same papal authority.[285]

For Roman Catholic leaders, the visibility, apostolic authority, and doctrinal unity of their church cannot be separated from the leadership of the pope, who embodies the supposed role given to Peter. The four Roman Catholic marks of the Church are:

1. One
2. Holy
3. Catholic
4. Apostolic.

These marks follow the terminology of the Nicene Creed, to emphasize the visibility of the Church of Rome. Unity, catholicity, and apostolicity are embodied in their concept of the papacy and its authority. The alien nature of the Roman Catholic doctrine of the Church is revealed in this definition by a theologian Martin Jugie, echoed by a host of others:

> Taken in its totality, the Church consists of three parts: the Church Militant on earth; the Church suffering in Purgatory; the Church Triumphant in Heaven.[286]

---

285 Baker, *Fundamentals*, III, p. 139.

286 Jugie, *Purgatory*, p. 39.

Roman Catholics react to Lutheran and Protestant objections by saying, "We have one pope, but they have a million popes, since they insist on the freedom of each person to interpret the Scriptures. The United States has a constitution, and Supreme Court to interpret the constitution. We have a Bible and an infallible pope to interpret it." Kueng is close to the Lutheran understanding of doctrinal authority when he states:

> It is this that has to remain vitally obligatory, binding, normative: Scripture, that is, as *norma normans* of an ecclesiastical tradition which may then also be taken seriously precisely as a *norma normata*.[287]

Lutherans call the *Book of Concord* the *norma normata* (ruled norm) of the faith while the canonical Scriptures are the *norma normans* (ruling norm) of the faith. From the Roman Catholic perspective, the *Book of Concord* is a summary of the Lutheran confession of faith. Lutherans are unique in having one set of confessions to unify them. Various Protestant groups have confessions, but those confessions do not all agree with one another.

For a Roman Catholic, tradition can include all kinds of material, such as apocryphal stories, visions, and worship services, all of which contribute to the formation of dogma. The multiplication of Protestant sects has offered justification for Roman Catholic criticism, but the Church of Rome prefers organizational unity to doctrinal agreement. The Church of Rome has the same variety of religious expression as the Protestants do, but they are under the roof of one, enormous, global tent. Liberal Protestants have worked toward cooperation and merger, slightly reducing the number of denominations. The result has not been more unity but alarming apostasy and rapid decline in those groups where mergers have been frequent. (See the author's *Liberalism: Its Cause and Cure*, published by Northwestern Publishing House, Milwaukee.)

---

[287] Kueng, p. 77.

In spite of a structure that allows many different styles to co-exist, not always peacefully, the Roman Catholic Church maintains a body of doctrine remarkably consistent since the early Medieval period.

> This Church, constituted and organized in the world as a society, subsists in the Catholic Church, which is governed by the successor of Peter and by the bishops in union with that successor.[288]

This is an important distinction, because many think the Church of Rome considers herself the only means of salvation. The old Latin saying is:

> *Extra ecclesiam nulla salus* – outside the Church there is no salvation.

The Vatican II definition, stated above, recognizes all Christian churches as subsisting or being part of the one true Church, which is the Church of Rome in their eyes. Father Baker explained:

> All means of salvation belong to the Catholic Church; even those that are found accidentally outside the social structure of the Church, such as, for example, Holy Scripture, Baptism, and Eucharist (see Vatican II, Constitution on the Church, no. 8). Therefore, all those who are supernaturally helped by God and all those who are saved outside the Catholic Church belong in one way or another to her and they are connected with her at least by an implicit desire....[289]

This explanation does not offer equality to other confessions, since Father Baker wrote:

> By this expression, [Constitution on the Church, no. 8] the Council affirmed that the fullness of the Church of Christ was to be found only in the Roman Catholic Church, while various

---

[288] *Lumen Gentium*, Constitution on the Church, no. 8, Vatican II, cited in *Fundamentals*, III, p. 93.

[289] Baker, *Fundamentals*, III, p. 148.

"elements" of sanctification and truth can be found in other Christian confessions.[290]

In a case which is little known outside the Roman Catholic Church, a priest named Father Leonard Feeney, Director of St. Benedict's Center in Cambridge, Massachusetts, taught that *extra ecclesiam* (outside the church) meant outside the confines of the Catholic Church. Feeney's view was condemned in 1949 by Pope Pius XII and he was excommunicated in 1953. Later, Feeney was received back into the Church of Rome after making a profession of faith.[291]

Ecumenical churches were shocked when Pope John Paul II issued a statement about the Church, labeling all denominations—even the Eastern Orthodox Church—defective.

> VATICAN CITY, Sept 5, 2000 (Reuters) (Condensed) - The Vatican on Tuesday rejected the concept that other religions could be equal to Roman Catholicism and ordered its theologians not to manipulate what it called the truth of the faith.
>
> The Vatican's restatement of its position was outlined in a complex theological document, the English title of which was "Declaration The Lord Jesus -- On the Unicity and Salvific Universality of Jesus Christ and the Church".
>
> The document repeated Church teachings that non-Christians were in a "gravely deficient situation" regarding salvation and that other Christian churches had "defects," partly because they did not recognise the primacy of the Pope.
>
> At a news conference to present the document, Cardinal Joseph Ratzinger [now Pope Benedict], the Vatican's doctrinal head, said some theologians were "manipulating and going beyond the limits" of tolerance when they put all religions on the same plane.
>
> "Therefore, there exists a single Church of Christ, which subsists in the Catholic Church, governed by the Successor of Peter and by the bishops in communion with him," it said.[292]

---

[290] *Ibid.*, I, p. 108.

[291] *Ibid.*, III, p. 186.

[292] Retrieved from http://www.cephasministry.com/catholicism_is_mother_church.html.

The statement caused a monumental uproar in all the ecumenical agencies. The Eastern Orthodox Church, long considered a sister church with Rome, was appalled at this new direction, which was really only the logical outcome of the Vatican II definition of the Church, the visible fulfillment of Christ's promise—in their view—"You are the Rock, and on this Rock I will build My Church." The Vatican basilica is called St. Peter's because the apostle is thought to be buried beneath the church. The continuity of history is emphasized in the concept of apostolic succession, that each succeeding generation of priests has been ordained by bishops in direct line with Peter.

> The situation of the Eastern Orthodox churches is different. They do have the apostolic succession of their bishops, going back to the Apostles, but they are defective in some teachings and, especially, they have broken communion with the pope, who is the legitimate successor of St. Peter and the source of unity in the Church.[293]

Rome's attitude toward other confessions is related to the outsiders' ability to claim apostolic succession. In addition, some within liberal Protestant and Lutheran circles want to establish apostolic succession within their own groups, placing apostolic succession above faithfulness to the Scriptures, adding an element to ordination not found in the Pastoral Epistles.

Lutherans and Protestants have taught the invisibility or hiddenness of the true Church, which means that membership in the body of Christ is determined by faith alone, which cannot be seen.

> For that is the true Church which embraces and confesses the true and sound doctrine of the Word of God.[294]

---

[293] *Ibid.*, I, p. 110. Baker said on the same page: "The only Church today that manifests the fullness of apostolicity is the Holy Roman Catholic Church. The Protestant churches lack the apostolic origin, since they did not appear until the sixteenth century. They are also defective in the doctrine of the Apostles and they do not have the necessary apostolic succession."

[294] *Examination*, I, p. 163.

Jesus described membership in terms of remaining faithful to His Word (John 8:31) rather than identifying with a visible structure or certain traditional rites. The Augsburg Confession, 1530, contains an eloquent statement about the Christian Church.

> It is also taught among us that one holy Christian church will be and remain forever. This is the assembly of all believers among whom the Gospel is preached in its purity and the holy sacraments are administered according to the Gospel. For it is sufficient for the true unity of the Christian church that the Gospel be preached in conformity with a pure understanding of it and that the sacraments are administered in accordance with the divine Word. It is not necessary for the true unity of the Christian church that ceremonies, instituted by men, should be observed uniformly in all places.[295]

For Lutherans, the marks of the Church are the Word and the Holy Sacraments.

> We are not dreaming about some Platonic republic, as has been slanderously alleged, but we teach that this church actually exists, made up of true believers and righteous men scattered throughout the world. And we add its marks, the pure teaching of the Gospel and the sacraments. This church is properly called the "pillar of truth" (1 Timothy 3:15), for it retains the pure Gospel and what Paul calls the "foundation" (1 Corinthians 3:12) that is, the true knowledge of Christ and faith.[296]

Thus we can see that the Roman Catholic doctrine of a visible Church with an infallible leader at her head is at odds with the Lutheran understanding of an invisible Church ruled first by the infallible Scriptures and guided by the Confessions. Protestants do not place the same emphasis upon their confessions as Lutherans do, but all

---

[295] Augsburg Confession, Article VII, Tappert, p. 32. German translation. Ephesians 4:4-5.

[296] Apology of the Augsburg Confession, Articles VII and VIII, the Church, #20, Tappert, p. 171.

Protestants do object to the infallibility and primacy of the pope. Those Roman Catholics who have studied the issue must wonder, as Kueng did:

> There is one last question left: Can a Catholic theologian who criticizes infallibility remain a Catholic?[297]

---

[297] Hasler, p. 2. "Introduction: The Infallibility Debate—Where Are We Now?" by Hans Kueng.

Papal Infallibility and Church Definition Summary

Roman Catholic View

The Church is visible:

- **One** – Unified under one pope with one doctrine.
- **Holy** – Administering God's grace.
- **Catholic** – Universal.
- **Apostolic** – Deriving her claims from the chief of the apostles, Peter.
- **Indefectible** – Unfailing, triumphing over trials, ill-will, dangers, and indifference.
- **Infallible** – Prevented by the Holy Spirit from failing.

The pope is the **Vicar of Christ**, with the authority of Peter

- **Possessing the keys** that bind or loose sins;
- **Infallible** *ex cathedra*, when defining doctrine or morals;
- **Judged by no one**, above the power of all Church Councils.

Bishops and priests are:

- **Infallible** when teaching in harmony with the pope.

Lutheran View

The Church is:

- **Invisible** – comprised of all people who trust only in Christ for their salvation.

- **Apostolic** – true to the teachings of Christ through His apostles, and therefore Catholic (universal) and orthodox.[298]

- **Marks of the Church** - The pure Word and Holy Sacraments.

- **Christ** is her only head.

- **Maintained and nurtured by the Holy Spirit** working through the Means of Grace.

- **The Holy Scriptures** judge all teaching, all Christian leaders, and all books.

---

[298] Lutherans are allergic to the term Catholic, but the term really means universal. Chemnitz took great pains to show that the Lutherans re-established the Catholic-orthodox-universal teaching of the Church. Aping Rome, however, does not make one Catholic in the true sense of the word.

Protestant View in General

- The Church is visible, comprised of those who have identified with the congregation's beliefs and practices.

- The Bible is inerrant and infallible. "No creeds but the Bible" is a commonly heard motto.

- Authority is vested in the teaching office, usually the local minister.

- Things associated with Roman Catholicism are normally avoided: creeds, liturgy, chanting, vestments, incense, genuflecting, individual confession, and paraments.

- The sacraments are normally called ordinances and have relatively little importance. Instead, prayer is emphasized.

- The worship service on Sunday may be overshadowed by the independent Sunday School or the home Bible study.

Chapter Six: Doctrines Concerning the Virgin Mary

The zeal and love of the Blessed Virgin Mary have such influence in obtaining God's help for us that, just as through her, God came down to earth, so through her, man mounts up to heaven. But just as man's iniquity often calls down God's indignation, God's Mother is the rainbow of the eternal covenant for mankind's salvation. For, while the prayers of those in heaven have certainly some claim on the watchful eye of God, Mary's prayers place their assurance on the right of a mother. For that reason, when she approaches the throne of her Divine Son, she begs as an advocate, she prays as a handmaid, but she commands as mother.[299]

The Virgin Mary has been the subject of many devotional works and now plays a role in the dogma of feminist theology. *Time* magazine's final cover story for 1991 was "The Search for Mary. Was the most revered woman in history God's handmaid—or the first feminist?"[300] The Bible mentions Mary's name rather frequently, especially in Matthew and Luke. The angel Gabriel announced to Mary that she would give birth to a Son, Who would be called "The Son of the Most High." (Luke 1:34) Mary asked how this could happen, "since I am a virgin." The Virgin Birth of Christ had been prophesied in Isaiah 7:14 –

Isaiah 7:14 Therefore the Lord himself shall give you a sign; Behold, a virgin shall conceive, and bear a son, and shall call his name Immanuel.

For thousands of years, no translator was troubled by this Isaiah passage. All of them translated the Hebrew word *almah* as virgin. The Septuagint in Greek and Jerome's Latin Vulgate used the words for virgin. However, in the 1950's, the liberal Revised Standard Version committee, associated

---

[299] Pope Pius X, *Apost. Consti, Tanto studio*, February 19, 1905. *Mary, Mother of the Church*, p. 9.

[300] Asking a question like this is a common journalism tactic to place the emphasis on the second alterative. Is this true journalism or just another partisan attack in the form of an innocent question?

with the National Council of Churches, suddenly discovered that all previous translations had been wrong for thousands of years, that Isaiah 7:14 was simply a prophecy of a normal pregnancy, so the RSV translated *almah* as young girl. Perplexity about the Virgin Birth of Christ is therefore a new phenomenon in the Church, a production of modern rationalism and its influence in the interpretation of the Bible. In this age of promiscuity, virginity rather than the birth of God's Son, is perceived as a miracle.

The Biblical Portrait

Although rationalists rebel against the Virgin Birth of Christ, the doctrine is clearly taught in Matthew and Luke, prophesied in Isaiah 7:14, and implied in other passages. The Holy Spirit overshadowed Mary (compare Exodus 40:34-38) who in a unique and miraculous way, conceived and gave birth

Luke 1:30 And the angel said unto her, Fear not, Mary: for thou hast found favour with God. 31 And, behold, thou shalt conceive in thy womb, and bring forth a son, and shalt call his name JESUS. 32 He shall be great, and shall be called the Son of the Highest: and the Lord God shall give unto him the throne of his father David: 33 And he shall reign over the house of Jacob for ever; and of his kingdom there shall be no end. 34 Then said Mary unto the angel, How shall this be, seeing I know not a man? 35 And the angel answered and said unto her, The Holy Ghost shall come upon thee, and the power of the Highest shall overshadow thee: therefore also that holy thing which shall be born of thee shall be called the Son of God.

No other historical person has been born of a virgin, so attacks upon the doctrine are really ways of undermining the Bible's revelation about Christ as Lord and Savior. Those who strain to find a myriad of supposed contradictions in the Bible are mute about Matthew and Luke being in agreement about the Virgin Birth.

Joseph, betrothed to Mary, did not understand the situation at first, when he learned she was pregnant, and resolved to cancel the marriage quietly, which seemed correct to him, given his lack of knowledge. An angel spoke to Joseph:

> Matthew 1:20 But while he thought on these things, behold, the angel of the Lord appeared unto him in a dream, saying, Joseph, thou son of David, fear not to take unto thee Mary thy wife: for that which is conceived in her is of the Holy Ghost.

So we see the shadow of the cross already in the midst of this holy event. The advent of Christ brought sorrow and heartache, not wealth and fame, to Mary and Joseph, the ones entrusted with the care of this special Child. Not only was the family denied a decent room at the inn for the birth of Jesus, but persecution soon set in from an enraged King Herod, forcing the family to hide in a foreign country until they could safely return (Matthew 2:13). The difficulties were many.

The Bible tells us of Mary's consternation at Jesus for remaining at the Temple and talking with the Elders.

> Luke 2:48 And when they saw him, they were amazed: and his mother said unto him, Son, why hast thou thus dealt with us? behold, thy father and I have sought thee sorrowing.

Later, people were scandalized that Jesus, a person they knew, assumed the role of a Teacher:

> Matthew 13:55 Is not this the carpenter's son? is not his mother called Mary? and his brethren, James, and Joses, and Simon, and Judas?

The Virgin Mary was present at the crucifixion of Christ. Jesus commended her to the care of the disciple He loved – John.

> John 19:25 Now there stood by the cross of Jesus his mother, and his mother's sister, Mary the *wife* of Cleophas, and Mary Magdalene. 26 When Jesus therefore saw his mother, and the

disciple standing by, whom he loved, he saith unto his mother, Woman, behold thy son!

After the resurrection of Christ, the Bible reveals that Mary played a visible role in the early Church.

Acts 1:14 These all continued with one accord in prayer and supplication, with the women, and Mary the mother of Jesus, and with his brethren.

In the first centuries of the Church, Mary's unique role was honored. All people did call her blessed, and she became a model for faithful followers of Christ, not only for her humble obedience to God, but also for her patient suffering as the mother of the crucified Savior. Nevertheless, the attention given Mary in the early Church's writing was relatively small, according to the former head of the theology department at the University of Notre Dame, Richard P. McBrien:

Even in the literature we do have, Marian references are extremely rare before the year 150 and are difficult to interpret in works written between 150 and 200.[301]

Ambrose and Augustine, who are Western Church fathers of the 4th century, were restrained in their treatment of Mary, associating her closely with the Church. The Eastern Orthodox Church, after the Council of Ephesus in 431 A.D., did the most to promote veneration of Mary in the early centuries of the Medieval Age, according to McBrien.[302]

Lutherans and Protestants have said less about the Virgin Mary in recent centuries, while the Roman Catholics and Eastern Orthodox have extended her role beyond what is revealed in the Scriptures and the earliest traditions. However, devotion to Mary among American Catholics has waned since Vatican II, according to Father Baker:

---

[301] McBrien, II, p. 869f.

[302] *Ibid.*, p. 873.

For example, Marian devotions in most parish churches are now either non-existent or very rare. There are still May devotions in some places, but they are not nearly as common as they were twenty years ago.[303]

This may have been a reaction against excessive Marian devotion, which began in the Medieval age. Because Christ was often portrayed as a severe judge in the Medieval Church, the mercy and love of Jesus were gradually transferred to Mary. A Carmelite priest, whose order is devoted to Mary, wrote:

> Even the Last Judgment scene of Michelangelo in the Sistine Chapel has led some to come away with the misguided impression that Jesus is a severe, unrelenting judge to be feared. Hence, the need of a merciful mother.[304]

Because of this, Mary was proclaimed as the intercessor between God and man, the branch by which one reaches Christ, the neck by which the Head of the Church is turned. In the worst of cases, Mary seems to supplant Christ altogether as the merciful Savior, making God's Son subordinate to His mother and dependent upon her will.

> It is lamentable that in the history of the people of God devotion to Mary sometimes got out of hand. For example, Mary was often pictured as the mother of mercy in opposition to Christ, the severe judge. The impression was given that one had to pray to Mary in order to temper the severity of the Lord. This distortion occurred especially in the Middle Ages when a very personal, affective devotion to Mary became prevalent.[305]

---

[303] Baker, *Fundamentals*, II, p. 315.

[304] Healy, *The Assumption of Mary*, p. 95.

[305] *Ibid.*

Since Mary plays such a distinct role in all aspects of Roman Catholic doctrine, the most important teachings need to be considered and compared to Lutheranism and Protestantism.

Roman Catholic Doctrines about Mary

Traditional Roman Catholic teaching is distinguished by special attention to the Virgin Mary and certain doctrines that are not accepted by Lutherans or Protestants:

A. The Immaculate Conception of Mary – According to this teaching, Mary was conceived without sin and did not sin at any time during her life. Some people confuse this with the Virgin Birth of Jesus, but the Immaculate Conception is a Marian doctrine related to Redemption.

A Marian priest explained the doctrine as follows:

> Supernaturally, however, there was accomplished in the womb of St. Anne the singular mystery known as the Immaculate Conception. From the first instant of Mary's existence in the womb of her mother, as a human creature, a daughter of Adam, she entered into life all pure, entirely free from the stain that mars every man coming into this world. And just as she did not know original sin at conception, neither would she ever experience actual sin, and her soul would always remain immaculate. Neither would she suffer the humiliating consequences of original sin, namely, ignorance and concupiscence.[306]

The Immaculate Conception is consistently taught within the Roman Catholic Church and has a lengthy history. One catechism states:

> Mary never committed the slightest sin. God made her full of grace. Mary never committed the smallest sin because she was very holy.[307]

---

[306] Peter A. Resch, S.M., S.T.D., *A Life of Mary, Co-Redemptrix*, Milwaukee: The Bruce Publishing Company, 1954, p. 31.

[307] Father Robert J. Fox, *The Marian Catechism*, Washington, New Jersey: AMI Press, 1983, p. 21.

History of the Immaculate Conception

Since the Bible is silent about the conception of Mary, even about the names of her parents, we find no clear references to the Immaculate Conception until Theodotus, Bishop of Ancyra in Galatia, who died in 430 A.D. Adolph Harnack said:

> If this truth is a revealed one, when was it revealed and to whom?[308]

The names of Mary's parents, Joachim and Anna, are supplied by the apocryphal book the *Protoevangelium of James*, dated approximately 150, and never accepted by the Church as Scripture. Likewise, the Immaculate Conception of Mary seems to have arisen from devotion to the Virgin, celebration of her conception, and imagined parallels between her and Eve. For instance, St. Justin (100-167) compared Mary to Eve, much as St. Paul compared Christ to Adam. St. Paul wrote:

> 1 Corinthians 15:21 For since by man *came* death, by man *came* also the resurrection of the dead.

St. Justin wrote:

> While still a virgin and without corruption, Eve received into her heart the word of the serpent and thereby conceived disobedience and death. Mary the Virgin, her soul full of faith and joy, replied to the angel Gabriel who brought her glad tidings, "Be it done to me according to thy word." To her was born He of whom so many things are said in the Scriptures.[309]

---

[308] Cited in Aidan Carr and G. Williams, "Mary's Immaculate Conception," *Mariology*, I, p. 333.

[309] *Ibid.*, p. 347. *Dialog cum Tryphone Judaeo*, No. 100, *PL*, 6, 710 D.

The Immaculate Conception was not explicitly taught in the Church centuries later, as can be seen in a passage from St. Augustine often quoted in favor of the doctrine:

> For we know that on her [Mary] more grace was conferred for vanquishing sin in every part, because she was worthy to conceive and bear Him of whom it is certain that He had no sin.[310]

Chemnitz responded to the use of this Augustine quotation to support the Immaculate Conception:

> This they slant, as if he thought that Mary is not included in the statements of Scripture which speak of original sin. However, because he clearly says that grace was conferred on Mary for vanquishing sin, it is quite clear that he does not think that Mary was conceived without sin....[311]

Chemnitz, a master of patristic knowledge, also cited many other passages in Augustine and Ambrose, proving Christ alone was born without original sin.

Because Nestorius confused the Two Natures (divine and human) of Christ, the Council of Ephesus in 431 defined Mary as the Bearer of God (*theotokos* in Greek). This title was given to combat the Nestorian opinion that Mary bore Christ, but not the Son of God, as if the Two Natures could be separated. *Theotokos* is often translated Mother of God, but the more common translation does not suggest that Mary generated God from her flesh. The title indicates instead that the Child born was truly human and truly divine, a union of the Two Natures that continues today. At this time, some Eastern church fathers began to extol Mary as:

---

[310] *Ibid.*, p. 350. Augustine, *De natura et gratia*, chapter 36.

[311] *Examination*, I, p. 377.

...immaculate; free from all guilt; spotless; undefiled; holy in spirit and body; a lily among thorns.[312]

The Council of Ephesus seems to have been a watershed regarding Mary's place in the Church:

> Before the Council of Ephesus there had been one liturgical feast of Mary, the feast of the Purification, and that was celebrated only in certain parts of the Eastern Church. But after Ephesus the feasts began to multiply.[313]

Many Church fathers did not write about the Immaculate Conception. John Damascene (676-749)...

> did not expressly teach the doctrine, nevertheless his whole treatment of Mariology points the way to it, and indeed presupposes it as an essential element in composite of her graces.[314]

Roman Catholic authors concede that the Immaculate Conception was not taught by Anselm (1033-1109) or even by St. Bernard of Clairvaux (1091-1153), who was nicknamed "Mary's Troubadour" for his Marian devotion. Thomas Aquinas (1225-1274), a prolific and brilliant theologian, considered one of the four doctors of the Roman Catholic Church "simply denied Mary's freedom from original sin." Thomas himself declared in his *Summa Theologica* that if one denies the Blessed Virgin's original sin, then he attacks the glory of Christ, who is Savior of all.[315]

Although the Feast of the Conception of Mary began to be celebrated in the 11th century, the Immaculate Conception did not have much theological support until John Duns Scotus (1270–1308)

---

[312] *Mariology*, I, p. 353. Theodotus, d. 430.

[313] McBrien, II, p. 873.

[314] *Mariology*, I, p. 355.

[315] *Summa*, II, q.27, a. 2 ad 2um, cited in *Mariology*, I, p. 366.

222

developed the idea of "anticipatory redemption" or "preredemption," that Christ preserved His mother from the stain of original sin before He was crucified for the sins of the world.[316] The Dominicans continued to resist the Immaculate Conception, following their greatest theologian, Thomas Aquinas. This had an effect on art for a period of time.

> It is interesting, however, that, as Millard Meiss has emphasized, the Dominicans were particularly instrumental in fostering the cult of the nursing Virgin. They were the only order in the Church that continually and vehemently opposed the growing belief in the Immaculate Conception of Mary. And if Mary was free from all stain of original sin, then lactation might not be her inheritance.[317]

Dominican clashes with the Jesuits were so frequent and violent that "in 1616 Pope Paul V forbade all discussion of the subject from the pulpit."[318] Nevertheless, support for the Immaculate Conception gathered strength, even among the Dominicans.

On December 17, 1830, St. Catharine Laboure, who died in 1876, had a vision of the Immaculate Conception standing on a globe, a frame around her reading, "Mary, conceived without sin, pray for us who have recourse to thee." A voice commanded Catharine to have a medal made, and many miracles were attributed to it. This sparked an interest in formally defining the Immaculate Conception.[319] The doctrine was declared to be the official dogma of the Church of Rome in 1854 by the papal bull *Ineffabilis Deus*, in the midst of opposition from Protestants and the Eastern Orthodox.

Pope Pius IX, who presided over Vatican I and had himself declared infallible in 1870, defined the Immaculate Conception on his own in 1854, without calling a Council of the Church.

---

[316] Baker, *Fundamentals*, II, p. 326.

[317] Marina Warner, *Alone of All Her Sex*, New York: Alfred A. Knopf, 1976, p. 204.

[318] *Ibid.*, p. 248f.

[319] McBrien, II, p. 879.

The Blessed Virgin Mary, in the first instant of her conception, by a singular grace and privilege granted by Almighty God, in view of the merits of Jesus Christ, the Savior of the human race, was preserved free of all stain of original sin.[320]

The apparition of the Virgin Mary to a poor shepherdess in France in 1858 is cited as proof of Mary's title:

Mary appeared to St. Bernadette in Lourdes, France, and said, "I am the Immaculate Conception."[321]

B. The Assumption of Mary – This doctrine teaches that Mary was taken, body and soul, into heaven before she died or immediately after she died.

The Assumption of Mary can be compared to the Ascension of Christ, recorded in Acts 1:8-11

Acts 1:8 But ye shall receive power, after that the Holy Ghost is come upon you: and ye shall be witnesses unto me both in Jerusalem, and in all Judaea, and in Samaria, and unto the uttermost part of the earth. 9 And when he had spoken these things, while they beheld, he was taken up; and a cloud received him out of their sight. 10 And while they looked stedfastly toward heaven as he went up, behold, two men stood by them in white apparel; 11 Which also said, Ye men of Galilee, why stand ye gazing up into heaven? this same Jesus, which is taken up from you into heaven, shall so come in like manner as ye have seen him go into heaven.

Mary's death is not recorded in the Bible, but the early Church marked the day of her death, the Dormition (falling asleep) of Mary, and from that festival arose the new teaching of the Assumption of Mary, starting around the 5th century after Christ.

---

[320] *Ineffabilis Deus, Acta Pii IX*, part L, vol. 1, p. 615. Cited in Healy, *The Assumption of Mary*, p. 73.

[321] *The Marian Catechism*, p. 20.

History of the Assumption of Mary

The Assumption of Mary is the most recently defined major doctrine of Mary, but it has been taught and celebrated in the Roman Catholic Church for centuries. The definition of the Immaculate Conception provided a basis for the Assumption to receive official approval from the Vatican. Like the Immaculate Conception, this formal declaration was promulgated by a pope with a singular devotion to Mary.

> Ever since the definition of the Immaculate Conception in 1854, a strong Assumptionist movement had begun to swell among the faithful, the pastors and even among some officials of nations. The constant petition that peaked at the time of Pius XII sought the definition of Our Lady's Assumption. Nearly two hundred bishops attending the First Vatican Council had signed a petition, although the Council did not take up the matter. After World War I the movement became stronger. Finally, all petitions that reached the Holy See between 1849 and 1940 were collected and edited at the Vatican in two big volumes.[322]

Not everyone approved of the new status of the Virgin Mary. Bishop Strossmayer (1815–1905) made a memorable speech in 1870 at the First Vatican Council against the concept of papal infallibility. Strossmayer, who remained a Roman Catholic, in spite of sympathies with the Old Catholics who left the Church of Rome after Vatican I, said:

> If He who reigns above wishes to punish us, making His hand fall heavy on us, as He did on Pharaoh, He has no need to permit Garibaldi's soldiers to drive us away from the eternal city. He has only to let them make Pius IX a god, as we have made a goddess of the blessed virgin. Stop, stop, venerable brethren, on the odious and ridiculous incline on which you placed yourselves. Save the church from the shipwreck which threatens her, asking from the Holy Scriptures alone for the rule of faith which we

---

[322] Healy, p. 19.

ought to believe and to profess. I have spoken: may God help me![323]

Strossmayer's reference to Garibaldi's troops indicated the growing suspicion that the military forces opposed to Vatican control of the papal states and in favor of Italian nationalism were poised to take the Eternal City away from the pope. This happened only a few months later.

In the first three centuries of the Church, no reputable Church father wrote about the death of Mary. St. Epiphanius wrote in his Medicine Chest, around 377: "Whether she died or was buried we know not."[324] In addition, the city of Ephesus was not considered Mary's final resting place until after the Council of Ephesus was completed in 431, when Marian devotion began to grow unchecked. One of the best examples is the apocryphal *Transitus Mariae* (Journey of Mary) writings, which established the Assumption. Below is one summary of the *Transitus Mariae*:

> Mary lives in Bethlehem. The archangel Gabriel makes known to her that her end is nigh. At her request all the apostles are brought from all the different countries of the world on a wondrous journey through the clouds to Bethlehem...the Holy Spirit carries Mary and the apostles off on a cloud to Jerusalem...The apostles carry her holy body on a bier to Gethsemane for burial. On the way a Jew rudely attempts to touch the corpse: Both his hands are cut off by an invisible sword and then immediately miraculously reattached by St. Peter. The Jew becomes a Christian. For three days the voices of unseen angels are heard. When the song ceases, the apostles conclude that the body of the Holy Virgin has been assumed into heaven.[325]

Although the *Transitus Mariae* legends seem crude and shocking, they are the only textual foundation for the Assumption of Mary. No historical

---

[323] Hudson, *Papal Power, Its Origins and Development*. Speech reproduced in *Christian News*, July 4, 1988, p. 15f.

[324] Lawrence P. Everett, C.SS.R., "Mary's Death and Bodily Assumption," *Mariology*, II, p. 463.

[325] Hasler, p. 98.

evidence exists, and the 5[326] or 6th century tales are not considered credible.[326] One expert in Mariology concluded:

> It is impossible to regard these accounts [*Transitus Mariae*] as reliable historical reports of the events described.[327]

The thirteenth century scholastics believed in the death of Mary because they denied her Immaculate Conception. Bonaventure wrote:

> Therefore Our Blessed Lady was subject to original sin.[328]

The promulgation of the Immaculate Conception of Mary led to a movement that denied Mary was subject to death because of her sinlessness.

> Today we have diametrically opposed views on the death of Mary supported by outstanding Mariologists.[329]

The feast of the Assumption began in the Eastern Orthodox Church in the 4th century as a day on which Mary's death was marked as Mary's "birthday" or entrance into heaven. The deaths of saints and martyrs are recognized and celebrated in the same way in liturgical churches to this day. The festival of Mary's Dormition or death was altered by the popularity of the *Transitus Mariae* literature of the 6th century, which influenced and changed the liturgy. The festival date was declared to be August 15th by the Byzantine Emperor Maurice (reigned 582 – 602). The Western Church began celebrating the Dormition of Mary around 690 and called it the Assumption of Mary in the 8th century.[330] Therefore, it is impossible to agree with Father Robert J. Fox

---

[326] Altaner, *Zur Frage der Definibilitaet der Assumption B.V.M, Theologische Revue*, 46, 1950, 17. Cited in Hasler, p. 264.

[327] Alfred Rush, "Mary in the Apocrypha of the New Testament," *Mariology*, I, p. 174.

[328] "Mary's Death and Bodily Assumption," *Mariology*, II, p. 465.

[329] *Ibid.*

[330] *Ibid.*, pp. 479ff.

that "The Catholic Church has always believed that Mary's body was assumed into heaven."[331]

Although the pope certainly led the effort to define the Assumption officially, we can see that years of effort went into achieving the final goal.

> On May 1, 1946, Pope Pius XII, following the method used by Pope Pius IX in preparation for the definition of the Immaculate Conception, sent a letter to the bishops asking their thoughts about the Assumption. He asked two questions: "Do you, Venerable Brethren, in your outstanding wisdom and prudence, judge that the bodily Assumption of the Blessed Virgin can be proposed and defined as a dogma of the faith? Do you, with your clergy and people, desire it?" The answer to both questions was affirmative, and by August 1950 the replies ran as follows: Affirmative, 1169 of 1181 resident bishops. Of the negative answers, only six hesitated on the revealed character of the Assumption; the others wondered whether a definition was opportune.[332]

The Vatican definition of the Assumption of Mary was titled *Munificentissimus Deus*. The work is called a papal bull because of the seal (*bulla*, Latin for seal) on the parchment. The act is also called an Apostolic Constitution because it legislates for the entire Roman Catholic Church and claims the supreme teaching authority of the apostles as well as guidance from the Holy Spirit.

C. Mary as Co-Redemptrix – This teaching claims that Mary participated in the work of redemption, by offering her Son on the cross.

Father Baker defined the title:

---

[331] *The Marian Catechism*, p. 60.

[332] Healy, p. 19f.

As members of the Church became more aware of Mary's cooperation with Jesus, starting in the fourteenth century various theologians and preachers coined a new title for her and began to refer to her as the "Coredemptrix" (= Coredemptress) of the human race. The basic justification for the title is to be found in the fact that both the Incarnation of the Son of God and the Redemption of mankind by the vicarious atonement of Christ were dependent on Mary's free assent.[333]

One of the standard texts on Mariology in the Roman Catholic Church states:

The title "Coredemptrix" first received Papal sanction under Pope Pius X, by his approval of its use in a decree of the Congregation of Rites concerning the feast of the Seven Dolors [seven sorrows of Mary].[334]

In 1918, Pope Benedict XV placed the greatest emphasis upon the role of Mary during the crucifixion of Christ, using the Roman Catholic terminology of the priest offering a Mass as a sacrifice:

Thus she suffered and almost died with her suffering and dying Son; thus she surrendered her maternal rights to save men and to placate the justice of God and, as far as it belonged to her, she immolated [sacrificed] her Son, so that it may deservedly be said of her that with Christ she redeemed the human race.[335]

History of Co-Redemption

The doctrine of Mary as the Co-Redeemer has almost no history, apart from this century. The editor of the three-volume *Mariology*, Juniper B. Carol, O.F. M., expected the teaching to be solemnly defined by the

---

[333] Baker, *Fundamentals*, II, p. 363.

[334] E Carroll, "Mary in the Documents of the Magisterium," *Mariology*, I, p. 35.

[335] [Pope Benedict XV, *Inter Sodalicia*, in *Acta Ap. Sedis*, vol 10, 1918, p. 182] Resch, *A Life of Mary, Co-Redemptrix*, p. 84.

pope.[336] However, the Church of Rome has stopped the progress of new Marian claims and titles for the time being. The era of greatest expansion was between 1854, when the Immaculate Conception was defined, and 1950, when the Assumption of Mary was affirmed. Pope Leo XIII (1878 – 1903) added to Marian devotion with his support of the Rosary and his description in 1894 (*Jacunda semper*) of Mary offering up Jesus as a sacrifice, a concept echoed by Pope Pius X in 1904 and repeated by Pope Benedict in 1918, as quoted above. Pope Pius XII, in *Mystici Corporis* (1943) also wrote that Mary

> ...offered Him up on Golgotha to the Eternal Father, together with the sacrifice of her maternal rights and love, on behalf of all the children of Adam, stained by the latter's shameful fall.[337]

Germanus (d. 733), who served as a patriarch of Constantinople, promoted the view that Mary had a maternal influence over God, and that she could turn away God's anger and vengeance.[338] Paul the Deacon (d. circa 799) translated the story of Theophilus, which has a man pleading with Mary to deliver him from a contract with Satan. According to Father Richard McBrien, the theology of the West became increasingly divorced from the Bible. The formula, *"Potuit, decuit, fecit,"* (*Potuit* – God could do it; *Decuit* – It was fitting to do it; *Fecit* – Therefore, He did it.) began to play a large role in Medieval Mariology.[339]

St. Bernard of Clairvaux (d. 1153) described Mary as together with Christ obtaining "a common effect in the salvation of the world." John Tauler (d. 1361) wrote that Mary offered herself along with her Son as a living victim for the salvation of all. ("...thou hast redeemed man together with thy Son.") The Jesuit Ferdinand de Salazar (d. 1646) made the same claim. These statements are so extravagant that Vatican II and subsequent pronouncements have been comparatively modest in tone. While the Immaculate Conception and Assumption may be seen as the

---

[336] "Our Lady's Coredemption," *Mariology*, II, p. 377.

[337] *Mariology*, II, p. 385.

[338] McBrien, II, p. 873.

[339] *Ibid.*, p. 874.

heritage of Medieval piety, the Coredemption of Mary is a frontal attack upon the sufficiency of the atoning death of Christ.[340]

D. Mary as Mediatrix – This doctrine teaches that Mary prays for believers, serving as a mediator between Christ and the sinner. This also parallels, and even supplants, the Biblical doctrine of Christ as the one mediator between God and man.

> 1 Timothy 2:3 For this *is* good and acceptable in the sight of God our Saviour; 4 Who will have all men to be saved, and to come unto the knowledge of the truth. 5 For *there is* one God, and one mediator between God and men, the man Christ Jesus; 6 Who gave himself a ransom for all, to be testified in due time.

Vatican II, the latest Council of the Church of Rome, stated:

> Therefore the Blessed Virgin is invoked by the Church under the titles of Advocate, Auxiliatrix, Adjutrix, and Mediatrix.[341]

Father Baker explained:

> In Catholic theology Mary is given the title "Mediatrix" for three reasons. First, because she occupies a middle position between God and his creatures...Second, because during her earthly life she contributed by her holiness, to the reconciliation between God and man brought about by Jesus. Third, because through her powerful intercession in heaven she obtains for her spiritual children all the graces that God deigns to bestow on them.[342]

Portraying Mary as a mediator between Christ and man serves to harden the role of the Savior into that of a judge and to make Mary the one who obtains grace, mercy, pardon, and peace. Thus, it is easy for a Protestant or Lutheran to agree wholeheartedly with Father Baker's conclusion:

---

[340] *Mariology*, II, pp. 397ff.

[341] *Lumen Gentium, Dogmatic Constitution of the Church*, VIII, 62. *Vatican II*, p. 91.

[342] Baker, *Fundamentals*, II, p. 360.

At first it may seem astonishing that no grace is imparted to mankind without the intercession of Mary.[343]

The Augsburg Confession states its objection:

> However, it cannot be proved from the Scriptures that we are to invoke saints or seek help from them. "For there is one mediator between God and men, Christ Jesus (1 Timothy 2:5), who is the only saviour, the only high priest, advocate, and intercessor before God (Romans 8:34). He has promised to hear our prayers. Moreover, according to the Scriptures the highest form of divine service is sincerely to seek and call upon this same Jesus Christ in every time of need. "If anyone sins we have an advocate with the Father, Jesus Christ the righteous." (1 John 2:1)[344]

The title Mediatrix also confers upon Mary a divine role in providing the faithful with spiritual blessings, which come from God alone. To these titles and roles can be added many more that are subordinate. Some indication of this may be found in the list of days honoring Mary, listed below.

Marian Devotion

Protestants and Lutherans agree that Roman Catholicism has maintained a singular devotion to the Virgin Mary, even if this devotion seems to have subsided somewhat in recent years. In contrast, Protestants and Lutherans are much more likely to invoke as examples the Apostles, martyrs, and Reformers of the Church, almost to the exclusion of St. Mary. These habits are illustrated in the naming of congregations. St. Paul is a common name for a Lutheran church, while St. Mary is common for a Catholic parish. St. Mary Lutheran Church is found in Kenosha, Wisconsin; St. Paul Lutheran everywhere.

---

[343] *Ibid.*, p. 366.

[344] Augsburg Confession, Article XXI, The Cult of Saints, Tappert, p. 47.

Because Lutherans and Protestants are unfamiliar with Marian devotion, some of the basic prayers and festivals focusing on Mary are described below.

The Christian Church was born liturgical, inheriting traditional Scripture readings, prayers, hymns, and observances from Judaism, while transforming them through the Word and Sacraments. The Psalms were kept as part of the worship service, but hymns were added. Although the Swiss Protestants broke with this liturgical tradition and created a new, Spartan form of worship, the Lutheran Church has continued the liturgical traditions of the Church, changing the wording when reform was required, not to add new teachings but to eliminate Medieval errors. Luther maintained a devotion to Mary, which he learned in the Church and continued most of his life. He did not turn away from Mary, but placed his emphasis upon the work of Christ. Nevertheless, many Lutherans today would be startled by Lutheran Marian devotion.

In the early centuries of the Western Church, Saturday was often observed as a day of fasting, to recognize and commemorate the sorrow of the Apostles after the crucifixion of Christ. By the eleventh century, Christians were celebrating Mass in honor of the Virgin Mary every Saturday, except during Lent. Therefore, Saturday is considered Mary's day, just as Sunday is called the Lord's Day. (Revelation 1:10) Moreover, the month of May is reserved for special devotions to Mary. This came about in the West to counter the orgiastic practices of pagan religion, such as the Roman rites in honor of the goddess Flora.[345] May devotions grew in popularity in the sixteenth, seventeenth, and eighteenth centuries. Influential books were *The Spiritual May*, by Wolfgang Seidl, O.S.B., (1549), *The Month of Mary, or the Month of May*, by A. Dionisi, S.J. (1725), and *The Month of Mary*, by F. Lalomia, S.J. (1758). The last-named work enjoyed 60 printings in several languages. Pope Pius XII, who pronounced the Assumption of Mary as official dogma in 1947, endorsed May devotions to Mary in his encyclical on the liturgy, *Mediator Dei*.[346] In addition, the month of October is dedicated to saying the Rosary, an emphasis that began with Pope Leo XIII in the 1880's in response to the capture of papal lands by the newly established Italian state, a conflict which lasted until the Lateran Treaty was signed in 1929 by the Vatican and Mussolini.

---

[345] *Mariology*, III, p. 58.

[346] *Ibid.*

Days honoring the Virgin Mary are numerous. The following observances vary in order of importance. The Roman Catholic Church distinguishes between solemnities, feasts, memorials, and optional memorials:

1. December 8 – The Immaculate Conception of Mary
2. February 11 – Feast of the Blessed Immaculate Virgin
3. March 25 – Feast of the Annunciation (Luke 1:26-38)
4. Friday following Passion Sunday – Our Lady of the Seven Dolors
5. May 31 – The Queenship of Mary
6. July 2 – The Visitation of the Blessed Mother (Luke 1:38)
7. July 16 – Our Lady of Mount Carmel
8. August 5 – Our Lady of the Snow
9. August 15 – The Assumption of Mary
10. August 22 – The Immaculate Heart of Mary
11. September 8 – The Nativity of Mary
12. September 12 – The Most Holy Name of Mary
13. September 15 – Feast of the Seven Dolors
14. September 24 – Our Lady of Mercy
15. October 7 – Our Lady of the Rosary
16. October 11 – Mary's Divine Maternity
17. November 21 – The Presentation of the Blessed Virgin

Many other Marian observances are celebrated in certain regions, such as Our Lady of Good Counsel, Mary Queen of Apostles, and Our Lady of Consolation. Two of the Roman Catholic Marian celebrations are shared by Lutherans because of their Biblical origin: the Annunciation and the Visitation, but with a greater emphasis by Lutherans upon Christ than Mary. Some mainline Lutheran calendars show August 15 as Mary, Mother of Our Lord rather than as Assumption Day, but special observance of that day is not common. Roman Catholic Marian festivals, many of them shared with the Eastern Orthodox Church, began as local celebrations and were raised to universal status as they grew in popularity.[347]

The Rosary

One of the distinguishing marks of Marian piety is saying the Rosary, a practice that seems quite mysterious to Lutherans and Protestants.

No form of extra-liturgical devotion to Mary is more widely practiced among the faithful or found by them to be more satisfyingly complete than the Rosary, which has come to be regarded as the very badge of Catholic piety.[348]

The Rosary of today originated in the fifteenth century with the priests of the Dominican Order, who were nicknamed the "Hounds of the Lord" (*Domini canes,* Latin) or prosecutors during the Roman Catholic Inquisition, during which people were tortured, tried, and executed. Their formal name is Order of Preachers but they are universally known as Dominicans.

The 15 beads on a traditional Rosary necklace are used to mark the devotions that are established. One decade means that ten Hail Mary's are said:

Hail Mary, full of grace, the Lord is with thee. Blessed art thou among women, and blessed is the fruit of thy womb, Jesus. Holy Mary, Mother of God, pray for us sinners now and in the hour of our death. Amen.

Before each decade the Lord's Prayer is said. After each decade, one mystery of redemption is the object of meditation. The fifteen mysteries are joyful, sorrowful, and glorious:

---

[347] Rev. Rene H. Chabort, "Feasts in Honor of Our Lady," *Mariology*, III, p. 117f.

[348] George W. Shea, "The Dominican Rosary," *Mariology*, III, p. 117f.

- Joyful – the Annunciation, the Visitation, the Nativity of Christ, the Presentation of Christ, the Finding of Christ in the Temple;

- Sorrowful – the Agony in the Garden, the Scourging at the Pillar, the Crowning with Thorns, the Carrying of the Cross, the Crucifixion;

- Glorious – the Resurrection, the Ascension, the Descent of the Holy Spirit, the Assumption of Mary, the Coronation of Mary as the Queen of Heaven.

A complete Rosary devotion in the old days included 150 Hail Mary's, a number corresponding to the 150 Psalms, so the Rosary was commonly called Mary's Psalter. The complete Rosary might be said in one day, and a plenary indulgence (release from Purgatory) is granted for those who do so under certain conditions. It is more common to say five decades or fewer on a given day. The Hail Mary's and Our Father's are to be spoken out loud. Although the Rosary beads are not required in most cases for the indulgence to be granted, the use of beads is common and has become part of our language.[349]

Pope John Paul II modernized the Rosary with a new set of mysteries, the mysteries of light:

They are: his baptism; the wedding feast at Cana, where according to the Bible, he transformed water into wine; his proclamation of the coming of the Kingdom of God; the Transfiguration, when God commanded the apostles to listen to Christ; and the institution of the Eucharist.[350]

---

[349] It was said of the first Roman Catholic presidential candidate, Al Smith, "Americans are not ready to have their president saying his beads in the White House." Decades later, when a Roman Catholic was elected president, voters would have been relieved if he had said his beads in the White House.

[350] Retrieved from http://frpat.com/Rosarymysteries.htm.

The new cycle of prayers is set as follows:

> Until now the Rosary's five joyful mysteries were recited on Mondays and Thursdays, the five sorrowful mysteries on Tuesdays and Fridays, and the five glorious mysteries on Wednesdays, Saturdays, and Sundays. The five new mysteries will be used on Thursdays. Joyful Mysteries will be prayed on Saturdays.

The new mysteries focus on the work of Jesus and help deflect criticism that Roman Catholicism is a religion of Mary and not of Jesus.

Marian devotion is closely connected with earning release from Purgatory, either for the individual or for the object of the individual's prayers. For instance, in one anecdote about a Roman Catholic priest noted for his piety, the widow of a suicide victim came to ask about her husband's soul, worried that he was spending eternity in Hell for killing himself. The priest, John Vianney, told the anxious widow:

> I tell you he is saved; that he is in Purgatory and that you must pray for him. Between the parapet of the bridge and the water, he had time to make an act of Contrition. He owes the grace to the Blessed Virgin Mary. You remember how your irreligious husband allowed you to keep the month of May in your room...how he sometimes joined with you in the prayers. That has merited for him the supreme pardon.[351]

Protestants and Lutherans cannot identify with this concept of the afterlife, nor harmonize it with justification by faith.

---

[351] (F. Trochu, L'admirable *Vie du Cure d'Ars*, Lyon, 1932) Cited in Jugie, p. 26. Vianney High School in St. Louis, devoted to Marian piety, sold some of its land on Kirkwood to the Lutheran Church-Missouri Synod, where the International Building (the Purple Palace) now stands.

Little known among Protestants and Lutherans is the use of the scapular and the doctrines concerning it. A scapular can be ordered for $1 from the Scapular Guild, P. O. Box 4651, Philadelphia, Pennsylvania, 19127. The modern scapular consists of two small cloth rectangles, white and brown, connected by two small brown ribbons.

On one rectangle is the statement: "Whoever dies wearing this Scapular shall not suffer eternal fire. Our Lady's Scapular Promise." On the other rectangle is printed a drawing of Mary holding the Infant Jesus, with St. Simon Stock kneeling before them. The caption reads: "Our Lady of Mt. Carmel, St. Simon Stock." One Carmelite priest wrote:

> Since the seventeenth century, the Brown Scapular has been a universal Catholic devotion, considered to be, together with the Rosary, a customary form of Marian devotional practice.[352]

One Carmelite described this devotion:

> The Scapular devotion takes its origin from the brown scapular worn by Carmelite religious who were founded at the beginning of the thirteenth century. The scapular is the most significant part of the Carmelite brown habit. It is a long narrow garment worn over a tunic...Carmelites wear it as a symbol of their consecration to Mary, and as a sign of their hope in her motherly protection. To accommodate the laity who wanted to affiliate themselves

---

[352] Christian P. Ceroke, "The Scapular Devotion," *Mariology*, III, p. 128.

with the spirit of the Order, the scapular was shortened to two small pieces of cloth joined by strings, placed over the shoulders and worn beneath the outer clothing. For the sake of convenience a medal as a substitute is often worn today or carried on one's person.[353]

The scapular promise was said to have been given to St. Simon Stock, an early leader of the Carmelite order, in 1251.

Surrounded by a great concourse of angels, the Queen of Heaven is descending towards him, holding forth the Brown Scapular of the friars and saying: "Receive, my beloved son, this habit of thy order: this shall be to thee and to all Carmelites a privilege, that whosoever dies clothed in this shall never suffer eternal fire."[354]

In the 1300's, Pope John XXII endorsed the scapular by decreeing:

...Those who wore the Brown Scapular, lived a life of chastity (purity) according to their state in life, and recited the Office of Our Lady, would through her intercession be released from purgatory on the first Saturday after death This is called the Sabbatine Privilege. Nine different Popes, besides Pope John XXII, have spoken of the Sabbatine Privilege and reconfirmed the teaching.[355]

To understand the scapular, which is sometimes replaced with a medal, we must begin with the Roman Catholic interpretation of Genesis 3:15, the Protoevangelium or First Gospel of the Bible. Until Vatican II, the Roman Catholic Church relied upon a mistranslation of the passage to suggest that Mary's heel would crush the head of the serpent, Satan.

---

[353] Healy, p. 153f.

[354] Hafert, p. 10. *Analecta Ordinis Carmelitarum*, VIII, 1932.

[355] Fox, *The Marian Catechism*, p. 85f.

I shall place enmities between thee and the Woman, thy seed and Her seed…thou shalt lie in wait for Her heel and She shall crush thy head…[356]

The Vulgate, or Latin version of the Bible, translated a clear masculine in Hebrew as a feminine in Latin. The original Hebrew is translated:

Genesis 3:15 And I will put enmity between thee and the woman, and between thy seed and her seed; it shall bruise thy head, and thou shalt bruise his heel.

The misinterpretation of the Latin Vulgate, which was made the official version of the Bible by the Roman Catholic Council of Trent, is connected with the aftermath of Elijah's experience with the Baal prophets on Mt. Carmel, when God brought an end to the seven year drought that had plagued the land.

1 Kings 18:44 And it came to pass at the seventh time, that he said, Behold, there ariseth a little cloud out of the sea, like a man's hand. And he said, Go up, say unto Ahab, Prepare *thy chariot*, and get thee down, that the rain stop thee not. 45 And it came to pass in the mean while, that the heaven was black with clouds and wind, and there was a great rain. And Ahab rode, and went to Jezreel.

The Carmelites, a Roman Catholic religious order devoted to the Virgin Mary, portray that cloud as a prophecy of Mary's future role.

Having ascended Mount Carmel and having met the monks there, Saint Louis [Louis IX of France] is astounded by the account of a most unusual tradition. The saintly monks say that they are the descendants of the Prophet Elias and call themselves "Hermits of Saint Mary of Mount Carmel" because the fiery prophet, whom they imitate, had beheld, in a foot-shaped cloud

---

[356] Haffert, p. 5.

that had divinely soared from the sea below them, a prophetic image of the Immaculate Virgin Mary who was to bring forth man's Salvation and to conquer the pride of Satan with Her heel of humility.[357]

Roman Catholic leaders are aware of the problem of using Genesis 3:15 as a prophecy of Mary, as shown by one well known author, St. Alphonsus of Liguori:

> She will crush your head: some question whether this refers to Mary, and not rather to Jesus, since the Septuagint translates it, He shall crush your head. But in the Vulgate, which alone was approved by the Council of Trent, we find She.[358]

One can find many excesses of Marian devotion and a host of miraculous claims for the scapular in such works as Haffert's *Mary in Her Scapular Promise*:

> Hence Pope Benedict XV – the celebrated World War Pontiff – granted five hundred days [release from Purgatory] for the kissing of the Scapular, every time it is kissed. And there are only one hundred days indulgence for making the Sign of the Cross with holy water!

A priest was granted a vision of Christ for giving a "somewhat worldly young girl" a scapular to wear. In 1656, one scapular extinguished a blazing fire in St. Aulaye, France, when it was hurled into the inferno at the command of the Blessed Virgin, only to be retrieved unharmed the next day. However, the core of the problem remains even in a modern, historical, scholarly treatment of the scapular:

---

[357] *Ibid.*

[358] St. Alphonsus Liguori, *The Glories of Mary*, (adapted), New York: Catholic Book Publishing, 1981, p. 88.

The particular value of the Scapular devotion consists in the special help of Mary, so that the grace of final perseverance, or of a "happy death," may be obtained through her intercession.[359]

Opus Dei, a secretive group made famous by *The Da Vinci Code*, promotes the scapular promise:

Wear on your breast the holy scapular of Carmel. There are many excellent Marian devotions, but few are so deep-rooted among the faithful, and have received so many blessings from the Popes. Besides, how maternal this sabbatine privilege is![360]

Organizations to Support Marian Piety

Marian devotion has been promoted through many different religious orders, which exist to honor the Virgin Mother. Some of the better known are the:

Carmelites (O.Carm.),

Discalced Carmelites (O.C.D.),

Mercedarians (O.D.M.),

Servites (O.S.M.),

Holy Ghost Fathers (C.S.Sp.),

Oblates of Mary Immaculate (O.M.I.),

Marist Fathers (S.M.),

Assuptionists (A..A.), and

Claretian Fathers (C.M.F.).

Veneration of Mary has also been spread through the work of the:

Benedictines (O.S.B.),

Cistercians (O.C.R.),

---

[359] Ceroke, *Mariology*, III, p. 138.

[360] *The Way*, p. 500. Cited at http://www.opusdei.us/art.php?p=17569. The author's hour-long meeting with the director of Opus Dei in St. Louis yielded no information.

Carthusians, (O.Cart.),

Dominicans (O.P.),

Jesuits (S.J.),

Franciscans (O.F.M.)

Redemptorists (C.Ss.R.), and

Salesians (S.D.B.).

These are only a few of the orders.

Mariology also lists 123 sisterhoods devoted to the doctrines of Mary, such as the Assumption (three orders) and the Immaculate Conception (24 orders). Before Vatican II, people would go to the University of Notre Dame and other Roman Catholic centers just to watch the armies of religious in the varied cassocks and habits. One nun told the author, "You would have loved our habit. The School Sisters of Notre Dame were the flying nuns." At that time Sally Field was starring in the improbable but popular television show, "The Flying Nun," in which her character used the winged, starched headpiece of her habit to fly to various places. After Vatican II, the number of men and women in religious orders dropped precipitously. The Second Vatican Council said relatively little about Mary, and subsequently American Catholicism has downplayed Marian doctrines. Today's attitude is more in keeping with St. Augustine's sentiments:

> They built temples to these gods of theirs, and set up altars, and ordained priests, and appointed sacrifices; but to our martyrs we build, not temples as if they were gods, but monuments as to dead men whose spirits live with God. Neither do we erect altars at these monuments that we may sacrifice to the martyrs, but to the one God of the martyrs and of ourselves.[361]

The decrease in Marian devotion in America highlights the power of the organizations that existed along with the religious orders to venerate Mary. Marian confraternities, or voluntary associations, gather people to promote the doctrines described earlier in this chapter: the Archconfraternity of the Rosary, the Confraternity of Our Lady of

---

[361] Augustine, *City of God*, XXII, 10, ed. Whitney. Oates, New York: Random House, II, p. 630. Cited in Jaroslav Pelikan, *The Riddle of Roman Catholicism*, New York: Abingdon Press, 1959, p. 136.

Mount Carmel, the Confraternity of Our Lady of Perpetual Help, and many others. One church historian reported about Luther's time:

> A great number of Confraternities of the Rosary sprang up whose members agreed to pray three rosaries a week for the salvation of the other members, the mendicant orders, and the universal church.[362]

In addition, another form of Marian association, the sodality, which began in 1563, has seen 16 members become pope and 43 canonized as saints. The original concept was to keep the Marian sodality selective, but eventually the group grew too large and became too much like a confraternity.[363]

Marian devotion has not ended. Some see an increase in Third World countries. The apparitions of Mary in Medjurgorje, Yugoslavia have been widely followed and supported in America. Apparitions are also claimed for certain sites in America, such as Bayside, New York. The conservative Roman Catholic magazine *Fidelity* has challenged the claims of Medjugorje and other shrines, while another periodical, *National Catholic Register*, has supported Medjugorje.[364] Pilgrimages to Marian shrines continue. *Fidelity* magazine printed a back-page ad for a trip to Fatima, containing this quotation from Pope John Paul II: "Here a man feels he is entrusted and confided to Mary; he comes here in order to be with Her, as with His mother."

Development of Marian Doctrine

For Lutherans and Protestants, the concept of doctrine developing is alien and difficult to comprehend. They expect Christian teaching to be based upon Scripture alone. In the history of doctrine, it is clear that the Church has defined more clearly those teachings which were under attack, but the doctrines in question were already taught with clarity in the Scriptures: the Two Natures of Christ, the Trinity, original sin, justification by faith. In contrast, Roman Catholic authors write freely

---

[362] Hillerbrand, p. 18.

[363] Richard L. Rooney, "The Sodalities of Our Lady," *Mariology*, III, pp. 241ff.

[364] Father James Nichols, "Mary's Peace and Grace," *National Catholic Register*.

about doctrines, which they admit have little or no evidence in the Scriptures and clearly arose centuries after Christ. The Immaculate Conception of Mary is a Roman Catholic doctrine that cannot be found in the Scriptures or the early traditions of the Church. In Roman Catholic thinking, widespread belief in a new doctrine, combined with worship practices adopting it, unite in validating the opinion as a revealed truth. Thus, many centuries may pass while a practice in one part of the world spreads to all parts of Roman Catholicism. Those who have written in favor of this doctrine, over a period of time, become the authorities used to support the teaching. The development of doctrine, apart from the Scriptures, is clearly described by a member of the Oxford Movement, whose Church of England members (most notably John Cardinal Newman) joined the Roman Catholic Church.

> Actually, the Catholic dogma of the Assumption does not rest on any scriptural account of her death, nor, for that matter, on any traditional account of her actual translation from earth to heaven. Rather, as one Anglican writer says of an apocryphal account of the Assumption: "The belief was never founded on that story. The story was founded on the belief. The belief which was universal, required a defined shape, and that shape at length it found"[365]

This is a completely different way of looking at Christian doctrine and remains a dividing line between Roman Catholics and other Christian confessions.

> This process is known as the development of doctrine. It is a gradual flowering under the guidance of the Holy Spirit, whereby doctrines that were but dimly perceived in early times are now seen as part of the harmonious pattern of revealed truth.[366]

---

[365] J. B. Mozley, *Reminiscences of Oriol College and the Oxford Movement*, II, 368. Cited in Paul F. Palmer, S.J., *Mary in the Documents of the Church*, Gerald G. Walsh, S.J., Westminster, Maryland: The Newman Press 1952, p. 64f.

[366] Eamon Carroll, "Mary in the Documents of the Magisterium," *Mariology*, I, p. 4f.

In Lutheranism we find the opposite trend, especially in doctrines concerning Mary: those doctrines that were fondly believed but not Scriptural were gradually abandoned. Luther, who was extremely conservative in his approach to church tradition, is a good example of that tendency.

Luther and Mary

Raised in the Medieval Church and trained as a theology professor, Luther believed at first in the Immaculate Conception of Mary and consequently in her sinlessness. He also accepted the perpetual virginity of Mary, which meant that Mary remained a virgin after the birth of Christ and never had sexual relations with Joseph. The perpetual virginity of Mary is discussed in the New Testament commentaries of Lenski, the sainted Lutheran professor from Capital Seminary (now Trinity Seminary) in Columbus, Ohio:

> Luther's *sempervirgine* [perpetual virginity of Mary] in the Smalcald Articles can neither be substantiated or denied from this "until" clause (Matthew 1:25 - And knew her not till she had brought forth her firstborn son: and he called his name Jesus.) The reason for assuming the full marital relation after the birth of Jesus between Joseph and Mary rests on other grounds, namely on the marriage itself. What Mary and Joseph revealed about their relation before the birth is what Matthew reports…The ordinary reader must take it that Matthew was unconcerned altogether about the intimacy after the birth, and that thus this normal intimacy followed.[367]

Richard McBrien considers the issue of Jesus having brothers and sisters an open question.[368] The perpetual virginity of Mary was first defined at the second ecumenical Council of Constantinople, 553, and re-emphasized at the Lateran Council of 649.

---

[367] Lenski, *Interpretation of Matthew*. Columbus: Lutheran Book Concern, 1932, p. 55f. The merged seminary has a Lenski room but does not sell Lenski in their student book store.

[368] McBrien, II, p. 896.

Luther wrote about the Immaculate Conception of Mary:

> We could not say to her: "Blessed art thou," if she had at any time been subject to malediction. Again it is only right and proper that the person from whom Christ was to take flesh which would vanquish all sin should herself be preserved free from sin. For "blessed" in its proper sense means that which is gifted with divine grace, namely, that which is without sin.[369]

Luther's 1521 commentary on the Magnificat, Mary's song in Luke, includes several prayers requesting the intercession of Mary, concluding:

> We pray God to give us a right understanding of this Magnificat, an understanding that consists not merely in brilliant words but in glowing life in body and soul. May Christ grant us this through the intercession and for the sake of His dear Mother Mary! Amen.[370]

Although the concluding sentence of the Magnificat commentary seems entirely out of place to a Lutheran, the rest of the work is a fine example of Luther's communication of the Gospel. Luther already rejected the Medieval concept that Mary's merit obtained her singular honors for her, yet he did not hesitate to call Mary sinless.

> Mary also freely ascribes all to God's grace, not to her merit. For though she was without sin, yet that grace was far too great for her to deserve it in any way. How should a creature deserve to become the Mother of God? Though certain scribblers make much ado about her worthiness for such motherhood, I prefer to believe her rather than them... She says her low estate was regarded by God, not thereby rewarding her for anything she had done, but, "He has done great things for me," he has done this of

---

[369] *Kirchenpostille, Sammtliche Werke*, Erlangen, ed. 1828, 15, 55. [Erlangen editor says on p. 54 of the edition that this section of the sermon was expunged after 1527, until restored by Luther himself.] Cited in Palmer, *Mary in the Documents of the Church*, p. 76.

[370] *The Magnificat*, trans. A. Steinhaeuser, Minneapolis: Augsburg Publishing House, 1967, p. 77.

his own accord without any doing of mine. For never in all her life did she think to become the Mother of God, still less did she prepare or make herself meet for it. The tidings took her all unaware, as Luke reports (Luke 1:29). Merit, however, is not unprepared for its reward, but deliberately seeks and awaits it.[371]

Luther did not shun the title "Mother of God," because the title was confirmed at an ecumenical council and taught in the Scriptures. A theological term like Mother of God or the Trinity can accurately summarize Scriptural teaching without the term itself being found in the Bible. Luther explained Luke 1:49 "For he that is mighty hath done to me great things; and holy *is* his name" as follows:

> The "great things" are nothing less than that she became the Mother of God, in which work so many and such great good things are bestowed on her as pass man's understanding.[372]

Luther has been portrayed as having a profound devotion to Mary, which one would expect of a Medieval monk. The popularity of the Virgin Mary reflected upon her mother, St. Anne.

> Toward the end of the fifteenth century Anne became more and more popular. In Saxony she was the patron saint of the miners-- the mining town Annaberg had received its name from hers. Elector Frederick the Wise had one of her thumbs in his collection of relics and Luther called upon her for help when he vowed to become a monk.[373]

In 1503, when he slashed his leg with a sword and endangered his life, Luther cried out to St. Anne to help him. However, Luther's Magnificat commentary warns against excessive Marian devotion:

---

[371] *Ibid.*, p. 44.

[372] *Ibid.*, p. 43.

[373] Hillerbrand, p. 18.

It is necessary also to keep within bounds and not make too much of calling her "Queen of Heaven," which is a true-enough name and yet does not make her a goddess who could grant gifts or render aid, as some suppose when they pray and flee to her rather than to God. She gives nothing; God gives all, as we see in the words that follow.[374]

Luther gradually pulled back from the celebration of the Assumption and the Immaculate Conception. He preached on the Feast of the Assumption in 1522, but abandoned it by 1544, according to Thomas O'Meara, O.P.[375] In 1532 he denied any notion of a special conception of Mary. "Mary is conceived in sin just like us..."[376] In his last sermon at Wittenberg, Luther preached:

I believe in Jesus Christ, for only of Christ is said "Behold the Lamb of God who takes away the sins of the world," not of Mary or of the angels.[377]

Even a critic of Luther's theology is forced to say:

The power and poetry of Luther's preaching needs no defense. Among his many sermons, those preached at Christmas are some of the very finest. They contain beautiful passages on Mary, lines where poetry and religious exaltation make him forget his polemic. His spirit and voice strive to describe the reality of God made man and the splendor of the woman who was His mother.[378]

---

[374] *The Magnificat*, p. 45. Luke 1:49.

[375] Thomas O'Meara, O.P., *Mary in Protestant and Catholic Theology*, New York: Sheed and Ward, 1966, p. 118. This work balances Luther's earlier Marian piety with his movement away from the extremes of the Medieval religion he was taught.

[376] *WA* 36, 41; cited in O'Meara, p. 116.

[377] American Edition 51, p. 376. Cited in Mario Colacci, *The Doctrinal Conflict between Catholic and Protestant Christianity*, Minneapolis: T. S. Dennison, 1962, p. 197.

[378] O'Meara, p. 124.

Although some may want to shock and titillate others with selected portions of Luther's writings, serious study will reveal a man who was blessed by truly meditating on God's Word day and night, as Psalm 1 promises:

> Blessed *is* the man that walketh not in the counsel of the ungodly,
>
> nor standeth in the way of sinners,
>
> nor sitteth in the seat of the scornful.
>
> 2 But his delight *is* in the law of the LORD;
>
> and in his law doth he meditate day and night.
>
> 3 And he shall be like a tree planted by the rivers of water, that bringeth forth his fruit in his season;
>
> his leaf also shall not wither; and whatsoever he doeth shall prosper.
>
> 4 The ungodly *are* not so:
>
> but *are* like the chaff which the wind driveth away.
>
> 5 Therefore the ungodly shall not stand in the judgment,
>
> nor sinners in the congregation of the righteous.
>
> 6 For the LORD knoweth the way of the righteous:
>
> but the way of the ungodly shall perish.

Lutherans and the Immaculate Conception

Since Luther was raised in the Medieval Church and served as an Augustinian monk, he was deeply influenced by Marian devotion and remained quite Roman in his statements about Mary during the early years of the Reformation. His study of Scriptures led him gradually away from the excesses of Marian piety, a tradition so strong that the *Book of Concord* dealt with it directly:

> Granting that the blessed Mary prays for the Church, does she receive souls in death, [the example of her faith and her humility]. What does Christ do if the blessed Mary does these things! Although she is most worthy of the most ample honors,

nevertheless she does not wish to be made equal to Christ, but rather wishes us to consider and follow her example [the example of her faith and her humility]. But the subject itself declares that in public opinion the blessed Virgin has succeeded altogether to the place of Christ. Men have invoked her, have trusted in her mercy, through her have desired to appease Christ as though He were not a propitiator, but only a dreadful judge and avenger...For we obtain remission of sins only by the merits of Christ, when we believe in Him.[379]

Another passage, from the Formula of Concord, might support the perpetual virginity of Mary, but only by inference:

On account of this personal union and communion of the natures, Mary, the most blessed Virgin, bore not a mere man, but, as the angel [Gabriel] testifies, such a man as is truly the Son of the most high God, who showed His divine majesty even in His mother's womb, inasmuch as He was born of a virgin, with her virginity inviolate. Therefore she is truly the mother of God, and nevertheless remained a virgin.[380]

Marian devotion seems to have waned in Lutherans after the Reformation. A more cautious attitude toward titles and honors for Mary is seen in the writings of Chemnitz:

But I think that the Virgin Mary is rightly proclaimed blest if those things are attributed to her which are both in agreement with the Scripture and can be proved from there, so that the name of the Lord may be holy. No other celebration can be pleasing to her.[381]

---

[379] Apology Augsburg Confession, XXI. #27. Saints. *Triglotta*, p. 349f. Tappert, p. 232f.

[380] *et tamen virgo mansit*. Formula of Concord, SD VIII. #23. Person of Christ. *Triglotta*, p. 1023. Tappert, p. 595. Comments from various Lutheran writers suggest that the perpetual virginity of Mary was assumed by most of them until recently, Lenski being an exception. Nevertheless, this remains a historical question that does not affect the Christian faith.

[381] *Examination*, I, p. 383.

Chemnitz rejected the Immaculate Conception of Mary, which Luther also came to deny as unscriptural:

> And when, in two questions concerning the Virgin Mary, the limits set by the Scripture had already been exceeded, some began to contend in the schools that also the Virgin Mary had been conceived without original sin. Of this opinion Scotus later became the patron...But many, like Thomas, Bonaventura, Gregory of Ariminium, etc., at that time contradicted this opinion, because it was not only set forth without the Word of God and the testimonies of antiquity but it also conflicted with clear testimonies of Scripture.[382]

John Calvin

John Calvin, the Swiss Reformer, gave great emphasis to Mary in his theological writings, according to Ross McKensie:

> His commentary on the infancy narratives is thorough and detailed, and his sermons on the Harmony of the Gospels which deal directly with Mary extend in the Brunswick edition of his works to no fewer than 500 columns. As a source of evangelical Marian spirituality, nothing quite like that is to be found in any of his contemporaries or his successors.[383]

Calvin believed in the perpetual virginity and the divine maternity of Mary. He avoided the term Mother of God, considering the term easily misunderstood, so he used other titles, such as Mother of our Lord. Calvin said: "To speak of the Mother of God instead of the Virgin Mary can only serve to harden the ignorant in their superstition."[384] Calvin did not accept the Immaculate Conception of Mary, writing that Christ's

---

[382] *Ibid.*, p. 179

[383] "Calvin and the Calvinists on Mary, " p. 6. Paper given at the Ecumenical Society of the Blessed Virgin Mary, Washington DC, 1980. Cited in Healy, p. 103.

[384] O'Meara, p. 129.

glory "Must not be obscured by excessive honor paid to His mother…"[385]

In subsequent years, Lutherans and Protestants were almost silent about Mary. This may have developed because a sermon or treatise about Mary would have struck some as proof of Romanizing and thus a topic to be avoided altogether. The excess of devotion to Mary by Roman Catholics has made any mention of her a point of confession, especially since those Lutheran pastors who became overly concerned with Mary ended up in the Church of Rome.[386]

---

[385] Ibid., p. 133.

[386] The author once asked, "How many Lutheran pastors have Rosaries?" A friend said, "I knew a Missouri Synod pastor who had them. He is a Roman Catholic priest now."

Summary - Doctrines about Mary[387]		
Doctrine	**Church Action**	**Accepted by**
Mary, the Mother of God (the divine maternity; *theotokos*)	Ephesus, 431	Roman Catholics, Lutherans, Protestants
Perpetual Virginity, May remained a virgin her entire life	Council of Constantinople, 533; Smalcald Articles, 1537	Roman Catholics, Some Lutherans, Luther, Calvin, Pieper's *CD*, II, p. 308
Immaculate Conception: Mary was conceived without sin and never sinned	Council of Trent; *Solicitudo omnium*, 1661; *Ineffabilis Deus*, 1854	Roman Catholics, Early Martin Luther
Assumption – Mary was taken into heaven, before or immediately after her death	*Munificentissimus Deus*, 1950	Roman Catholics, Eastern Orthodox
Co-Redemptrix – Mary cooperated in redeeming mankind	*Inter Sodalicia*, 1918, *Miserentissimus Redemptor*, 1928	Roman Catholics
Mediatrix of All Graces – all blessings and forgiveness come through Mary	*Ad Diem*, 1904	Roman Catholics

[387] Father Francis Ripley summarized the collection of 385 recent official Roman Catholic statements about Mary thus: "In their official statements the Popes have emphasized in many other ways Our Lady's action in the Church. They tell us that her holiness has a great influence over all the Church, that she takes part in the work fulfilled in the Church by Christ and that she always intercedes for the Church. She never ceases to spend herself for the Church. She is the base, the centre and the link of union between Christians. She enrolls us in the Church and there strives for union in love. As the Seat of Wisdom, she illuminates the Bishops and helps them and renders all people docile to them. As Queen of the Apostolate, she inspires Doctors and promotes the zeal of the religious. She procures the dominion and extension of the Church and is its stronghold, help, support, constant refuge, hope and guiding star. She watches over the Church, defends it in its dangers and brings to it peace, victory, and freedom." *Mary, Mother of the Church*, p. 76.

Queen of peace, pray for us!

Our gaze is directed toward you in great
fear, to you do we turn with ever-more
insistent faith in these times marked by
many uncertainties and fears for the
present and future of our planet.
Together we lift our confident and
sorrowful petition to you, the first fruit of
humanity redeemed by Christ, finally freed
from the slavery of evil and sin: hear the
cry of the pain of victims of war and so
many forms of violence that bloody the
earth. Clear away the darkness of sorrow
and worry, of hate and vengeance. Open
up our minds and hearts to faith and
forgiveness!

Mother of mercy and hope:

Help every human being
of every race and culture
to find and embrace Jesus,
who
came to earth in the
mystery of Christmas to
give us 'His' peace.

Mary, Queen of peace, give us Christ, true peace in the world!

Chapter Seven: Luther versus the Papacy

A few years ago, it would have seemed unnecessary to defend Luther against the old charges leveled against his character during his lifetime and repeated ever since. Roman Catholics in this century have grown to appreciate Luther, even if they continue to disagree with his doctrine. For good cause, traditional Roman Catholics have suspected that their brothers who defend Luther are also sympathizers with his doctrine of justification by grace through faith alone. They are not imagining this. During a theology class at the University of Notre Dame, Father Oliver Williams, a Holy Cross Father, said, "Luther was right" about justification. During a lecture at Waterloo Lutheran Seminary, Father Harry McSorley answered the question of his book *Luther: Right or Wrong?* He concluded his lecture about the unfree will, in which Erasmus took a position against Luther, by saying, "Luther was right." Traditional Roman Catholics are well aware of their liberal theologians who share the spirit, if not the doctrine, of Luther. Although liberal Roman Catholic theologians like Charles Curran have more in common with the Unitarian and social activist thoughts of liberal Protestants, Luther is still being blamed for the current American rebellion against papal authority, papal doctrine, and papal infallibility.[388]

Fidelity Magazine

Luther has come under attack again by traditional Roman Catholics, represented by *Fidelity* magazine (now *Culture Wars*) and its expert editor, E. Michael Jones, Ph.D., author of *Is Notre Dame Catholic?*[389] The magazine grew out of his experience of being fired as a theology professor at St. Mary's College, the nearby associated women's college, for being pro-life.

---

[388] In a graduate seminar at Moreau Seminary, University of Notre Dame, Kueng's book on *Infallibility* was discussed. Most of the Roman Catholic priests and seminarians agreed with Kueng. A local priest looked around the room and asked angrily, "Why are you priests?" He was ignored.

[389] E. Michael Jones, *Is Notre Dame Catholic?* South Bend, Fidelity Press, 1989. The book examines such contradictions as: two atheists teaching in the liturgy department, both homosexual; fetal experimentation at Notre Dame; and the liberal stance of Notre Dame President Ed Malloy, CSC. The typesetting was done by the Ultramontane Associates. Ultramontane is the name of the 19th century movement for asserting papal authority and infallibility.

Jones' attack against Luther came in the form of the Fidelity cover story, "Luther: The First Modern," (May, 1991). The article begins as a book review of *The Ragamuffin Gospel* by Brennan Manning, a former priest from Charismatic Renewal. Jones and Manning are still active in their respective efforts today. The article briefly reviews the doctrine of free will, then describes Manning's career as a former priest, now married with children. The next section, truly a *non sequitur*, starts with the escape of nuns from Nimbschen in 1523, quoting Luther's open letter about freeing the nuns. Jones writes about the remarks of Amsdorf, not Luther:

> Such was the women's liberation practice by the Protestant Party in Germany in the sixteenth century. Actually, since it involved the programmatic breaking down of sexual restraints, it was not much different than its twentieth century variety.[390]

This is the traditional Roman Catholic argument, that the current problems in Catholicism are the result of Luther's revolt (not reform), a rebellion based upon his theological justification for an immoral life. In fact, a definite sign of a Roman Catholic author's perspective can be identified in his choice of "Protestant revolt" over "Protestant Reformation." Moreover, Luther is generally portrayed as unstable and unworthy of serious theological debate. Therefore, Jones' adroit use of the logical fallacy, guilt by association, linking the charismatic ex-priest to Luther and his "apostate nuns," effectively condemns both men at the same time, since conservative Roman Catholics have been trained against Lutheran doctrine in particular. Luther is blamed for Brennan, and Brennan is a typical example of Luther's influence and teaching in this era.

The effort to convince the world that Luther was a degenerate and false teacher began with Johannes Cochlaeus (1479–1552).[391] According to Adolf Herte, all Roman Catholic books attacking Luther have been dependent upon the citations and argumentation of Cochlaeus, including the works in the last century of Father Heinrich

---

[390] Jones, "Luther: The First Modern," review of *The Ragamuffin Gospel* by Brennan Manning, Portland: Multnomah Press, 1990. Fidelity, May, 1991, pp. 37-46. Hereafter cited as "Luther: The First Modern."

[391] W. H. T. Dau, *Luther Examined and Reexamined*, St. Louis: Concordia Publishing House, 1917, p. 6.

Denifle and Father Hartmann Grisar.[392] An American proponent of the personal attack against Luther (the ad hominem fallacy) is Monseignor O'Hare in his classic *The Facts about Luther*, which is still available from conservative Catholic booksellers.[393] When Pope John Paul II visited Germany in 1980, Remigius Baeumer published a defense of Cochlaeus and portrayed him as a reformer and defender of the Church.[394] This line of reasoning by Roman Catholics, which has been resuscitated by Jones, is critiqued by the Roman Catholic scholar Sebastian Merkle, as summarized by Stauffer:

> From the outset they must refrain from belittling and detracting from Luther, recognize the religious motives for his action, perceive that he was the father of the freethinkers or a revolutionary, and in sum admit that the movement he started was solely spiritual.[395]

To understand Luther, we must remember what Origen said:

> Let him therefore who is concerned about his life not be taken in by the friendliness of heretics to agree with their doctrine. Neither let him be offended at my faults, who am a teacher, but let him consider the doctrine itself.[396]

---

[392] *Das katholische Lutherbild in Bann der Luther-kommentare des Cochlaeus*, 3 vols., Muenster: 1943; cited in Gotthelf Widerman, "Cochlaeus as a Polemicist," in *Seven-Headed Luther, Essays in Commemoration of a Quincentennary*, 1483-1983, pp. 195-206, ed. Peter Newman Brooks, London: Clarendon Press, 1983, p. 203.

[393] Msgr. Patrick F. O'Hare, *The Facts about Luther*, Rockford: TAN Books and Publishers, 1987. Original edition, 1916.

[394] Baemler, Johannes Cochlaeus, (1479 – 1552). Katholische Leben und Kaempfen im Zeitalter der Glaubensspaltung, Heft 40, Aschendorff, 1980. Baeumler's essay is in *Kleine deutsche Kirchengesichte*, ed. B. Koetting, 1980. "Cochlaeus as a Polemicist," p. 204.

[395] Richard Stauffer, *Luther as Seen by Catholics*, London: Lutterworth Press, 1967, p. 38.

[396] Cited in *Examination*, I, p. 154.

Conclaeus published his *Seven-Headed Luther* (*Septiceps Lutherus*) in 1529, with a title page illustrating Luther as a seven-headed man keen on novelties, raging furiously, looking for violence, and eager to set up a new papacy for himself. The image is from the Book of Revelation:

> Revelation 13:1 And I stood upon the sand of the sea, and saw a beast rise up out of the sea, having seven heads and ten horns, and upon his horns ten crowns, and upon his heads the name of blasphemy.

Surrounded by unreliable associates, Cochlaeus became increasingly wild and undiscerning in his attacks, publishing another work in 1534. One scholar wrote:

> For the personal element in this history of the Lutheran Reformation is so dominant, the reader finds it difficult to avoid the impression that, for Cochlaeus, the Reformation was exclusively to be blamed on Luther...No good was to be expected of such a man, and no defamation seemed too base to be left unmentioned.[397]

---

[397] "Cochlaeus as Polemicist," p. 198.

Cochlaeus spread the rumor that Satan conceived Luther, that Luther's mother was a prostitute, that Luther's marriage was forced by his immoral activity with Katherine, one of many lovers. By gathering and misrepresenting many of Luther's statements, Cochlaeus made it possible for Roman Catholic leaders to avoid Luther.

> Although Cochlaeus no doubt always attempted to quote faithfully, and never willingly distorted Luther's statements, *Septiceps Lutherus* is nevertheless a masterpiece of distortion, misrepresentation, and also stupidity.[398]

The Jones review continues with a survey of Luther's character, not his doctrine, taking up the cause of Brennan again with this caustic summary:

> Given all of this, it is not hard to understand why Brennan Manning would find Lutheran theology attractive. He, like Luther and his followers, is a priest who has broken solemn vows by attempting marriage. Like Luther's followers in the sixteenth century, he needs a theological justification for what he has done. Similarities abound.[399]

Then we learn that Manning and Luther were heavy drinkers, another false accusation against Luther, although it is true that Manning was treated for alcoholism. Manning, says Jones, is like Luther, wanting the Gospel on his own terms. "His is the theology of Frank Sinatra."[400] Jones concludes:

> "Was Luther Right?" asks Professor Alan Schreck of Steubenville University in an article not quite as brainless as the first. To which we respond, Is the pope the antichrist? Conventional wisdom is all but unanimous in seeing ecumenism as the project whereby Catholics concede that Protestants were right all along. Charismatics, as the article by Professor Schreck shows, are particularly prone to this intellectual deficiency.[401]

---

[398] *Ibid.*, p. 200.

[399] "Luther: The First Modern," p. 45.

[400] *Ibid.*, p. 46.

[401] *Ibid.*, p. 47.

Jones' review is ideal for its restatement of the traditional Roman Catholic view of Luther, which has not changed since the Reformation. Luther remains officially excommunicated and condemned to Hell by the Church of Rome.

What is the evidence shown for discussing Luther's character in the Jones review? Is it *Here I Stand*, the best-selling biography of Luther by Yale University historian Roland Bainton? Or is it the lesser known but more valuable *This Is Luther*, by Ewald Plass? Or did he use Roman Catholic authorities like F. X. Kiefl or Sebastian Merkle? Or Anton Fischer? These authors are not cited at all. Instead, the Jones review of Luther's character relies almost completely upon two Roman Catholic authors, Father Heinrich Denifle and Father Hartmann Grisar, who are both dependent upon Cochlaeus.[402]

Comparing Luther to Hugh Hefner, Jones claims that the Reformer attracted apostate priests and nuns by rationalizing "sexual license and broken vows."[403] The stated evidence against Luther consists of:

- The Reformer's admission of carnal desire, which one can find in St. Paul's writings, not to mention those of the Church fathers;

- Slanderous remarks against Luther in the letters of his opponents;

- Selective quotations too weak for anything but a sly insinuation.

One case in particular is a letter from one physician to another, suggesting that perhaps Luther was being treated for "the pain of the French disease." Grisar, no friend of Luther, admitted that this is the only letter in the entire corpus that mentions the disease, but speculates that the letter must refer to syphilis.[404] Luther's illnesses were well known to everyone at that time, so a battle with syphilis would have been general knowledge, since many figures in public life, secular and religious, were

---

[402] Roland Bainton., *Here I Stand, A Life of Martin Luther*, New York: Mentor Books, 1950. Ewald Plass, *This Is Luther*, St. Louis: Concordia Publishing House, 1984. F. X. Kiefl, *Martin Luthers religioese Psyche*. Sebastian Merkle, *Gutes an Luther und Uebles an seinem Tadlern*. Anton Fischer, *Was der betende Luther der ganzen Christenheit zu sagen hat*. The Roman Catholic books are mentioned in Stauffer, *Luther as Seen by Catholics*, p. 38

[403] "Luther: The First Modern," p. 42.

[404] *Ibid.*, p. 43.

known for having venereal disease.[405] Yet word of Luther's alleged case of syphilis failed to get out and the Reformer somehow failed to transmit the disease to his wife, or secondarily, to his children. To quote Bainton's debunking of the Erik Erikson's psychoanalysis of Luther in *Young Man Luther*: "The first step is to make the utmost effort to get the facts straight."[406]

A couple of Jones' assertions about Luther need to be addressed. One is that "Libido culminating in broken vows was the engine that pulled the Reformation train."[407] Jones' proof, from Grisar, is that Luther wrote about being a famous lover, having relations with women, having three wives, and barely able to hold on to Katherine, his third wife.[408] The letter itself is valid, but Jones' use of it is absurd. Jones dignifies his tactics by including the fact that Luther said he was joking in the letter, but then Jones insinuates the opposite. Luther wrote to encourage Spalatin to marry. Luther's reference to relations with women (*sic misceor feminis*) is repeated by Jones with the insistence that Luther must have really meant sexual intercourse. However, Boehmer pointed out already in 1916 that the word *sic* in the phrase does not allow such an interpretation, that it is a humorous reference to Luther's many articles about marriage. He wrote so much about marriage, "*sic misceor feminis* – and in this way have to do with women."[409] Boehmer's excellent work is found in Roman Catholic and Lutheran theological libraries, in English and German. Luther was simply goading Spalatin to marry and was showing how quickly the nuns were finding husbands. Luther was not in love with Katherine when they were first married, as he admitted, but he later became so enamored of her that he worried about his love for her supplanting his love for Christ.

Jones has another witness against Luther, his close associate Philip Melanchthon, who wrote an agitated letter immediately after he found out that Luther married without his knowledge. Melanchthon had many fine qualities and deserved the high esteem Luther had for him, but Philip was often mastered by his fears and qualms, especially after

---

[405] Heinrich Boehmer, *Luther in Light of Recent Research*, New York: *The Christian Herald*, 1916, p. 215.

[406] Roland Bainton, "Psychiatry and History: An Examination of Erikson's *Young Man Luther*," in *Psychohistory and Religion*, ed. Roger Johnson, Philadelphia: Fortress Press, 1977, p. 56.

[407] "Luther: The First Modern," p. 42.

[408] *Ibid.*, p. 42.

[409] Boehmer, p. 217.

Luther's death in 1546. Many bachelors bemoan the loss of their best friend to marriage and at first speak tragically about scheming women. But Philip gladly attended Luther's public ceremony a few weeks later. We know from the historical record that Luther married Katherine after a young man jilted her. When she refused to marry an old man, Pastor Glatz, she said she would only marry Luther or Amsdorf. Luther repeated the joke to his father, who approved of his son being married. The thought of premarital sex between Luther and Katherine existed only in the minds of Cochlaeus and his modern Amen Corner.

The faults of Luther are well documented, since he conducted his work in the view of so many people, published an enormous body of work, occasionally autobiographical in nature, and spoke freely at a large dinner table, enjoying the unique experience of having his conversation recorded by guests and printed as the Table Talks. Some critics of Luther, according to Bainton, have not been careful at examining the reliability of the various contributors to the Table Talks. Luther could be coarse, but he lived in an era when other authors were far worse. He is often faulted for his polemics, although he confined his attacks to false doctrine, instead of impugning the motives or character of the false teachers. After all, the Scriptures command religious teachers to use the Word of God as a shield and weapon against false doctrine.

With so many primary and secondary sources available, more than any other historical figure except Christ, a writer can easily produce a work with an enormous number of quotations without drawing an honest portrait of Luther. On the other hand, a defense of Luther can strike the non-Lutheran as hagiography, as naïve as the saints' biographies in the devotional literature of the Roman Catholic Church. Other works seek to make a political point, using just one aspect of Luther's life, to make him the first charismatic, the first Pietist, the first revolutionary, the first psychoanalysis patient, or the first liberal doubting the Bible. Looking down a well, these writers see a reflection of their own faces and call it a Luther biography.

Luther is properly the object of much discussion among all denominations, but he does not receive the serious attention he deserves among Lutherans and non-Lutherans. Non-Lutherans attack Luther without studying his works. Lutherans defend him with the same shallowness. The best biography of Luther is by Ewald Plass, *This Is Luther*, and the best collection of his writings, What Luther Says, edited by Plass. A collection of his writings, edited as daily meditations, is entitled *Day by Day We Magnify Thee*. In addition, the eight volume *Sermons of Martin Luther* (republished in four volumes) are an invaluable tool for studying the doctrine of the Reformer and learning the meaning of the Word. C. F. W. Walther's Luther lectures were published as *The Proper Distinction between Law and Gospel.* Another resource is Siegbert Becker's *The Foolishness of God*, which deals with the proper use of reason in Luther's doctrine. Luther's works are also published on CD.

The best approach to studying Luther is to read his work, especially his sermons. The following quotations are meant to give a sample of Luther's genius as a Doctor of the Bible and to outline his thought. The treatment is entirely inadequate and will be followed by a book of his best sayings, but the collection is meant to serve as a sampler, to encourage a thorough study, appreciation, and love of Luther's thought, which was always intended to be faithful to the Holy Scriptures.[410]

Luther Quotations

First, to understand Luther's theology correctly, and this is rare, we must take into account his absolute fidelity to pure doctrine, as defined by the Scriptures, the ruling norm of all faith and practice.

In philosophy an error that is small at the beginning becomes very great in the end. So a small error in theology overturns the

[410] Martin Luther, *The Sermons of Martin Luther*, 8 vols. (now published in 4 vols.), ed. John Lenker, Grand Rapids: Baker Book House, 1983. *What Luther Says, An Anthology*, 3 vols. ed. Ewald Plass, St. Louis: Concordia Publishing House, 1959. Martin Luther, *Day by Day We Magnify Thee*, Philadelphia: Fortress Press, 1982. Siegbert Becker, *The Foolishness of God, The Place of Reason in the Theology of Martin Luther*, Milwaukee: Northwestern Publishing House, 1982. C.F.W. Walther, *The Proper Distinction between Law and Gospel*, ed. W. H. T. Dau, St. Louis: Concordia Publishing House.

whole body of doctrine...That is why we may not surrender or change even an iota (*apiculum*) of doctrine.[411]

Comparing pastors to the angels of Christmas, Luther emphasized that those who preach must proclaim the pure Word of God, no matter what may happen as a result.

> The preachers are to be angels, that is God's messengers, who are to lead a heavenly life, are to be constantly engaged with God's Word that they under no circumstances preach the doctrine of men. It is a most incongruous thing to be God's messenger and not to further God's message.[412]

Luther was called a trouble-maker for insisting on complete agreement about the teachings of the Bible. To this day, such an attitude is considered unloving and divisive, but Luther wrote:

> Therefore, do not speak to me of love or friendship when anything is to be detracted from the Word or the faith; for we are told that not love but the Word brings eternal life, God's grace, and all heavenly treasures.[413]

Those called by God must not only teach the truth, but also condemn error, or they are not true shepherds.

> For nothing can feed or give life to the soul, which is not the doctrine of Christ. Although the hireling does not himself slay and destroy he does not restrain the wolf. Therefore, because you neither point out nor teach this shepherd, you shall not and ought not to be heard, but you shall be shunned as a wolf.[414]

---

[411] *What Luther Says*, III, p. 1365.

[412] *Sermons of Martin Luther*, I, p. 153.

[413] *What Luther Says*, III, p. 1411f.

[414] *Sermons of Martin Luther*, III, p. 58f.

Luther on Conversion

In writing about conversion, Luther taught that the human will is passive, receiving both contrition for sin (through the Law) and faith in Christ (through the Gospel) as the Holy Spirit acts effectively through the Word and Sacraments. Arguing from the Scriptures, he asserted that human merit and human will play no part in God's work of conversion.

> Man's own merit or holiness can contribute nothing toward getting out of the old birth of flesh and blood or achieving the new birth. Man is not born again of his own choice and idea; but a new birth must take place through Holy Baptism, without man's contributing anything. The Holy Spirit is bestowed through the divine will and grace by means of the externally preached Word and the water.[415]

> For you do not find Him; He finds you. For the preachers come from Him, not from you. Your faith comes from Him, not from you. And everything that works faith within you comes from Him, not from you.[416]

> But, as has often been said, faith changes the person and makes out of an enemy a child, so mysteriously that the external works, walk and conversation remain the same as before, when they are not by nature wicked deeds.[417]

Law and Gospel

The proper distinction between the demands of the Law and the comforting promises of the Gospel pervades Luther's doctrine. His honesty about all carnality, that is, all sins of the flesh, have led people to

---

[415] *What Luther Says*, I, p. 344.

[416] *Ibid.*, I, p. 345.

[417] *Sermons of Martin Luther*, I, p. 210.

condemn him for endorsing a condition he saw as evidence of the old Adam at work:

> You may tie a hog ever so well, but you cannot prevent it from grunting, until it is strangled and killed. Thus it is with the sins of the flesh.[418]

Contrary to some casual observers, Luther did teach the Law in all its severity, acknowledging at the same time that sorrow for sin is a work of God, not man.

> A penitent heart is a rare thing and a great grace; one cannot produce it by thinking about sin and hell. Only the Holy Spirit can impart it.[419]

Luther did not practice hedonism or encourage it, nor did he promote cheap grace - forgiveness without repentance.

> True is the proverb and better than everything they have hitherto taught about remorse: Never to sin again is repentance at its best; and a new life is the best of repentance.[420]

> All preaching of sin and God's wrath is a preaching of the Law, no matter how or when it may be done. On the other hand, the Gospel is such preaching as sets forth and bestows nothing but grace and forgiveness in Christ. And yet it is true that the Apostles and preachers of the Gospel sanctioned the preaching of the Law, as Christ Himself did, and began with this in the case of those who had not yet acknowledged their sins and had felt no fear of God's anger.[421]

---

[418] *Ibid.*, II, p. 247.

[419] *What Luther Says*, III, p. 1212.

[420] *Ibid.*, p. 1214.

[421] *Sermons of Martin Luther*, IV, p. 158.

Luther dealt with a Medieval form of situation ethics or values clarification in a society no less degenerate than our own.

> Today nothing is so common as turning right into wrong and wrong into right by employing all sorts of clever expedients and strange tricks.[422]

In situation ethics, invented by Joseph Fletcher, an avowed atheist, one can and should commit adultery to save a life. Not so in Luther's doctrine:

> You must never do evil so that good may come of it. To kill a woman is a sin; yet if her life could be saved by adultery this sin should never be committed.[423]

Evangelism

Luther is supposed to have been silent about evangelism, according to some poorly educated Protestants, but his teaching focused on the Biblical doctrine of growth through the Means of Grace. He did not worry about the results God would surely provide from the Holy Spirit at work through the Word and Sacraments. Although Luther did not promote hokey evangelism gimmicks, he did teach that all Christians should teach Christ to their neighbors.

> Hence I send you into the world as my Father hath sent me; namely, that every Christian should instruct and teach his neighbor, that he may also come to Christ. By this, no power is delegated exclusively to popes and bishops, but all Christians are commanded to profess their faith publicly and also to lead others to believe.[424]

---

[422] *What Luther Says*, III, p. 1294.

[423] *Ibid.*, p. 1304.

[424] *Sermons of Martin Luther*, II, p. 359.

Luther had great confidence in the value and effect of preaching the Gospel, which is evangelism at its best.

> The preaching of this message may be likened to a stone thrown into the water, producing ripples which circle outward from it, the waves rolling always on and on, one driving the other, till they come to the shore. Although the center becomes quiet, the waves do not rest, but move forward. So it is with the preaching of the Word. It was begun by the apostles, and it constantly goes forward, is pushed on farther and farther by the preachers, driven hither and thither into the world, yet always being made known to those who never heard it before, although it be arrested in the midst of its course and is condemned as heresy.[425]

The Means of Grace

Those who opposed infant baptism prompted Luther to praise the value of this sacrament as proof of God's grace:

> There are the infants, bare and naked in body and soul, having neither faith nor works. Then the Christian Church comes forward and prays, that God would pour faith into the child; not that our faith should help the child, but that it may obtain a faith of its own. If it has faith, then after that whatever it does is well done, whether it suckle its mother's breast, or whether it soil itself, or whatever it may please to do.[426]

Luther had no patience for the *Schwaermer* (named for the way bees buzz) or Enthusiasts who imagined that the Holy Spirit came to people apart from the Means of Grace. According to Luther, the Pentecostal tears down the path to God, Holy Baptism and the Word, while talking about how to get in touch with God.

---

[425] *Ibid.*, III, p. 202.

[426] *Ibid.*, IV, p. 378.

He wants to teach you, not how the Spirit is to come to you but how you are to come to the Spirit, so that you learn how to float on the clouds and ride on the wind.[427]

It is a glory which every preacher may claim, to be able to say with full confidence of heart: "This trust have I toward God in Christ, that what I teach and preach is truly the Word of God." Likewise, when he performs other official duties in the Church—baptizes a child, absolves and comforts a sinner—it must be done in the same firm conviction that such is the command of Christ. He who would teach and exercise authority in the Church without this glory, "it is profitable for him," as Christ says, (Matthew 18:6), "that a great millstone should be hanged about his neck, and that he should be sunk in the depths of the sea." For the devil's lies he preaches, and death is what he affects.[428]

Humor

Luther's sense of humor, keen ability to observe human nature, and gift of creating vivid analogies are indications of his knowledge of the human condition and man's relationship to God. For example, he compared false teachers to the vainglorious peacock:

The peacock is an image of heretics and fanatical spirits. For on the order of the peacock they, too, show themselves and strut about in their gifts, which never are outstanding. But if they could see their feet, that is the foundation of their doctrine, they would be stricken with terror, lower their crests, and humble themselves. To be sure, they, too, suffer from jealousy, because they cannot bear honest and true teachers. They want to be the whole show and want to put up with no one next to them. And they are immeasurably envious, as peacocks are. Finally, they have a raucous and unpleasant voice, that is, their doctrine is bitter and sad for afflicted and godly minds; for it casts consciences down more than it lifts them up and strengthens them.[429]

---

[427] *What Luther Says*, II, p. 916.

[428] *Sermons of Martin Luther*, VIII, p. 227.

[429] *What Luther Says*, II, p. 642.

Luther used hyperbole, or exaggeration, to make a good point about our lack of trust in Christ.

> Therefore, I hold that the German proverb is true, that more souls go to heaven from the gallows than from the cemetery; for criminals have not so greatly practiced lack of confidence in the goodness of Christ.[430]

Luther often contrasted the message of human reason and the world to that of faith and God's Word:

> Note that when that wise harlot, natural reason (whom the heathen have followed when they wanted to be very wise), looks at married life, she turns up her nose and says: Ah, should I rock the baby, wash diapers, make the bed, smell foul odors, watch through the night, wait upon the bawling youngster and heal its infected sores, then take care of the wife, support her by working, tend to this, tend to that, do this, do that, suffer this, suffer that, and put up with whatever additional displeasure and trouble married life brings? Should I be so imprisoned? O you poor, miserable fellow, did you take a wife? Shame, shame, on the trouble and displeasure. It is better to remain free and to lead a quiet life without care.[431]

Noticing the power of wealth in his day, Luther commented on the difficulties caused by affluence:

> For whom the devil cannot overcome with poverty, want, need and misery, he attacks with riches, favor, honor, pleasure, power and the like, and contends on both sides against us; yea, he "walketh about," says St. Peter in 1 Pt. 5:8....[432]

---

[430] *Ibid.*, III, p. 1275.

[431] *Ibid.*, II, p. 885f.

[432] *Sermons of Martin Luther*, II, p. 145.

A good eye for man's failings enabled Luther to give us many wise observations.

> The nice, envious person who is sad when another prospers, and would gladly have one eye less if thereby his neighbor had none, is the product of Satan.[433]

Good Works

Luther is often brutalized for not being liberal enough, for not caring about the poor and encouraging good works. One passage indicates Luther's proper emphasis on good works, not as a cause of salvation, but as a fruit of God's gracious work of conversion.

> In order to keep your faith pure, do nothing else than stand still, enjoy its blessings, accept Christ's works, and let him bestow His love upon you. You must be blind, lame, deaf, dead, leprous and poor; otherwise you will stumble at Christ. That Gospel which suffers Christ to be seen and to be doing good only among the needy, will not belie you.[434]

Trials

Luther is remembered justly for his theology of the cross, the emphasis upon the role of suffering for the Word in the Christian life. Luther did not promise mansions and boundless health for believers, a theology of glory common among the televangelists of today. Instead, he offered real comfort for the afflicted soul.

> For the devil will not allow a Christian to have peace; therefore Christ must bestow it in a manner different from that in which the world has and gives, in that he quiets the heart and removes

---

[433] *Ibid.*, III, p. 102.

[434] *Ibid.*, I, p. 110.

from within fear and terror, although without there remain contention and misfortune.[435]

Luther found value and purpose in suffering.

> One Christian who has been tried is worth a hundred who have not been tried for the blessing of God grows in trials. He who has experienced them can teach, comfort, and advise many in bodily and spiritual matters.[436]

Although human reason and the world tell us that unpopularity is a sign of failure in the ministry, Luther argued another perspective from Romans, one that every believer should memorize.

> But when our good work is followed by persecution, let us rejoice and firmly believe that it is pleasing to God; indeed, then let us be assured that it comes from God, for whatever is of God is bound to be crucified by the world. As long as it does not bring the cross, that is, as long as it does not bring shame and contempt as we patiently continue in it, it cannot be esteemed as a divine work since even the Son of God was not free from it--(suffering for the sake of the good He did) --but left us an example in this. He Himself tells us in Matthew 5:10, 12: "Blessed are they which are persecuted for righteousness sake...Rejoice, and be exceeding glad: for great is your reward in heaven."[437]

Because of his bouts with severe depression, Luther was able to warn others against making their depression worse and how they might find relief from the dark night of the soul.

---

[435] *Ibid.*, II, p. 380.

[436] *What Luther Says*, III, p. 1381.

[437] *Commentary on Romans*, trans. J. Theodore Mueller, Grand Rapids: Kregel Publications, 1976, p. 55.

The deeper a person is sunk in sadness and emotional upheavals, the better he serves as an instrument of Satan. For our emotions are instruments through which he gets into us and works in us if we do not watch our step. It is easy to water where it is wet. Where the fence is dilapidated, it is easy to get across. So Satan has easy access where there is sadness. Therefore one must pray and associate with godly people.[438]

In an era when emotions are sacramental, governing our words and actions, ruling over the Word and practical reason, Luther provides a good prescription against salvation by feelings.

Therefore, let God's Word be of more authority to you than your own feelings and the judgment of the whole world; do not give God the lie and rob yourself of the Spirit of truth.[439]

The Gospel is the greatest comfort to those who are weighted down by guilt, despair, and anxiety.

Whoever now believes the Gospel will receive grace and the Holy Spirit. This will cause the heart to rejoice and find delight in God, and will enable the believer to keep the law cheerfully, without expecting a reward, without fear of punishment, without seeking compensation, as the heart is perfectly satisfied with God's grace, by which the law has been fulfilled.[440]

Luther had to fight many battles within his own group, as leaders strayed, and also from without, attacked by the papacy and alarmed by the growing menace of the Muslim invasion of Europe. Yet we can find many accounts of his joyous evenings of relaxation with his family and friends, his tender moments with his beloved children, his sorrow at the loss of his daughter Magdalena, who died in his arms, and his great love

---

[438] *What Luther Says*, III, p. 1243.

[439] *Sermons of Martin Luther*, III, p. 304.

[440] *Ibid.*, I, p. 99.

for Katherine, one of the nuns who escaped from the convent at Nimbschen. If we wonder why Luther's sayings still cause hilarity today, so much that a Luther quotation in a solemn theological paper can make a room full of pastors rock with laughter, we only need to remember what he said:

You have as much laughter as you have faith.[441]

The Antichrist

When Lutherans and Roman Catholics discuss doctrine, they cannot avoid one aspect of traditional Lutheran doctrine, that the institution of the papacy bears the clearest evidence of being the Antichrist. Some writers have sought to prove their case by showing how immoral and dishonest certain popes have been. The abuse of children by Catholic priests became a scandal in America and various other countries, causing many to question Roman Catholicism or Christianity itself. Luther cautioned his own allies not to engage in such comparisons, since the comparisons fail when Lutheran pastors fall into sin. The ultimate issue involves the First Table of the Ten Commandments, since those three commandments concern our relationship with God and His revealed Word. Sins against the First Table are far more serious, since they destroy the soul ultimately and continue without the awareness of the sinner. People are far more aware of their sins against the Second Table: stealing, murdering, and committing adultery. An immoral pastor hurts himself and sends himself to Hell, said Luther, but a false teacher hurts everyone and murders souls. That reasoning does not offer anyone a license for breaking any commandment, but emphasizes the absolute necessity of adhering to the pure Word of God. False doctrine will finally destroy one's confidence in salvation through the merits of Christ alone (the First Table) while offering a broad, diverse, pluralistic path of destruction paved with good intentions and broken commandments (the Second Table).

Lutherans are not unique in viewing the papacy as the Antichrist. Before the advent of ecumenism, which requires doctrinal indifference,

---

[441] *What Luther Says*, II, p. 692.

Protestants and Lutherans were not shy in pointing out the dangers of the papacy. The Anglican Church, now toying with recognition by the Church of Rome, was once a severe critic of the papacy. Those theologians who have identified the papacy with the Antichrist are: Luther, Melanchthon, Calvin, Zwingli, Hugh Latimer, William Tyndale, Thomas Cramner, John Foxe, John Knox, and John Wesley. The English poets Herbert Spenser, John Donne, and George Herbert also called the papacy the Antichrist.[442]

Antichrist in the New Testament

The word Antichrist is limited to five occurrences and appears only in the Johannine epistles (1 John 2:18, singular and plural; 2:22; 4:3; 2 John 7), but the doctrine itself involves more passages. In the Johannine epistles, Antichrist means an opponent of Christ, a person within the Church. The prefix *anti* in Greek is commonly used to signify a substitute, so the Antichrist should be viewed as a Christ-like figure. A non-Christian like Hitler or L. Ron Hubbard cannot be the Antichrist because a mark of the Antichrist is "…the fact that they originate in the Church."[443] In each case, the Antichrist begins an opposition to the Gospel that is continued until the coming of Christ. The spirit of the Antichrist already existed in the Apostolic era, with Cerinthus, for instance, teaching against the Two Natures and the Virgin Birth of Christ from within the Church.[444] Although many heresies have been defeated, such as that of Cerinthus, they continue today in various forms within the Church. Some of the earlier heresies and their modern forms are:

- Gnosticism (liberals claim a secret knowledge of what the Bible really teaches);

- Montanism (Pentecostalism and the charismatic movement);

- Nestorianism (Reformed problems with the Two Natures).

Luther condensed all heresies into three categories of attacks: on the human nature of Christ, the divine nature of Christ, and justification.

---

[442] R. C. H. Lenski, *The Interpretation of St. Paul's Epistles to the Colossians, Thessalonians, Timothy, Titus, Philemon,* Columbus: The Wartburg Press, 1937, p. 433. Hereafter cited as Thessalonians

[443] R. C. H. Lenski, *The Interpretation of the Epistles of St. Peter, St. John, and St. Jude,* Columbus: The Wartburg Press, 1945, pp. 429ff.

[444] *Thessalonians,* p. 408.

Modern substitutions for Christianity that still use the name of Christ are: The Masonic Lodge, Christian Science, Adventism, Jehovah's Witnesses, and Mormonism. Since liberals of all denominations are scandalized by most Biblical doctrines, they consistently fall into one heresy or another, or many at once. They are part of the herd of Antichrists and the flood of anti-Christian propaganda leading up to the revelation of the great Antichrist at the end of time. The opposition to Christ that began so early in the Church will be manifested in the last days. The chief passage about this is found in 2 Thessalonians 2:1-11 –

> 2 Thessalonians 2:1 Now we beseech you, brethren, by the coming of our Lord Jesus Christ, and *by* our gathering together unto him, 2 That ye be not soon shaken in mind, or be troubled, neither by spirit, nor by word, nor by letter as from us, as that the day of Christ is at hand. 3 Let no man deceive you by any means: for *that day shall not come*, except there come a falling away [apostasy in Greek] first, and that man of sin be revealed, the son of perdition; 4 Who opposeth and exalteth himself above all that is called God, or that is worshipped; so that he as God sitteth in the temple of God, shewing himself that he is God. 5 Remember ye not, that, when I was yet with you, I told you these things? 6 And now ye know what withholdeth that he might be revealed in his time. 7 For the mystery of iniquity doth already work: only he who now letteth *will let*, until he be taken out of the way. 8 And then shall that Wicked be revealed, whom the Lord shall consume with the spirit of his mouth, and shall destroy with the brightness of his coming: 9 *Even him*, whose coming is after the working of Satan with all power and signs and lying wonders, 10 And with all deceivableness of unrighteousness in them that perish; because they received not the love of the truth, that they might be saved. 11 And for this cause God shall send them strong delusion, that they should believe a lie:

Apostasy, 2 Thessalonians 2:3

Like many passages about the end of the world, this lesson explains the delay of Christ's coming. Two things must happen before the end. One is the apostasy (falling away) of the church. Apostasy does not mean the rejection of the Gospel by unbelievers, but the turning away from the Gospel by those within the visible church, those who previously believed the Word of God. The apostasy is not the same as the Antichrist, but the Antichrist is the fruit and ultimate result of the apostasy. Although unbelief has always prevailed in the world, our modern era is the first one where the vast majority of ordained clergy, professors of religion, and church leaders reject salvation through Christ while calling themselves sincere—even Bible-believing—Christians. Marketing the Gospel by selling it as a product is just one example of apostasy, far more subtle than openly denying the Trinity or the divinity of Christ. The early Church preserved the apostolic Gospel in the face of violent opposition and defended the truth using the ruling norm of the Scriptures, but gradually, as was shown in the previous chapters, new doctrines were added, enforced, and made mandatory for salvation: the Immaculate Conception and Assumption of Mary, Purgatory, papal infallibility, and—most importantly—salvation by works added to faith. Thus the largest, most ancient, and most visible confession of faith is apostate, having turned away from the One True Faith of the Scriptures.

The Man of Sin, Son of Perdition

The second sign of the end is the revelation of the Man of Sin, who sets himself up as a god within the visible church. The Man of Sin is literally the Son of Perdition (2 Thessalonians 2:3 and John 17:12), the same term used for Judas. He is not Satan, as some suppose, but a man. Several phrases define the Man of Sin:

1. He opposes and sets himself up against everyone who is God's representative;

2. He sits in God's temple;

3. He proclaims himself God.

This does not define one particular man, but an institution, the papacy. No man, however pious or moral, can fill the office of pope without taking on the characteristics pointed out in 2 Thessalonians 2. At first the Bishop of Rome was one of many church leaders. When the Roman Empire began collapsing in the 400's, the Bishop of Rome and the clergy filled a power vacuum created by state officials deserting their posts, people clamoring for leadership. The Bishop of Rome began to assert his authority over that of the other bishops, as the "first among equals." Increasingly the popes asserted their power and prerogatives. During the Reformation, church councils still provided some leverage against papal tyranny; nevertheless, the Council of Trent enforced the worst new doctrines of the Medieval Church. The complete lack of councils until Vatican I demonstrates how power accumulated in the papacy. Vatican I was completely controlled by Pope Pius IX, who made himself infallible, like God. The latest council, Vatican II, affirmed and extended the infallibility decree of Vatican I. At the end of Vatican II, the pope, not the assembled delegates, declared Mary to be the Mother of the Church.

The papacy opposes the representatives of God by declaring that they are genuine teachers of the Gospel only to the extent they agree with the Bishop of Rome. Vatican II softened the image of the papacy in its definition of the Church, but the substance of the Roman Catholic claim to be the visible Church remains as deceptive as ever. For that reason, many people cannot accept the Medieval perversions of the gospel, which remain official dogmas, and yet cannot imagine leaving the Church of Rome. The confusion between institutional loyalty and faithfulness to God's Word culminates in people withdrawing from church altogether. They become cynical about the Christian faith, and ultimately lose faith in the merits of Christ, which alone provide our salvation as a gift, through faith, apart from any works or worthiness on our part.

The papacy certainly is set up within the temple of God and the pope proclaims he is God through his infallibility. At first, in the Apostolic Church, the leaders met and solved doctrinal problems as a brotherhood. St. Peter did not preside over the first council, Acts 15, the Council of Jerusalem. The Word of God shows that St. Peter "was completely wrong" in caving in to one faction, after the council, Galatians 2:11. The divine prerogatives of the papacy were absent for centuries, since no papacy existed, but gradually certain men claimed power and authority over other bishops, their successors consolidating that power. When the papacy was at its weakest point, Pope Pius IX allowed himself to be called God Incarnate by the Ultramontanes, permitting decrees to capitalize the personal pronouns referring to "Him." The infallibility decree of 1870, which is official dogma, disclosed his divine posturing. Ominously, the whole concept of papal definition of doctrine—apart from and opposed to the Word of God—made the infallible Scriptures irrelevant. Except for Pope John XXIII, every pope since Pius IX has added to the application of papal infallibility. Although the papacy has declared that the Bible is divine revelation, recent decrees, such as *Divino Afflante Spiritu*, have opened the door for the apostasy of the Historical Critical Method, making any definition of the Biblical text possible.

Those who search out the intention of the sacred writers must, among other things, have regard for "literary forms." For truth is proposed and expressed in a variety of ways, depending on whether a text is history of one kind of another, or whether its form is that of prophecy, poetry, or some other type of speech. The interpreter must investigate what meaning the sacred writer intended to express and actually expressed in particular circumstances as he used contemporary literary forms in accordance with the situation of his own time and culture.[445]

Thus the standard edition for the Documents of Vatican II has this introduction to *Verbum Dei* by R. A. F. McKenzie, SJ:

More precisely, Scripture contains revelation, namely, in the form of a written record; but not all of Scripture is revelation. Much of it is the record of revelation's effects, of the human reactions to it, of men's faith or lack of it. All of Scripture is inspired, but not all is revealed.[446]

Thus, in an ultra-conservative magazine like *The Fatima Crusader*, we can read about a Roman Catholic priest saying that the Bible:

…was a work of the Holy Spirit. But it is a book nonetheless, and any book has its limitations. It does not contain all of God's workings. No book could.[447]

Recent popes have assumed a more modest stance as religious leaders, but papal doctrine still exalts the Bishop of Rome as God. He is still regarded as the Vicar of Christ, holding the key to heaven's store of merits. These merits can be passed down by the pope to shorten one's future stay in Purgatory or to relieve the souls of friends and relatives

---

[445] Note: "Art. 12 insists on two of the main points made in Pius XII's *Divino Afflante Spiritu*." *Verbum Dei*, Dogmatic Constitution on Divine Revelation, II, 12, *Vatican II*, p. 120.

[446] Introduction to *Verbum Dei*, Dogmatic Constitution on Divine Revelation, *Vatican II*, p. 108.

[447] *Wolves of the World*, cited in an interview with Father Josyp Terelya, *Fatima Crusader*, Spring, 1992, p. 20. This is the Roman Catholic doctrine of the insufficiency of the Scriptures.

already suffering in this intermediate Hell. As a false god, the pope offers people terror instead of comfort, fear instead of trust, and uncertainty instead of assurance through the Means of Grace. Roman Catholics are further confused by the papacy's embrace of other religions, including Judaism, as if salvation came from good diplomatic relations with the Vatican rather than through Christ alone, the Way, the Truth, and the Life (John 14:6). Pope John Paul II was an appealing figure, but he has expressed unity with all religions through various gestures that are widely reported in the press but apparently ignored by the public.[448] Lutherans hold that the lamb-like beast (Revelation 13:11-18) who speaks as a dragon represents the papacy. The beast speaks blasphemies, dishonors God, as the papacy does today, and performs deceiving miracles, reminding us of 2 Thessalonians 2:1-11. Therefore, Melanchthon wrote, and all traditional Lutherans confess:

> Now, it is manifest that the Roman pontiffs, with their adherents, defend [and practice] godless doctrines and godless services. And the marks [all the vices] of Antichrist plainly agree with the kingdom of the Pope and his adherents. For Paul, 2 Thessalonians 2:3, in describing to the Thessalonians Antichrist, calls him "an adversary of Christ, who opposeth and exalteth himself above all that is called God, or that is worshiped, so that he as God sitteth in the temple of God." He speaks therefore of one ruling in the Church, not of heathen kings, and he calls this one the adversary of Christ, because he will devise doctrine conflicting with the Gospel, and will assume to himself divine authority.[449]

Some Christians think that the heroic qualities of John Paul II, his stance against Marxism, his endurance after the murder attempt in St. Peter's Square, and his charisma as a spokesman for Christianity should prevent any declaration that the papacy is the Antichrist.

This teaching shows forcefully that the Pope is the very Antichrist, who has exalted himself above, and opposed himself

---

[448] Extensive coverage of the pope's travels can be found in the media.

[449] Treatise on the Power and Primacy of the Pope, #39. *Triglotta*, p. 515. Tappert, p. 327

against Christ, because he will not permit Christians to be saved without his power, which, nevertheless, is nothing, and is neither ordained nor commanded by God. That is, properly speaking, to exalt himself above all that is called God, as Paul says, 2 Thessalonians 2:4. Even the Turks or the Tartars, great enemies of Christians as they are, do not do this, but they allow whoever wishes to believe in Christ, and take bodily tribute and obedience from Christians.[450]

One must remember that this doctrine is not directed against a man but against an office and an institution. The office is used to set aside the teachings of Christianity and the institution is used to promote these man-made dogmas required for salvation. Luther wrote:

> There is a vast difference between the sovereignty which the Pope has and all other sovereignties in the whole world. To put up with these, be they good or bad, may do no harm, but the Papacy is a sovereignty that exterminates faith and the Gospel...Therefore what we condemn is not the wickedness of the sovereign, but the wickedness of the sovereignty, for it is so constituted that it cannot be administered by a pious, upright sovereign, but only by one who is an enemy of Christ.[451]

In contrast, others want to emphasize the doctrine of the Antichrist in terms of political power and the corruption that results from ecclesiastical power in the civil realm. Oddly enough, many conservative Evangelicals vie for the same kind of power, since Protestantism started in Switzerland with theocratic principles not unlike the Roman Catholic Church. Zwingli fought and died as a soldier on the battlefield, with hundreds of Protestant ministers, at Kapel in 1530. As heir to Zwingli's Swiss Reformation, Calvin had the city council of Geneva pass laws that required attendance at church. However, Luther emphasized the two regiments (or kingdoms), one to rule over civil affairs with the sword, the other to govern spiritual matters with the Word of God. The civil

---

[450] Smalcald Articles, Part II, Article IV. #10-11. The Papacy. *Triglotta*, p. 475. Tappert, p. 300.

[451] Luther, quoted in Francis Pieper, *Christian Dogmatics*, III, p. 468f. John 8:31 2 Thessalonians 2:3ff; 1 Peter 4:11; 1 Timothy 6:3f; Matthew 28:20.

authorities were not to interfere with the church, which degenerates into caesaropapism, and the church was not to use the powers of government, the sword, which degenerates into theocracy. The danger of the papacy is not from its worldly power, political plans, or secret diplomacy. God can bring down the mightiest empire. The papacy is dangerous because of its requirement of human merit for salvation, its implicit denial of the Atonement of Christ in the doctrine of Purgatory, its definition of the Virgin Mary and the Roman pontiff. St. Paul prophesied that the rebellious one would deceive believers with the Satanic power of phony miracles and miraculous signs. These have multiplied rather than declined in the last era, with vast business networks set up around Lourdes, Fatima, and Medjugorje. The traffic in indulgences to release people from Purgatory is simply horrible to consider, since people are asked to pay for the sins that were redeemed on the cross.

> I resolve to sin no more, not even venially; for I know that nothing defiled can enter Heaven. I will do penance for my sins, even those that have been pardoned in Confession, so that I will not be detained in Purgatory.[452]

What is this prayer, if not the spirit of deception, taking away the comfort of forgiveness through Christ, urging a perfection that can only increase guilt, holding up the threat of Purgatory in spite of sins being pardoned? Will not the souls of sincere believers, who trust in the merits of Christ alone, regardless of church affiliation, be taken to heaven by the angels, since Christ washes us and makes us pure through His innocent blood? Will not the souls of unbelievers—regardless of religious affiliation, theological education, or ordination—be taken to Hell? In God's Word there is no middle ground, no mini-Hell for those too good for Hell and too bad for Heaven. Thus, considering the vast amount of evidence, we must conclude that the papacy is the very Antichrist, supplanting the true Gospel, with an imitation of it. Luther wrote, and Lutherans confess:

> Lastly, it is nothing else than the devil himself, because above and against God he urges [and disseminates] his [papal] falsehoods concerning Masses, purgatory, the monastic life, one's own works

---

452 "The Glory of Heaven," *The Fatima Crusader*, Spring, 1992, p. 17.

and [fictitious] divine worship (for this is the very Papacy [upon each of which the Papacy is altogether founded and is standing]), and condemns, murders, and tortures all Christians who do not exalt and honor these abominations [of the Pope] above all things. Therefore, just as little as we can worship the devil himself as Lord and God, we can endure this apostle, the Pope, or Antichrist, in his rule as head or lord. For to lie and to kill, and to destroy body and soul eternally, that is wherein his papal government really consists, as I have very clearly shown in many books.[453]

Warning and Hope

Lutherans cannot afford to rest upon their denominational affiliation and say, "O God, we thank you that we are not like these." The time of apostasy has struck at all of Christianity. So many Christian leaders have turned away from their own heritage that the gravitational pull of their apostasy threatens us all. We are tempted to say to ourselves and to one another, "At least we don't..." only to find ourselves doing and saying the same things a few years later, comforted by our relative faithfulness. But God's Word does not admonish us to be somewhat better than apostates. We have only one standard, the pure Word of God. We must measure our doctrine and practice against the ruling norm of the Scriptures rather than against the standing of another denomination.

Even if all the people in the world ceased to believe in all the doctrines of the Bible, they would still be true.

Mark 13:31 Heaven and earth shall pass away: but my words shall not pass away.

The granite mountains that hide our U.S. president and top-secret installations during a time of crisis; the flexing skyscrapers that hold up against furious storms by rooting themselves in bedrock; the steel blast doors fashioned to guard military targets from nuclear explosions too

---

[453] Smalcald Articles, Part II, Article IV. #14. The Papacy. *Triglotta*, p. 475. Tappert, p. 301.

intense to imagine or describe: all these are nothing in comparison with the eternal value and power of God's Word. They will vanish. God's Word will remain forever.

A Final Word – The Gospel

The purpose of this book has been to provide a way for people to understand, study, and discuss three distinctive Christian confessions. Pastors, seminarians, and college students may also benefit from doctrinal comparisons and a study of the sources, especially the Scriptures. Many confirmation students have used this book, but this is not intended to be an intellectual exercise. Instead, the research has been done in order to make clear the blessings and benefits of Christ's atoning death on the cross, how we obtain complete and free forgiveness of our sins through the Gospel in Word and Sacrament. No one can master all of the sources concerned with Christian doctrine, but one can marvel at this simple truth, which we receive in faith, beyond all human reason: God became man, was born of a Virgin, taught with authority, blessed the children, performed miracles, raised the dead, died on the cross for the sins of the world, and rose bodily from the sealed tomb. Whether we start with the Creation or the Two Natures of Christ, or final judgment, the central message is still the same: on the cross Christ exchanged His righteousness for our sinfulness, to give us forgiveness and eternal life as a gift, to motivate our good works with thankfulness instead of obligation, to give us the peace that passes all human understanding. Luther wondered how all this took place, and answered, in his commentary on 2 Peter 1:3

> Thus: God permitted His holy Gospel to go forth into the world and to be made known. Consequently, no human being had ever before labored to secure it, or sought after it or prayed for it. But before man ever thought of it, God offered, bestowed, and shed forth such grace richly beyond all measure, so that He alone has the glory and the praise for it, and we ascribe the virtue and the power to Him alone, for it is not our work but His alone.[454]

When does this matter? If we take seriously John Bunyan's Biblical allegory, *Pilgrim's Progress*, then the central points of doctrine matter each

---

[454] Luther, *Commentary on 1 and 2 Peter*, Grand Rapids.

and every day, as we struggle toward the end of life's journey, remaining faithful to God's Word. Each day we are tempted by such false guides as – Flatterer, Worldly Wiseman, Legality, Hypocrisy, and Formalist – to rely on our own merits and stray from the way of salvation. Satan and our sinful nature draw us into sin and away from the comfort of God's promises. Along the way, in the rugged wilderness and on the rocky plain, the Gospel of Christ guides and sustains us, defeating the power of sin, death, and the devil. Beyond us we see the saints in heaven, all those who died trusting in the merits of Christ alone. The daughters I baptized, Bethany and Erin Joy, are gathered around the throne of the Lamb, where we will one day join their eternal doxology. We can pray, with Christian, the narrator of *Pilgrim's Progress*,

O God Complete my pilgrimage, Conduct me safely there.

Bibliography

Baepler, W. A. "Doctrine, True and False," *The Abiding Word*. ed., Theodore Laetsch, St. Louis: Concordia Publishing House, 1946.

Bailey, Raymond. *Thomas Merton on Mysticism*. New York: Doubleday and Company, 1974.

Baker, Kenneth, S.J. *Fundamentals of Catholicism*. 3 vols., San Francisco: Ignatius Press, 1982.

Baldwin, Louis. *The Pope and the Mavericks*. Buffalo: Prometheus Books, 1988.

Becker, Siegbert. "Objective Justification." Chicago Pastoral Conference, WELS, Elgin, Illinois, November 9, 1982.

Bente, F. *American Lutheranism., The United Lutheran Church, General Synod, General Council, United Synod in the South*. 2 vols. St. Louis: Concordia Publishing House, 1919.

_____. *Concordia Triglotta, Historical Introductions to the Symbolical Books of the Evangelical Lutheran Church*. St. Louis: Concordia Publishing House, 1921.

Bunyan, John. *The Pilgrim's Progress*. New York: Limited Editions Club, 1941, first published in 1673.

Burghardt, Walter J., S. J. *The Testimony of the Patristic Age Concerning Mary's Death*. Newman Paperback, n.d.

Caroll, E. "Mary in the Documents of the Magisterium." *Mariology*, 3 vols. ed., Juniper B. Carol, O.F.M., Milwaukee: The Bruce Publishing Company, 1961.

Carr, A., and G. Williams. "Mary's Immaculate Conception." *Mariology*, 3 vols., ed., Juniper B. Carol, O.F.M., Milwaukee: The Bruce Publishing Company, 1961.

Chemnitz, Martin. *Examination of the Council of Trent*, trans., Fred Kramer, St. Louis: Concordia Publishing House, 1986.

_____. *Loci Theologici*, 2 vols. trans. J. A. O. Preus, St. Louis: Concordia Publishing House, 1989.

_____. *The Lord's Supper*, 1590, trans. J. A. O. Preus. St. Louis: Concordia Publishing House, 1979.

_____. _The Two Natures of Christ_, 1578, trans. J. A. O. Preus. St. Louis: Concordia Publishing House, 1971.

Cho, Paul Yonggi. with a foreword by Dr. Robert Schuller. _The Fourth Dimension_, 2 vols. South Plainfield, NJ: Bridge Publishing, 1979.

Chytraeus, David. _A Summary of the Christian Faith_ (1568), trans., Richard Dinda, Decatur: Repristination Press, 1994.

Cole, William J., S.M., _Was Luther a Devotee of Mary?_ Reprinted from Marian Studies, 1970.

Collin, Remy. _Evolution._ New York: Hawthorn Books, 1959.

Cranny, Titus. S.A., Is Mary Relevant, A Commentary on Chapter 9 of Lumen Gentium, The Constitution on the Church from Vatican II, New York: Exposition Press, 1970.

Crossroads Community Church Statement of Faith 594 N. Lafayette South Lyon, MI 48178 810-486-0400.

Commission on Theology and Church Relations "Theses on Justification" St. Louis: May, 1983.

Curia, Rick Nicholas. _The Significant History of the Doctrine of Objective or Universal Justification._ Alpine, California: California Pastoral Conference, WELS. January 24-25, 1983.

Douay Reims version, _Holy Bible._ Translated from the Latin Vulgate, Version Rockford: TAN Books, 1899.

Drevlow, Arthur H. "God the Holy Spirit Acts to Build the Church," _God The Holy Spirit Acts_, ed., Eugene P. Kaulfield, Milwaukee: Northwestern Publishing House, 1972.

Echternach, W. "Word and Words," _The Lutheran Encyclopedia_, 3 vols. ed., Julius Bodensieck, Minneapolis: Augsburg Publishing House, 1965.

Engelder, Theodore. "Objective Justification." _Concordia Theological Monthly_, 1933, Ft. Wayne: Concordia Seminary Press, n.d.

_____. W. Arndt, Th. Graebner, F. E. Mayer. _Popular Symbolics_, St. Louis: Concordia Publishing House, 1934.

Fox, Father Robert J. _The Marian Catechism_, Washington, New Jersey: AMI Press, 1983.

Genet, Harry. "Big Trouble for the World's Largest Church," _Christianity Today_, January 22, 1982.

Gerberding, G. H. *The Lutheran Pastor*, Philadelphia: Lutheran Publication Society, 1902.

_____. *The Way of Salvation in the Lutheran Church*, Philadelphia: Lutheran Publication Society, 1887.

Gerhard, Johann. *A Comprehensive Explanation of Holy Baptism and the Lord's Supper, 1610.* ed. D. Berger, J. Heiser, Malone, Texas: Repristination Press, 2000.

"Grace, Means of," *The Concordia Cyclopedia.* ed., L. Fuerbringer, Th. Engelder, P. E. Kretzmann, St. Louis: Concordia Publishing House, 1927.

Graebner, A. L. *Outlines of Doctrinal Theology.* St. Louis: Concordia Publishing House, 1910.

Haferd, Laura. "A Place Where Men Can Go, People Not Creeds, Attract, Churches Told." *Akron Beacon Journal*, October 8, 1988,p. C-3.

Haffert, John Mathias. *Mary in Her Scapular Promise.* Sea Isle City, NJ: The Scapular Press, 1942.

Harley, Pastor Vernon "Synergism--Its Logical Association with General Justification." 511 Tilden, Fairmont, Minnesota 56031, August, 1984.

Hasler, August Bernhard. *How the Pope Became Infallible, Pius IX and the Politics of Persuasion.* Garden City: Doubleday and Company, 1981.

Healy, Kilian, O.Carm. *The Assumption of Mary.* Wilmington, Delaware: Michael Glazier, 1982.

Heick, Otto W. *A History of Christian Thought*, 2 vols. Philadelphia: Fortress Press, 1966.

Hill, Napoleon. *Think and Grow Rich.* New York: Fawcett Crest Books, 1937, revised 1960.

Hillerbrand, Hans J., ed. *The Reformation, A Narrative History Related by Contemporary Observers and Participants.* New York: Harper and Row 1964.

Hoenecke, Adolph. *Evangelisch-Lutherische Dogmatik*, 4 vols., ed., Walter and Otto Hoenecke, Milwaukee: Northwestern Publishing House, 1912, now being translated into English.

Hove, E. *Christian Doctrine*, Minneapolis: Augsburg Publishing House, 1930.

Hubbard, David Allan." What We Believe and Teach," Pasadena, California: Fuller Theological Seminary.

Hudson, Henry T. *Papal Power, Its Origins and Development.* Hertfordshire, England: Evangelical Press, 1981.

Hunter, Kent R. (D.Min., Fuller Seminary). *Launching Growth in the Local Congregation, A Workbook for Focusing Church Growth Eyes.* Detroit: Church Growth Analysis and Learning Center, 1980.

Jackson, Gregory L. "Figs From Thistles," Rev. Steve Spencer, *Orthodox Lutheran Forum,* September 27, 1991.

_____. *Liberalism: Its Cause and Cure.* Milwaukee: Northwestern Publishing House, 1991.

_____. *Thy Strong Word,* Glendale: Martin Chemnitz Press, 2000.

Jacobs, Henry Eyster. *A Summary of the Christian Faith,* Philadelphia: General Council Publication House, 1913.

Jedin, Hubert. *Ecumenical Councils of the Catholic Church,* New York: Paulist Press, 1960.

The Jerusalem Bible, New York: Doubleday and Company, 1966,

Jugie, Martin. *Purgatory and the Means to Avoid It,* New York: Spiritual Book Associates, 1959. This classic can be ordered from http://www.marianland.com/romancatholicbooks/purgatoryma nstoavoid.html.

Kallestad, Walter P. (D. Min., Fuller Seminary) "Entertainment Evangelism," *The Lutheran,* (ELCA), May 23, 1990.

Kelm, Paul. "How to Make Sound Doctrine Sound Good to Mission Prospects."

Koehler, Edward W. A. *A Short Explanation of Dr. Martin Luther's Small Catechism.* Fort Wayne: Concordia Theological Seminary Press, 1946.

_____. *A Summary of Christian Doctrine,* St. Louis: Concordia Publishing House, 1952.

Kolb, Robert. *Andreae and the Formula of Concord.* St. Louis: Concordia Publishing House, 1977.

Koren, U. V. "An Accounting," *Grace for Grace: Brief History of the Norwegian Synod,* ed., Sigurd C. Ylvisaker, Mankato: Lutheran Synod Book Company, 1943.

Krauth, Charles P. *The Conservative Reformation and Its Theology*. Philadelphia: United Lutheran Publication House, 1913 (1871).

Kretzmann, Paul E. *Popular Commentary of the New Testament*, 2 vols. St. Louis: Concordia Publishing House.

Kueng, Hans. *Infallible? An Inquiry*. trans. Edward Quinn, Garden City: Doubleday and Company, 1971.

Lawrenz, Carl. Chairman, Commission on Doctrinal Matters, *Fellowship Then and Now, Concerning the Impasse in the Intersynodical Discussions on Church Fellowship*.

Le Goff, Jacques. *The Birth of Purgatory*. trans. Arthur Goldhammar, Chicago: University of Chicago Press, 1984.

Lenski, R. C. H. *New Testament Commentaries*. Columbus: The Wartburg Press, 1945.

Liguori, St. Alphonsus. *The Glories of Mary*. (adapted), New York: Catholic Book Publishing, 1981.

Lindbeck, George A. *Infallibility*. Milwaukee: Marquette University Press, 1972.

Lindsell. Harold. *The Battle for the Bible*. Grand Rapids: Zondervan, 1976.

_____. *The Bible in the Balance*, Grand Rapids: Zondervan Publishing House, 1979.

Loy, Matthias. *Sermons on the Gospels*, Columbus: Lutheran Book Concern, 1888.

Luther, Father Benjamin. *Catholic Twin Circle*, November 4, 1990.

Luther, Martin. *Commentary on Peter and Jude*, ed. John N. Lenker, Grand Rapids: Kregel Publications, 1990.

_____. *Commentary on Romans*. trans. J. Theodore Mueller, Grand Rapids: Kregel Publications, 1976.

_____. *Lectures on Galatians*, 1535, ed., Jaroslav Pelikan, St. Louis: Concordia Publishing House, 1963.

_____. *The Magnificat*, trans. A. T. W. Steinhaeuser, Minneapolis: Augsburg Publishing House, 1967.

_____. *Sermons of Martin Luther*, 8 vols. ed. John Nicolas Lenker, Grand Rapids: Baker Book House, 1983.

_____. *Sermons of Martin Luther, The House Postils*, 3 vols., ed. Eugene F. A. Klug, Grand Rapids: Baker Book House, 1996.

_____. *What Luther Says, An Anthology*, 3 vols. ed. Ewald Plass, St. Louis: Concordia Publishing House, 1959.

Lutheran Church Missouri Synod. *Kleiner Katechismus.* trans. Pastor Vernon Harley, LCMS, St. Louis: Concordia Publishing House, 1901.

Lutz, Martin W. "God the Holy Spirit Acts Through the Lord's Supper." *God The Holy Spirit Acts.* ed., Eugene P. Kaulfield, Milwaukee: Northwestern Publishing House, 1972.

Madson, Norman A. *Preaching to Preachers*, Mankato: Lutheran Synod Book Company, 1952.

Marquart, Kurt. *"Church Growth" As Mission Paradigm, A Lutheran Assessment.* Our Savior Lutheran Church, Houston: Luther Academy Monograph, 1994.

_____. "Robert D. Preus," *Handbook of Evangelical Theologians.* ed., Walter A. Elwell, Grand Rapids: Baker Book House, 1995.

Maurer, Wilhelm "Formula of Concord," *The Lutheran Encyclopedia.* 3 vols. ed., Julius Bodensieck, Minneapolis: Augsburg Publishing House, 1965.

Mayer, F. E. *American Churches, Beliefs and Practices.* St. Louis: Concordia Publishing House, 1946.

McBrien, Richard P. *Catholicism*, 2 vols. Minneapolis: Winston Press, 1980.

McGavran, Donald A. *Understanding Church Growth*, Grand Rapids: William B. Eerdmans, 1980.

_____. and Winfield C. Arn, *Ten Steps for Church Growth.* New York: Harper and Row, 1977.

Meyer, John P. *Ministers of Christ, A Commentary on the Second Epistle of Paul to the Corinthians.* Milwaukee: Northwestern Publishing House, 1963.

Miles, Delos *Church Growth, A Mighty River*, Nashville: Broadman Press, 1981.

Milner, Benjamin Charles Jr. *Calvin's Doctrine of the Church.* Leiden: E. J. Brill, 1970.

Murphy Paul I. with R. Rene Arlington. *La Popessa.* New York: Warner Books, 1983.

Nazarene Publishing House. *Manual of the Church of the Nazarene*. Kansas City: Nazarene Publishing House, 1932.

Neuhaus, Rev. Richard (ELCA at the time), *Forum Letter*, 338 E 19th Street New York, NY 10003 November 26, 1989.

Nichols, James Hastings. *History of Christianity. 1650-1950*, New York: The Ronald Press Company, 1956.

Nyman, Helge. "Preaching (Lutheran): History," *The Encyclopedia of the Lutheran Church*. 3 vols., ed. Julius Bodensieck, Minneapolis: Augsburg Publishing House, 1965.

O'Hare, Msgr. Patrick F. *The Facts About Luther*. Rockford, Illinois: TAN Books and Publishers, 1987.

O'Meara, Thomas O.P. *Mary in Protestant and Catholic Theology*. New York: Sheed and Ward, 1966.

Ortiz, Juan Carlos. *Call to Discipleship*. Plainfield: Logos International, 1975.

Palmer, Paul F., S.J. *Mary in the Documents of the Church*. Gerald G. Walsh, S.J., Westminster, Maryland: The Newman Press 1952,.

Pelikan, Jaroslav. *The Riddle of Roman Catholicism*, New York: Abingdon Press, 1959.

Pieper, Francis. *Christian Dogmatics*, 3 vols., trans., Walter W. F. Albrecht, St. Louis: Concordia Publishing House, 1953.

_____. The Difference Between Orthodox And Heterodox Churches, and Supplement, Coos Bay, Oregon: St. Paul's Lutheran Church, 1981.

Pieplow, Edwin E. "The Means of Grace." *The Abiding Word*. ed., Theodore Laetsch, St. Louis: Concordia Publishing House, 1946,

Pope Paul VI, *Marialis Cultus*, Washington D.C.: U. S. Catholic Conference, 1974.

Preus, J. A. O. *The Second Martin, The Life and Theology of Martin Chemnitz*. St. Louis: Concordia Publishing House, 1994.

Preus Robert D. *Justification and Rome*. St. Louis: Concordia Academic Press 1997.

Preuss, Eduard. "The Means of Grace," *The Justification of the Sinner before God*. trans., Julius A. Friedrich, Chicago: F. Allerman, 1934.

Resch, Peter A. S.M., S.T.D. *A Life of Mary, Co-Redemptrix*. Milwaukee: The Bruce Publishing Company, 1954.

Reu, Johann Michael. *In the Interest of Lutheran Unity*. Columbus: The Lutheran Book Concern, 1940.

Ripley, Father Francis J., *Mary, Mother of the Church*. Franciscan University. Rockford: TAN Books, 1969.

Rush, Alfred. "Mary in the Apocrypha of the New Testament," *Mariology*. 3 vols., Juniper B. Carol, O.F.M., Milwaukee: The Bruce Publishing Company, 1961.

Sasse, Hermann. *Here We Stand*. trans. Theodore G. Tappert, Minneapolis: Augsburg Publishing House, 1946.

Schlink, Edmund. *Theology of the Lutheran Confessions*. trans. Paul F. Koehneke and Herbert J. A. Bouman, Philadelphia: Fortress Press, 1961.

Schmauk Theodore E. and C. Theodore Benze. *The Confessional Principle and the Confessions, as Embodying the Evangelical Confession of the Christian Church*. Philadelphia: General Council Publication Board, 1911.

Schmid, Heinrich. *Doctrinal Theology of the Evangelical Lutheran Church*. trans., Charles A. Hay and Henry E. Jacobs, Philadelphia: United Lutheran Publication House, 1899.

Schmidt, Martin. "Pietism," *The Encyclopedia of the Lutheran Church*, 3 vols. ed. Julius Bodensieck, Minneapolis: Augsburg Publishing House, 1965.

Schouppe, Rev. F. X., S.J., *Purgatory, Illustrated by the Lives and Legends of the Saints*, Rockford: TAN Books and Publishers,1973 (1893).

Setzer, J. Shoneberg. *What's Left to Believe*. Nashville: Abingdon Press, 1968.

Sharrock, David John. C.SS.R., *The Theological Defense of Papal Power by St. Alphonsus de Liguori*. Washington D.C.: Catholic University of America Press, 1961.

Shea, V.R.M. George W. "The Dominican Rosary." *Mariology*, 3 vols. ed., Juniper B. Carol, O.F.M., Milwaukee: The Bruce Publishing Company, 1961.

Shotwell, John T. and Louise Ropes Loomis, *The See of Peter*, New York: Columbia University Press, 1927.

Sidey, Ken. "Church Growth Fine Tunes Its Formulas," *Christianity Today*, June 24, 1991.

Sitz, E. Arnold. *Entrenched Unionistic Practices, A Record of Unionistic Practice in the LCMS*. Authorized by the Commission on Doctrinal Matters, Wisconsin Evangelical Lutheran Synod.

Sommer, Martin S. *Concordia Pulpit for 1932*. St. Louis: Concordia Publishing House, 1931.

Sungenis, Robert. *Not by Faith Alone: The Biblical Evidence for the Catholic Doctrine of Justification*, Santa Barbara: Queenship Publishing, 1997.

Tappert, Theodore, ed. *The Book of Concord*. Philadelphia: Fortress Press,

_____, ed. *Lutheran Confessional Theology in America, 1840-1880*. New York: Oxford University Press, 1972.

Tierney, Brian. *Origins of Papal Infallibility, 1150-1350*, Leiden: E. J. Brill, 1972.

Tillmanns, Walter G. "Means of Grace: Use of," *The Encyclopedia of the Lutheran Church*, 3 vols. Julius Bodensieck, Minneapolis: Augsburg Publishing House, 1965.

Valleskey, David J. "The Church Growth Movement: An Evaluation," *Wisconsin Lutheran Quarterly*, Spring, 1991.

_____. "The Church Growth Movement, Just Gathering People or Building the Church?" The Northwestern Lutheran, May 5, 1991.

_____. *We Believe--Therefore We Speak, The Theology and Practice of Evangelism*. Milwaukee: Northwestern Publishing House, 1995.

Vatavuk, William M. *Catholic Twin Circle*, December 3, 1989.

Vatican, *Liberia Editrice Vaticana, Catechism of the Catholic Church*, St. Paul Books and Media, 1994.

Wagner, C. Peter, ed. with Win Arn and Elmer Towns, *Church Growth: The State of the Art*, Wheaton: Tyndale House, 1986.

Walther, C. F. W. "Christ's Resurrection--The World's Absolution. "*The Word of His Grace, Sermon Selections*, Lake Mills: Graphic Publishing Company, 1978.

_____. *The Proper Distinction between Law and Gospel*, trans. W. H. T. Dau, St. Louis: Concordia Publishing House 1897.

Warner, Marina. *Alone of All Her Sex*. New York: Alfred A. Knopf, 1976.

Wendland, Ernst H. "Church Growth Theology." *Wisconsin Lutheran Quarterly*, April, 1981.

_____."Missiology—And the Two Billion," Wisconsin Lutheran Quarterly, Wisconsin Lutheran Quarterly, January, 1974.

Werning. Waldo J. *The Radical Nature of Christianity, Church Growth Eyes Look at the Supernatural Mission of the Christian and the Church.* South Pasadena: William Carey Library, 1975.

_____. *Renewal for the 21st Century Church*, St. Louis: Concordia Publishing House, 1988.

_____. *Vision and Strategy for Church Growth*, Second Edition, Grand Rapids: Baker Book House, 1983.

Subject Index